A TREKKER'S GUIDE
to Collectibles
WITH VALUES

Jeffrey B.
Snyder

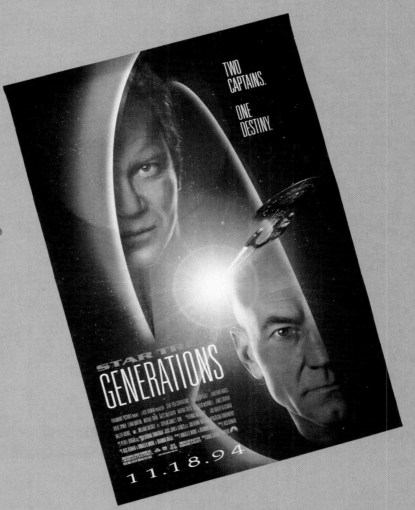

TWO
CAPTAINS.

ONE
DESTINY.

STAR TREK
GENERATIONS

11.18.94

Schiffer
Publishing Ltd

77 Lower Valley Road, Atglen, PA 19310

Dedication

To Marc and Marti — your talents, energy, and creativity are inspirational to me.

Acknowledgments

I wish to express my heartfelt gratitude to all the people who made this book possible. Collectors and dealers generously allowed me to photograph their collections. When necessary, I was permitted into their homes and places of business with my tangle of photographic equipment. They made the photographs for this book possible and were generous with their knowledge, stories, and advice as well. I offer my thanks to: John E. Balbach; Bob Hoag; Jeff Maynard, New Eye Studio, along with Jill Dzinski and Kate Berning; Marc A. Snyder; Michael W. Snyder; and Sherry L. Snyder.

A special thanks to the men and women of the space program, real heroes blazing a trail to the stars for all humanity. May we have the foresight to continue to support you and your efforts.

Printed in Hong Kong

Library of Congress Cataloging–in–Publication Data

Snyder, Jeffrey B.
    A trekker's guide to collectibles / by Jeffrey B. Snyder.
       p.   cm.
    Includes bibliographical references and index.
    ISBN 0-88740-965-2
    1. Star Trek television programs--Collectibles--Catalog. 2. Star Trek films--Colletibles--Catalogs.   I. Title.
    PN1992.8.S74S68 1996
    791.45'72--dc20
                            95-25792
                                    CIP

Published by Schiffer Publishing, Ltd.
77 Lower Valley Road
Atglen, PA 19310
Please write for a free catalog.
This book may be purchased from the publisher.
Please include $2.95 postage.
Try your bookstore first.

We are interested in hearing from authors
with book ideas on related subjects.

Table of Contents

Introduction

"On big screen or small, Star Trek has a gravitational force that reliably pulls in the audience. The movies and TV shows reassure us that there will be a future, and that it will be fun if we don't mind a couple of pesky Klingons in the passing lane."
— Carrie Rickey, Philadelphia Inquirer Movie Critic[1]

"There remain among us many still who are unmoved by what Goethe called 'the best part of man'. These [the incurious and uninspired in the face of the unknown] remain, even now, in the condition of those prehuman apes who are concerned only with economics, sociology, and politics, hurling bricks at each other and licking their own wounds."
— Joseph Campbell[2]

In the early 1960s, the science fiction genre was scorned by most television and movie directors, their critics, and most of the viewing public. Television network executives considered "sci-fi" the stuff of children's programming. Equally unappreciated, drama had withered and died on television's vine; all thirteen of the serious anthology shows which had been available to the networks were dropped by 1965 in favor of "family-oriented programming." So, in the early 1960s, when former police officer turned scriptwriter Eugene Roddenberry tried to sell the networks on a serious, dramatic adult series dealing with socially relevant issues, cloaked in the trappings of science fiction, the networks were skeptical at best.[3]

Star Trek's concept - a one hour serial science fiction show for adults with continuing characters (except for the red-shirted security guards, who came and went in alarming numbers) - was a new one. The original episodes were often allegories for real-world problems facing society in the 1960s, from the Vietnam War to race relations. The problems were to be solved with reason rather than violence by the crew of a United Federation of Planets starship. The episodes presented an optimistic and exciting view of the human future.

For the networks, Gene Roddenberry billed Star Trek as a "Wagon Train to the stars." He kept the show affordable by taking his starship's crew primarily to "M Class" planets (planets similar to Earth or Mars but always featuring "shirt sleeves" working environments) and by creating inexpensive, reusable special effects.

The U.S.S. Enterprise NCC-1701 moving at warp speed. *Courtesy of the Collection of Jeff Maynard — New Eye Studio*

The starship Enterprise itself was unlike any other space ship on film at that time; a roomy craft carrying 430 crew members in comfortable, unintimidating interiors, all centered on a bridge designed to become as familiar to the viewers as their own living rooms. The plain exterior of this starship was instantly recognizable from any angle.

CBS was the first to express interest in the series in 1964. They met with Roddenberry, went over his ideas for cutting costs, made notes, thanked him kindly, and aired Irwin Allen's *Lost in Space* (a 1965-1968 family-oriented science fiction series) instead. NBC then picked up Roddenberry's series.[4]

NBC broadcast Star Trek in the fall of 1966, after numerous changes to script and personnel alike. Reviews for the first season were mixed and - far worse - ratings were low. Despite first season Emmy awards nominations and the high artistic standard maintained despite a shoestring budget, NBC decided to cancel Star Trek in its second season.

A Taste of Armageddon city scape. Star Trek Galore, 1976. *Courtesy of the Collection of Jeff Maynard — New Eye Studio*

Mr. Spock's evil alter-ego from the episode "Mirror, Mirror" was no match for NBC executives determined to cancel the series. *Courtesy of the Collection of Jeff Maynard — New Eye Studio*

The show was saved from the axe by fans who sent in thousands of letters of complaint. Star Trek ran for a second and a third season. The crew of the Enterprise repeatedly fended off their arch enemies (the Romulans and the Klingons), reasoned with alien species of all shapes and sizes, and deflected every threat facing the Federation; however, with continuing low

ratings and advertisers complaining that the largely teenage audience would never buy their prime-time products, the starship Enterprise never completed its original five year mission. The series was canceled at the end of its third season in 1969 with a total of seventy-eight season episodes aired.

For most series this would have been a fatal blow, but not so for Star Trek. Seventy-eight episodes was just enough to rerun the series in syndication. Fan loyalty was intense; their numbers grew every year. More viewers watched the original series in syndication than ever saw it when it ran in prime time. Fan clubs, "fanzines" (magazines produced by and for fans), and Star Trek conventions soon followed in the early 1970s.

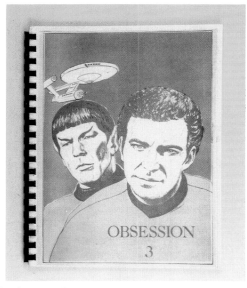

Obsession 3 fanzine, 1984. *Courtesy of the Collection of Jeff Maynard — New Eye Studio*

Reruns, magazines, conventions, and - of course - collectibles related to the original series sustained Star Trek fans until the Paramount movie studio offered Roddenberry the opportunity to remake his series for the big screen. Once *Star Trek: The Motion Picture* was released in 1979 and became a box office hit, Star Trek came back with a vengeance.

As of this writing, Star Trek is a rapidly growing and enduring pop-culture phenomenon. From that short-lived, late '60s series suffering from poor ratings sprang seven movies (with another just around the corner), three television series, and an audience of loyal "Trekkers" in some seventy-five nations around the planet. Many of those states, republics, provinces and territories have been swept by a "Trek mania."

None of the descendants of the original series have faced their progenitor's problems. The second television series, *Star Trek: The Next Generation,* was the first series sold directly into syndication. It became the highest rated syndicated show in television history. The Next Generation surpassed the originally stated "five year mission" of the starship Enterprise by two years. The show was cancelled as a series solely to move it to the silver screen, picking up where the original *Star Trek* cast left off at the end of the first six feature films. *Star Trek: Deep Space 9* has not done as well as *The Next Generation*, yet it has been rated the top drama in syndication. The most recent addition, *Star Trek: Voyager,* has been well-received and at this time is the one-and-only star attraction of a fledging television network, UPN (United/Paramount Network).

No longer a series watched mostly by teenagers, Paramount claims Star Trek now attracts more college educated professionals than almost any other show. Among the average twenty million weekly viewers today, some of the better-known fans include Robin Williams, Mel Brooks, General Colin Powell, and

Star Trek The Motion Picture. There Is No Comparison. 1979 movie poster. *Courtesy of the Collection of Jeff Maynard — New Eye Studio*

Star Trek has become part of the culture and may be seen almost everywhere! *Courtesy of the author's collection*

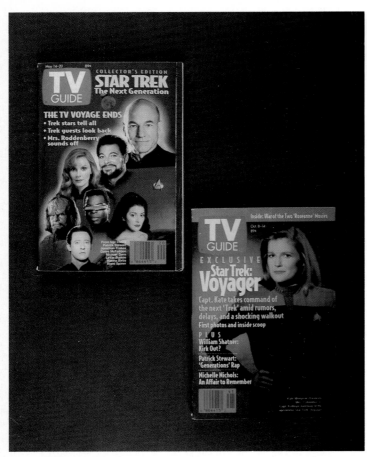

TV Guides: heralding the end of Star Trek: The Next Generation, May 14-20, 1994 and the imminent arrival of Star Trek: Voyager and Star Trek's first woman in the captain's chair, October 8-14, 1994. *Courtesy of the author's collection*

physicist Stephen Hawkings. Needless to say, there are no longer complaints from the advertisers about Star Trek's viewership lacking financial clout.[5]

Along with the television shows and the movies has come an avalanche of collectible merchandise of all sorts, from buttons and books to toys and models. Even brass replicas of *Star Trek: The Next Generation*'s Enterprise-D, selling for over $2000 each, are to be found. Between 1990 and 1995 alone, Star Trek merchandise has created over one billion dollars in total revenue. Over sixty-three million Star Trek books have been printed, with more than thirty new titles appearing every year. Many video stores now dedicate entire sections to Star Trek videocassettes, containing every television episode and movie, a testimony to their popularity.[6]

Star Trek has managed to endure and grow for over a quarter century by presenting a detailed and consistently optimistic view of the human future, in which our present difficulties and prejudices of every sort have been put behind us - a future in which our own handiwork allows us to bend the laws of physics and tear off across the cosmos wherever we wish to go. As one conventioneer put it, "A lot of science fiction shows the future just like now, only worse. I like [Star Trek] because it shows us a future I could live in." Jonathan Frakes (who played Commander William Riker) adds, "This is a show that doesn't insult the audience. It is intelligent, literate, and filled with messages and morals — and that's what most of the people who watch it are interested in."[7]

Endnotes

1. Carrie Rickey. "A Couple of Captains, Trekking Together." *Philadelphia Inquirer*. November 18, 1984. On Screen, 3.
2. Joseph Campbell. *Myths To Live By*. (New York: Bantam Books, 1972), 248.
3. Gordon F. Sanders. *Serling. The Rise and Twilight of Television's Last Angry Man*. (New York: Dutton Books, 1992), 5.
4. William Shatner with Chris Kreski. *Star Trek Memories*. (New York: Harper Paperbacks, 1993), 39-40.
5. Richard Zoglin. "Trekking Onward." *Time, Inc.* (transmitted to America On Line, November 20, 1994).
6. Zoglin. "Trekking Onward."
7. Ursula K. LeGuin. "My Appointment with the Enterprise. An Appreciation." *TV Guide* 42(20) 2146, May 14-20, 1994, 32 & Zoglin. "Trekking Onward."

Star Trek's consistently optimistic view of the future continues to attract viewers over the years. Kirk meets Harry Mudd. *Courtesy of the Collection of Jeff Maynard — New Eye Studio*

The Space Shuttle Orbiter 101 Enterprise, so named at the request of thousands of Star Trek fans, at its first unveiling on September 17, 1976 and during a test flight on October 12, 1977. With growing numbers and great enthusiasm, these well-educated Star Trek fans wield considerable influence. *Courtesy of the National Aeronautics and Space Administration*

Chapter I. Science Fiction, Science, and the Road to the Twenty-Third Century

"Science fiction pretends to look into the future, but it's really looking at a reflection of the truth immediately in front of us."
— Ray Bradbury[1]

How was it possible to offer up a low-budget science fiction serial in 1966, lose it to cancellation in three seasons time, and have that very same show go on to become a highly profitable, internationally known, multimedia hit, a cultural icon spinning off sequels, toy lines and collectibles of all sorts decades after the first episode was aired? The answer lies in a tangled web of science fiction story-telling, real world technological advancement, social change, mass media entertainment, and current events.

Science and Fiction: Creating a Genre, Spawning the Series

Star Trek, while enduring, is only a recent addition to a long line of films in the science fiction genre. This genre, whether created for the movies or television, at its core asks the simple question "What if?" It is well defined by the author Gene Wright as, "a celebration of the possibilities of being human in a universe at once mysterious and hostile." Science fiction films question our everyday reality - our view of the world - and speculate on the future world we will one day inhabit. The views of the future in film are generally less caustic or extreme than those portrayed in novels, and their effects - being visual - are more immediate and resonant with a large, general audience.[2]

Devotees of science fiction literature and film critics alike frequently ridicule science fiction films for replacing a literary tradition stretching back well into the nineteenth century with special effects trickery and fast-paced action sequences. The critics claim most of these films are actually either Westerns or detective stories skulking behind futuristic facades. While true, the critics fail to recognize that science fiction has revitalized these popular genres with a much broader scope, offering almost infinite possibilities for future story lines.

The future predictions of science fiction films are regularly overrun and discredited by reality. There has been, for example, no race of genetically engineered supermen produced to be led into a Eugenics War by a twisted genius named Khan Noonien Singh during the 1990s as envisioned in the first *Star Trek* series. Nor will the now defunct Pan American Airlines (spacelines?) be making any trips to orbiting doughnut-shaped space stations at the turn of the twenty-first century as seen in *2001-A Space Odyssey*. Science fiction films fall far short as soothsayers; however, these films do, at times, project the very real human concerns and fears of the day into those future worlds, revealing much about the times in which they are produced. Since Hollywood has made most of these futuristic films, American anxieties have been predominantly portrayed over the years in this genre. We have already touched on several of the areas of concern which manifest themselves in Star Trek and will do so again later.[3]

The special effects in 2001 A Space Odyssey changed the look of science fiction. Art from the motion picture soundtrack record by MGM. *Courtesy of the author's collection*

Films with science fiction elements began to be made in about 1902, shortly after the introduction of the early short films themselves, in the form of short trick films by the French special-effects innovator Georges Méliès, with additional contributions by Louis Lumière, Stuart Blackton, Ferdinand Zecca and Segundo de Chomon. These were generally lighthearted, funny pieces based on the simple notion that all of the new technological gadgetry available in the early twentieth century was just as likely to break down (with amusing results) as it was to work on any given occasion.[4]

There is irony here, the story telling techniques these men employed to poke fun at technology were those dictated to them by the new cinematic technology available; the restrictions they faced where not those of literary tradition but those imposed by these limited machines, forcing each director to tell his story in black and white pictures alone. Of all the film genre, science fiction films are the most closely related to and dependent on the technology that first generated them.

As films grew in length and film makers had more time to think about all that new technology, more ominous science fiction films were produced. The first films dealt with the dangers of new technologies unleashed in war and would become a growing theme prior to World War I. In 1909, *The Airship Destroyer*, inspired by H.G. Wells' novel *War in the Air* which had been released the year before, speculated on the use of aircraft in future warfare. Films about future war appeared before both World War I and II. When the imagined future battles met with the harsh realities of the modern warfare of their days, these movies ceased to be popular.

Along a similar vein (but far less potent as a theme because the threat was not of our own creation) were films of life in the aftermath of a cosmic collision with either a comet or a wandering planet. The first film of this sort was *The Comet,* produced in 1910. This film reflected and expanded upon the fears raised in 1908 when astronomers revealed that the Earth would pass through the tail of Halley's Comet in 1910 and that the tail contained cyanogen gas, a component of cyanide. Some feared that the atmosphere would be poisoned, leading to mass extinctions with humanity at the top of the endangered species list. Thoughts turned to spaceflight and getting off before the dreaded passage. Illustrations and postcards poked fun, showing people using lad-ders, balloons, flimsy experimental airplanes, and cannons to leave Earth for the moon.[5]

Renewed interest in cometary collisions arose in June of 1994 when the shattered comet Shoemaker-Levy 9 bombarded Jupiter in twenty-one fragments. This comet graphically illustrating for us all just how destructive the bodies of these "dirty ice balls" could really be. Several of the resultant explosions from individual fragments (closely observed from space by both NASA's Hubble space telescope and their Galileo space probe) were powerful enough to raise dust clouds the size of Earth. Times have changed since 1908. No amusing illustrations or postcards were inspired by the comet this time. Shortly after the collisions, astronomer Carl Sagan suggested in his 1994 book *A Pale Blue Dot* that getting off Earth, spreading ourselves out among the planets and the stars, would be a wise way to avoid being caught with all of our eggs in one fragile basket should a similar comet strike the Earth. More serious depictions of leaving home are regularly produced in science fiction shows and people actually do leave the planet on occasion with American Space Shuttles and Russian rocketry. No doubt more than a few Trekkers even wished they could hail a passing starship and move off-world after Shoemaker-Levy 9's destructive performance.

All twenty-one fragments of Comet Shoemaker-Levy 9 impact with Jupiter, leaving several Earth-sized dark spots on the planet's surface (seen near the southern pole of the planet). *Courtesy of the National Aeronautics and Space Administration*

A third motif developed in the early films depicted man tinkering with nature itself, with frightening results. These dark melodramas combined science and magic, beginning with *Homunculus* in 1916 and *Alraune* in 1918. All three of these early themes (dangerous man-made technologies, natural dangers from space, and unnatural man-made perversions) recur throughout the history of science fiction film making and can be readily found in Star Trek episodes.[6]

No doubt inspired - in part - by American scientist Robert H. Goddard's determined efforts to reach space with his early liquid fueled rockets, adventure serials had silvery art deco styled rockets fizzing, popping, and sparking across the screen during the 1930s and 1940s. Silver suited heroes and heroines armed with ray guns pitted themselves against megalomaniacal villains bent on world domination - villains wielding an array of exotic weaponry produced by eccentric and often misunderstood scientists. Flash Gordon and Buck Rogers — first in comics and magazines and then in films — vanquished their foes and kept their audiences on the edges of their seats. These films, while very light entertainment, would influence the look and action in many a space adventure to come.[7]

The portals to the science fiction universe were thrown wide open to rapidly growing audiences with the introduction of television. The small screen brought other-worldly adventures directly into living rooms across America and around the globe. Science fiction's first television broadcast was the 1949 *Captain Video* teleseries. Beginning with these early shows, wherever there were popular TV shows - particularly shows of interest to children - toys, models, gadgets, and costumes related to them were soon to follow. Thus began a booming future collectibles market.[8]

Television had been around in an experimental form in the 1920s and 1930s. Moviegoers watched as Ming the Merciless glared evilly into his own television screen to take in the action around him, but TV would have to wait until after World War II to arrive as a product for mass-market consumption.

When it came, television conquered America with staggering speed. In 1946 only two-hundredths of one percent of American homes had a television set. In 1956, front porch swings were abandoned and fireflies winked through the night unchased as seventy-two percent of America's households gathered around to take in the shows on their very own sets. It had taken five hundred years for printing press technology to get books into the hands of the general public, the broadcasting industry had television technology widely distributed in less than a single generation.[9]

In the 1950s, science fiction came strongly into its own as a full-blown film genre, incorporating the various elements developed throughout the previous four decades. Television continued to provide its fast-paced action adventures for the kids, including Captain Video and his Video Rangers, Tom Corbet Space Cadet, Space Patrol with Commander Buzz Corry, and Rocky Jones Space Ranger. Neighborhoods were filled with children carrying space toys and armed with ray guns.[10]

Movies took a darker turn, tackling the nagging fears of the post-World War II decade. Realizing we were living in an atomic age and for the first time had the ability to wipe out the human race in one stroke was traumatizing. The successful test explosions of hydrogen bombs by both the United States and the Soviet Union in 1952 and 1953 worsened the fears. Many science fiction films of the 1950s dealt with the fear of living in the nuclear age. These films displayed again and again the almost unimaginable consequences of the misuse of modern technology (or the use of similar technologies on us by malevolent aliens) and the resultant struggle to regain control of human destiny in a chaotic, shattered world.

Driving many 1950s science fiction films onward was that all pervasive fear of the atom bomb and the destruction of which it was capable. However, while modern technology was capable of reducing the human race to ashes, it was also essential for the survival of a modern society. Therefore, in the period

films, scientists were not portrayed as evil, their inventions were simply misused. The military, necessary to defend against the "Red Menace," played the role of the rescuer, never the destroyer. The large numbers of science fiction films produced during this decade, with these themes, underscores the depth of the dread felt during this decade.

Teenagers flocked to the movies while their parents generally stayed home around their TV sets in the 1950s. Science fiction films appealed to the teens and movie-makers responded to them as well. By this time an old studio system in Hollywood had broken down, releasing actors and actresses from the major studios and presenting independent film makers with better opportunities to finance their projects. Many of the independents took aim at the youthful market. By the middle of the decade, many of the science fiction films were targeted directly at the teenagers including *The Blob* (1958) and *Teenagers from Outer Space* (1959). They appeared most often at the drive-ins. The exceptions were big-budget spectaculars including *The War of the Worlds* (1953) and *1984* (1956).[11]

During the 1960s, science fiction faced the realities of the space age. On October 4, 1957, a race was begun between the world's two largest nations with a beep, or rather a series of them. The Soviet Union successfully launched their Sputnik satellite, with its beeping transmissions heard around the globe, to the amazement of the world and the consternation of the United States. The United States had been believed to be the leader in rocket technology until that day in 1957. For years afterwards, America would play catch up while sales of American technology overseas slipped as the Soviets pulled ahead. The launch also had ugly implications for a nation all too aware of the potential disaster of nuclear war. If the Soviets could launch a satellite, they could launch a ballistic missile with an nuclear warhead as well. Children were taught in school to "Duck and Cover" in case of a nuclear attack while America's rocket scientists scrambled to catch up.[12]

The United States seemed to be stuck one step behind the Soviets in the race to space. On April 12, 1961 the Soviets successfully launched their first test pilot, Yuri Gagarin and recovered him unharmed; the United States followed with Alan Shepards successful fifteen minute flight aboard Freedom 7 in May.

In between those two launches, a course of events would change the history of the two nations' space programs. On April 15, 1961, CIA trained Cuban exiles attempted a coup beginning with air strikes against Fidel Castro's air force. These were followed two days later by the failed Bay of Pigs invasion attempt. Within two days the world knew this was an American fiasco and America's reputation was in desperate need of a lift.[13]

Following the advice of his science adviser that a "space spectacular" would shift the focus from current events, President John F. Kennedy delivered a speech to Congress on May 25, 1961 laying out his vision for the immediate future of the space program. He declared, "that this Nation should commit itself to achieving the goal, before this decade is out, of landing a man on the moon and returning him safely to earth." This program also had the benefit of creating a task America's space scientists believed the Soviet Union could not handle. With little debate, Congress approved the plan. NASA's Mercury and Gemini manned space flights paved the way. Less than ten years after the goal was set, the crew of Apollo 11 (Neil Armstrong, Buzz Aldrin and Michael Collins) completed the task. On July 20, 1969, Neil Armstrong and Buzz Aldrin successfully landed the American lunar module Eagle on the moon. The Soviets, beaten to the moon, turned the attentions of their manned program toward prolonged orbital flights and space station development. Landing on the moon remains a feat no other nation on Earth has been willing or able to accomplish.[14]

Unlike the future war films prior to both world wars, science fiction films flourished in the face of the realities of the burgeoning American and Soviet space programs. During the 1960s, science fiction films began to gain more respect, to draw

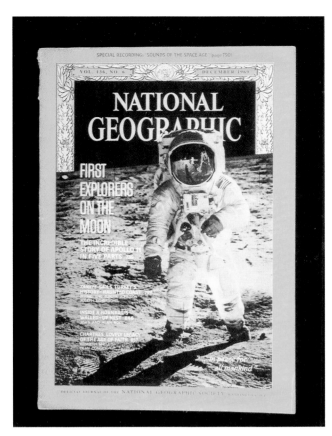

The Moon Landing, National Geographic, December, 1969. *Courtesy of the author's collection.*

Star Wars 20th Century Fox poster from the soundtrack album, 1977. *Courtesy of the Collection of Sherry L. Snyder*

some preeminent directors and stars, and to garner bigger budgets. The successful 1959 film *On the Beach* began the trend. *Star Trek* would not receive its due on the small screen, however, or gather a sizable following until it reached a larger audience in syndication in the 1970s. No doubt *Star Trek* received a boost from two films produced in 1968. That year *2001-A Space Odyssey* and *Planet of the Apes* were released and really made people sit up and take notice of science fiction films. *2001* gave the genre a new look and a bigger budget; *Planet of the Apes* brought new respect to the serious science fiction film that questioned where human misdeeds, if carried forth into the future unchecked, would lead us.[15]

By 1970, with the success of the Apollo program to the moon, Americans were convinced they or their children would one day walk where Armstrong and Aldrin had walked. That optimism would fade as the program was brought to a halt two missions short of its intended goal in 1974. Science fiction films, however, prospered — climaxing with the late 1970s sensations *Star Wars, Close Encounters of the Third Kind* (both in 1977) and *Star Trek-The Motion Picture* (1979). In fact, the success of *Star Wars* convinced Paramount to drop its plans for a second *Star Trek* television series in the late 1970s and instead place the original cast in a major motion picture.

These films represented a sharp departure from the films of the decades before which had presented and dealt with societal fears and ills. Star Wars, Close Encounters and Star Trek movies would shift their focus to escapism, heroics and innocence combined with stunning visual effects.[16] In the decade when Americans were traumatized by Richard Nixon's resignation from the presidency under threat of impeachment and by the less-than-victorious American withdrawal from the Vietnam war (with all of the social unrest and shaken faith in the nation's abilities that accompanied these events) this was undoubtedly a welcome relief.

Close Encounters of the Third Kind. *Courtesy of the Collection of Sherry L. Snyder*

In the 1980s and 1990s, science fiction films continue to grow, following the path blazed by the big hits of the late 1970s with films such as *E.T. The Extraterrestrial* (1982). While successful, many of these films have been popular in their avoidance of issues of social relevance rather than for facing up to and presenting them in imaginative ways. This desire to avoid issues and the topics presented in present day films still reveal a great deal about modern society to the careful viewer.

Star Wars completed its trilogy, topping itself with ever more complex special effects in each movie. To the delight of Star Trek fans, the series has enjoyed continued success on both the large and small screens.

Whether science fiction continues to head predominantly down a path of escapism, returns to its old questioning ways, or swerves down some other as yet unblazed trail in response to new events and issues facing society at large remains to be seen. Recent reports indicate Hollywood films now depend on the world market as much as on the American box office for profits. Their biggest money-makers rely on action and effects over stories — style over substance. This may indicate the future trends for most film genre to come. However, as things stand now, whatever movie trends come next, it appears that Star Trek will be there.

The Birth & Effect of Star Trek

Star Trek first aired in confusing and turbulent times. The idealistic stories presented by a diverse cast, peppered with morals and antiviolence themes, were an appealing alternative to daily events for those who enjoyed the show between 1966 and 1969.

The world into which Star Trek was born

Americans who grew up during the 1940s and took control of the nation in 1960 were raised with the expectation that they would win at any endeavor undertaken. The victories of World War II and the growth of American industry and technology taught them so. That belief helped propel the Apollo missions to the moon. Americans expected technology to take them there when President Kennedy proposed the expedition. Following World War II, military leaders expected to win. Doctors felt it was only a matter of time before they found the cure for disease. The public began to expect that in time those same doctors would conquer death itself. Social scientists expected to be able to explain how society worked and politicians believed they could use that knowledge and the wealth it created to vanquish poverty without taxing the middle or upper classes. It was believed a national consensus could be reached between the disparate populations in America. Events of the 1960s would shatter those beliefs.[17]

The election of John F. Kennedy to the presidency in 1961 launched a period of high optimism in the United States. He challenged Americans in his inaugural address, "Ask not what your country can do for you; ask what you can do for your country." Kennedy's track record was impressive despite the Bay of Pigs debacle. His "New Frontier" social program proposed that Americans, like their predecessors on the frontier in the nineteenth century, would have to rise to new challenges including the creation of equal opportunity for everyone. He pushed for civil rights. The president led the nation through the Cuban Missile Crisis and negotiated the Nuclear Test Ban Treaty with Britain and the Soviet Union in 1963. The young and vigorous image he and his wife Jacqueline projected dazzled much of the nation. Many felt that optimism died with him when he was assassinated on November 22, 1963.[18]

The African-American civil rights movement led by Dr. Martin Luther King, Jr. in the 1950s and 1960s worked to shatter the "Jim Crow" laws in force in the 1960s. African-Americans were denied the vote, were kept from all but the lowliest jobs, and were set apart from the rest of American society in as many ways as was possible. Pivotal events in the movement occurred in the spring of 1963 when Dr. King carried his drive to eliminate segregation laws to Birmingham, Alabama, the largest industrial city of the South. Thousands of young Americans marched into downtown, picketing stores closed to them. Squads of police attacked the nonviolent marchers with fire hoses and dogs, arresting many. News cameras caught the horrific scenes and broadcast them across the nation, stirring an uproar against such flagrant brutality. Birmingham's business leaders, under overwhelming public pressure, repealed the Jim Crow practices in their stores. This event was followed on August 28, 1963, the one hundredth anniversary of the Emancipation Proclamation, with a Freedom March for Jobs and Freedom on Washington, D.C. to demonstrate for full and equal citizenship. One quarter of a million people, African-American and white alike, peacefully demonstrated for new civil rights legislation.[19]

President Kennedy was struggling with how to persuade a reticent Congress to pass the much needed new civil rights legislation when he was assassinated in Dallas, Texas. No event had so devastated the nation since the bombing of Pearl Harbor in 1941.

Vice President Lyndon B. Johnson assumed the presidency following the assassination and, in 1964, persuaded Congress to pass the Civil Rights Act. Johnson also pushed through the Voting Rights Act and launched proposals to aid the poor in a package dubbed his "War on Poverty."[20]

However, Vietnam overshadowed Johnson's social legislation. A former colony in the French Empire, the northern half of Vietnam, under a nationalist-Communist regime, threw off French rule in 1954. President Eisenhower refused to send American combat troops in to aid the French. Instead, during the late 1950s, several thousand American military advisers were sent to South Vietnam, a country run by proud but weak leaders who were especially good at making enemies for themselves. President Kennedy upped the ante in the early 1960s, sending 13,000 more advisers as conditions worsened. Early in the Johnson administration, the president reported North Vietnam had fired on two American warships in the Gulf of Tonquin. The president responded by bombing North Vietnam. In 1965, Johnson sent in combat ground troops. By 1968 more than half a million Americans were fighting in the cities and jungles of South Vietnam. America was ensnared in a war that would bitterly divide the nation at home, a war it would not win.[21]

Reflecting on the years Star Trek first appeared, Dorothy (D.C.) Fontana — one of the writers and story editors for the original series — stated, "It seemed like there was a hell of a lot of trouble in the world and it was a time there might not have been a whole lot of hope in America. And here comes this series that says mankind is better than we might think."[22]

Star Trek arrives

These were the turbulent times during which Eugene Wesley Roddenberry (1926-1991) conceived of and first developed Star Trek in 1963. Gene Roddenberry, the son of an army sergeant, flew eighty-nine B-17 bombing missions in the Pacific during World War II. Following the war, Roddenberry signed on as a pilot with Pan American Airlines, flying internationally. In his spare time, he wrote articles predominantly for a variety of aviation magazines.

In 1949 Gene Roddenberry returned to Los Angeles, this time to write television scripts. However, being ahead of his time in an industry that had yet to move to the west coast, Roddenberry joined the Los Angeles Police force to make ends meet. In this position he was promoted to sergeant and speech writer for the Police Chief.[23]

In 1951, Roddenberry would sell his first television script. By 1954, he had become successful enough as a script writer to leave his position on the police force for a full-time writing career. At that point he had written for Dragnet, the Four Star Theater, The Goodyear Theater, and the Kaiser Aluminum Hour, among others. Between 1957 and 1963, he wrote for the Have Gun, Will

Travel series — two of those years as the head writer. In the early 1960s, he also married Majel Barrett (who would play Nurse Christine Chapel on Star Trek, Lwaxanna Troi in Star Trek: The Next Generation, and provide the voice of Federation computers everywhere throughout the various Star Trek series to come).[24]

In 1963, Roddenberry would have accrued a substantial enough reputation for NBC to pick up a show of his own creation about American Marines entitled The Lieutenant. By the time The Lieutenant premiered, Gene Roddenberry had run afoul of television network executive's reticence to deal with substantive or political issues on the air. NBC repeatedly refused to allow Roddenberry to air social commentary of any sort. In the middle of the first season, NBC refused to broadcast, or pay the production costs of, an episode on racism within the armed services. Roddenberry came to the conclusion that the only way he was going to be able to take on important issues of the day — while having them both paid for and aired — was to disguise them within the trappings of a science fiction series.[25]

Later that year, Roddenberry developed the Star Trek series and spent ten months trying to interest studios and television networks in the project. Ironically, it would be NBC that would pick up the new series. The show centered its attentions on the crews' interactions, dealing with present day issues in a science fiction setting, and grounded as much as possible in present day reality. Characters with abilities far beyond the human norm were avoided since these were beyond the audiences ability to empathize with.

Roddenberry strove to keep the interactions of the crew believable and hoped the audience would be caught up in their lives. If the audience actually cared about what became of the crew, the series had a stronger chance for survival. He also was determined not to have the series tampered with and rewritten in concept by the network itself, or anyone else. This would create problems between Roddenberry and his writers during the early episodes of Star Trek: The Next Generation, as will be seen later.[26]

Journey to Babel party scene. Note the Saurian brandy bottle. Star Trek Galore, 1976. *Courtesy of the Collection of Jeff Maynard — New Eye Studio*

The look of the ship was to be different from any previously conceived. The interiors were to be familiar and unintimidating, a place viewers could get to know and recognize as they traveled through it. As for the exterior, Gene Roddenberry described what he was looking for to Matt Jefferies, the artist responsible for the ship's design in the following way, "I don't want to see any rockets. I don't want to see any flying saucers. I don't want to see any planes. I don't want to see any jets. I don't want to see any wings. Just make her look like she's got

power."[27] The exterior of this starship was also to be kept plain. That way a variety of colored lights could be projected onto its surface to represent different environments through which the ship travelled.

Roddenberry's starship and her crew were to steer clear of situations and machinery which did not have some grounding in the present day laws of physics. For his first pilot attempt, "The Cage," Roddenberry went so far as to have professional scientists — ranging from aeronautical engineers to physicists — read the early drafts and provide their input concerning how to tell a reasonably accurate future tale of space travel.[28]

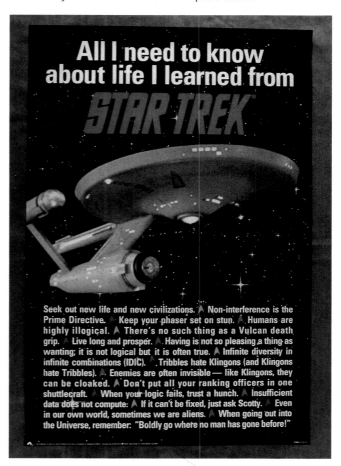

"All I need to know about life I learned from Star Trek" poster by Portal Publications, 1992. *Courtesy of the Collection of Jeff Maynard — New Eye Studio*

The first pilot was outlined June 29, 1964, filmed in late November and December of 1964 and submitted to network executives at NBC in February of 1965. The cast and names used were very different from the one fans would come to know and love. Captain Christopher Pike (Jeffrey Hunter) commanded the starship Yorktown and was supported by Number One (Majel Barrett) as his first officer. The ship's science officer was the familiar Mr. Spock (Leonard Nimoy), but the physician was an older man named Philip Boyce (John Hoyt) who never once uttered the familiar line "Damn it Jim - or Chris in this case - I'm a doctor, not a ..."

Network executives thoroughly enjoyed watching the pilot, applauding when it concluded. They all proclaimed it to be a fine piece of work with strong creative and technical qualities. Then they turned it down. Well written and produced it was, but the executives felt "The Cage" lacked action and was far too intellectual for their viewers. This pilot was too highbrow for the "Wagon Train to the stars" Roddenberry had promised them in his pitch.

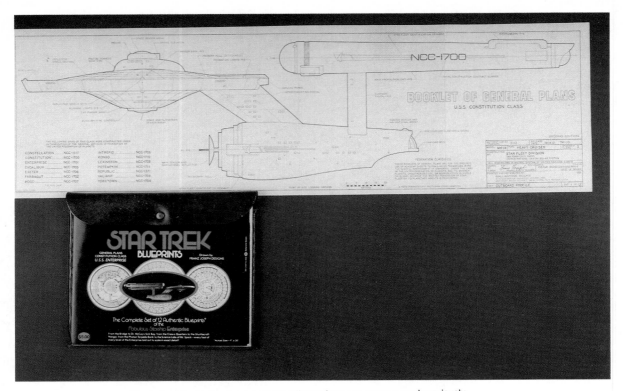

The look of the Enterprise was to be different from any space vessel previously conceived. Franz Joseph designed the first licensed Star Trek blueprints, by Ballantine in 1975, which inspired a tidal wave of imaginative variations. *Courtesy of the Collection of Marc A. Snyder*

Postcards with Captain Kirk (William Shatner) & Mr. Spock (Leonard Nimoy). Gene Roddenberry had first thought Spock should have red skin to enhance his exotic look; however, in the late 1960s there were many black & white TVs on the market. That red skin would appear as if Nimoy were wearing blackface makeup. Once this technical difficulty was pointed out, the idea of a red-faced Spock was dropped. *Courtesy of the Collection of John E. Balbach*

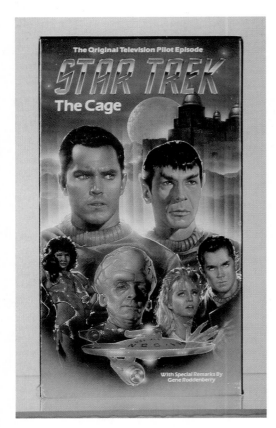

"The Cage," the Star Trek series premier that wasn't. *Courtesy of the Collection of Jeff Maynard — New Eye Studio*

NBC had also been uncomfortable with some of the show's characters. In test screenings, the commanding presence of Number One portrayed by a woman was roundly rejected by men and women alike. Women felt Number One was too annoying and pushy. Mr. Spock also gave the network qualms. His appearance, with the pointy ears and arched brows, was so devilish they feared their sponsors would be frightened off. However, on the merits of the show they sent Roddenberry back to take a second crack at it.[29]

Roddenberry went back and delivered three scripts as potential second pilots, "The Omega Glory," "Mudd's Women," and "Where No Man Has Gone Before." Roddenberry wrote the first two himself. The third was penned by Samuel Peeples. All three were action packed episodes and much more to NBC's liking. In June of 1965, they selected "Where No Man Has Gone Before" as the script for the second pilot.

Casting and name changes came with the second pilot. Jeffrey Hunter was unavailable and William Shatner replaced him as Captain James T. Kirk commanding the starship Enterprise. Number One disappeared and Mr. Spock remained. James Doohan was presented as Chief Engineer Mongomery Scott and George Takei as Sulu (with all of two lines to deliver) in this episode. The doctor, Dr. Piper, was played by Paul Fix. No special relationship existed between doctor and captain in that first episode. This would change during the first season with the arrival of DeForest Kelley as Dr. Leonard "Bones" McCoy.

The appearance of the show changed some. Mr. Spock was given a more exotic look. Special effects animation including glowing eyes, phaser fire, and the resultant blasts produced were upgraded as well.

In January of 1966 the completed effort was sent to NBC, thoroughly enjoyed, and accepted. This time the executives were given the action, adventure, explosions and special effects that they believed would sell, captivate the public, and gather sponsors. Gene Roddenberry was satisfied as well. He had his chance to make the socio-political statements he desired.

Star Trek's effect

Network enthusiasm would fade as the series ran and failed to produce the ratings or the type of audience NBC needed. However, in three years Star Trek was able to accomplish quite a bit.

On the surface, the series was more fully conceived and far more sophisticated than any previously televised science fiction offering. Ratings issues aside, Star Trek would set the standard against which future efforts in TV sci-fi would be judged.

On a deeper level, the series often dealt with issues substantially more difficult and pertinent than the standard fair of family oriented programming offered in its day. Elements of the show even provided social commentary. For example, the Federation's Prime Directive, insisting on "noninterference" with the natural development (or the wars) of an alien culture, was Roddenberry's negative response to American involvement in Vietnam.

Star Trek also delivered a message of optimism about the future of the human condition which had not long before been commonly felt in America but which during the 1960s was being eroded by brutal events at home and abroad. The public's confidence in a bright future where great things could be accomplished was slipping away in the 1960s and continues to drop off in the 1990s. Star Trek's unfailingly positive outlook continues to be attractive in this climate.

Finally, Star Trek offered an integrated crew with men and women of different nationalities and races working well together. This image, presented during the height of both the Cold War and the Civil Rights movement, had an impact on both the actors and the viewing public alike.

George Takei (Lieutenant Sulu) felt the multi-ethnic casting was significant, "At the time, it was very hard for Asian actors to get cast in anything other than the role of a servant, and I'd made a vow to myself that I'd never play that sort of demeaning character." Nichelle Nichols, who played the black communications officer Uhura, reported a remarkable experience during her tenure. She was ready to quit the show early on; her role was extremely limited. According to Nichols, she was asked to meet a big fan of hers the evening she made that decision at an NAACP meeting. This Star Trek fan was Dr. Martin Luther King, Jr. Hearing she planned to quit, Dr. King advised against it, "Nichelle, you can't do this. Don't you know that the world, for the first time, is beginning to see us as equals? Your character ...is... intelligent, strong, capable, and a wonderful role model, not just for black people, but for all people. What you're doing is very, very important, and I'd hate to see you walk away from such a noble task."[30]

Whoopi Goldberg remembers watching the original series, "As a teen, I was a fan. I recognized the multicultural, multiracial aspects, and different people getting along together for a better world. Racial issues have been solved. Male-female problems have been solved. The show is about genuine equality."[31]

This combination of qualities presented during troubled times created a fervent fan loyalty which carried the series seventy-eight episodes on into syndication. These fans (first termed "Trekkies" and now — as many of them have grown older and more respected — "Trekkers") went on to hold large conventions in the 1970s, write innumerable stories based on the series, spawn their own magazines ("fanzines"), collect every bit of Star Trek merchandise they could find, and often created some very convincing props and costumes of their own. This carried the series on into the movies and additional series unprecedented in television history to date.

Endnotes

1. Gene Wright. *The Science Fiction Image. The Illustrated Encyclopedia of Science Fiction in Film. Television, Radio and the Theater.* (New York: Facts On File Publications, 1983), 56.
2. Gene Wright. *The Science Fiction Image.* i-ii.
3. Phil Hardy (ed.). *Science Fiction. The Complete Film Sourcebook.* (New York: William Morrow & Company, Inc., 1984), xiv.
4. Hardy. *Science Fiction.* xi; Wright. *The Science Fiction Image.* i-ii.
5. Hardy. *Science Fiction.* xi.
6. ibid. xi.
7. ibid. xii.
8. Stuart Schneider. *Collecting the Space Race.* (Atglen, PA: Schiffer Publishing Ltd., 1993), 8; & Ted Hake. *Hake's Guide to TV Collectibles.* (Radnor, PA: Wallace-Homestead, 1990), 5.
9. Elizabeth L. Newhouse (ed.) *Inventors and Discoverers. Changing Our World.* (Washington, D.C.: The National Geographic Society, 1988), 212.
10. Schneider. *Collecting the Space Race.* 8.
11. Hardy. *Science Fiction.* xiv.
12. ibid. xiv.
13. Daniel J. Boorstin. *The Americans. The Democratic Experience.* (New York: Vintage Books, 1974), 595.
14. ibid. 594-595.
15. Hardy. *Science Fiction.* 196.
16. ibid. 290; Andrew Chaikin. *A Man On The Moon. The Voyages of the Apollo Astronauts.* (New York: Penguin Books, 1994), 583.
17. Godfrey Hodgson. *America In Our Time: From World War II to Nixon. What Happened And Why.* (New York: Vintage Books, 1978), 463.
18. John Anthony Scott. *The Story of America.* (Washington, D.C.: The National Geographic Society, 1992), 306; E.D. Hirsch, Jr., et al. The Dictionary of Cultural Literacy. (Boston, MA: Houghton Mifflin Company, 1993), 282.
19. Scott. *The Story of America.* 306.
20. ibid. 306.
21. ibid. 308.
22. Zoglin. "Trekking Onward."
23. Wright. *The Science Fiction Image.* 271.
24. ibid. 271.
25. Shatner, et al. *Star Trek Memories.* 26.
26. ibid. 29-30.
27. ibid. 46.
28. ibid. 53.
29. ibid. 79-82.
30. ibid. 104 & 287-288.
31. Zoglin. "Trekking Onward."

Chapter II. Details, Details. Life in the Twenty-Third Century and Beyond

"We're living in a science fiction time. We're swimming in an ocean of technology, and that's why Star Trek, Star Wars and ninety percent of the most successful films of last ten years are science fiction."

— Ray Bradbury[1]

Star Trek, 1966-1969, The Small Screen

The original Star Trek television series, and all of its progeny for that matter, required some extra attention from the viewers. The audience had to take in more than a couple episodes to get a good grasp on who the regulars were among the crew (and which newcomers were just phaser-fodder), which aliens crossed paths with the Enterprise most often, what their affiliation with the Federation was, and which shipboard gadget was doing what at any given moment. This being the case, a brief review of some of the pertinent details of the various shows and movies here should prove helpful when plunging deeply into the collectibles which follow.

The Enterprise was sent forth on its missions by Starfleet Command (the navy of the twenty-third century) for the United Federation of Planets, an alliance of worlds with their central governing body located on Earth. The ship's company included the following cast and crew of regulars: Captain James T. Kirk (William Shatner), First Officer/Science Officer Mr. Spock (Leonard Nimoy), Dr. Leonard McCoy — "Bones" (DeForest Kelley), Chief Engineer Montgomery Scott — "Scotty" (James Doohan), Lieutenant Sulu at the helm (George Takei), Communications Officer Lieutenant Uhura (Nichelle Nichols), Ensign Pavel Chekov (Walter Koenig), Nurse Christine Chapel (Majel Barrett), and Yeoman Janice Rand (Grace Lee Whitney). Dr. McCoy, Lieutenant Uhura,

Spock, Kirk, & McCoy, looking for "A Piece of the Action." *Courtesy of the Collection of Jeff Maynard — New Eye Studio*

Kirk with Tribble troubles. *Courtesy of the Collection of Jeff Maynard — New Eye Studio*

The Crew of the U.S.S. Enterprise, 1991. *Courtesy of the Collection of Jeff Maynard — New Eye Studio*

Mr. Spock in dress uniform. *Courtesy of the Collection of Jeff Maynard — New Eye Studio*

William Shatner and Leonard Nimoy out of uniform and out of character. *Courtesy of the Collection of Jeff Maynard — New Eye Studio*

Mr. Chekov's back, Dr. McCoy, Chief Engineer Scott, & Lt. Uhura. *Courtesy of the Collection of Jeff Maynard — New Eye Studio*

and Yeoman Rand were added during the first season. Mr. Chekov made his appearance at the beginning of the second. Of these characters, the show came to focus on the interactions of the captain, Mr. Spock, and Dr. McCoy. The banter between these three still provide some of the best moments for many fans.

The starship U.S.S. Enterprise, NCC-1701, was the device which propelled the crew across the cosmos throughout the series and was the most costly of special effects. Twenty technicians from the Howard A. Anderson optical effects company produced at least three miniatures for the series. These ranged from a four inch wooden scale model, to a more detailed three foot model, and finally an elaborate fourteen foot model produced from sheet plastic with hardwood engine "nacelles." The fourteen foot model was supported from below with a pipe mounted on a tripod, allowing it to be tipped and turned for the camera. This third model currently hangs in the National Air and Space Museum in Washington, D.C.

The Enterprise vaulted across the cosmos at speeds faster than light on warp engines run by matter-antimatter reactions fueled by dilithium crystals. Ship defenses included phasers, photon torpedoes, and deflector screens or "shields" which saved the crew from certain incineration at the hands of their enemies many times. However, in difficult moments shield number four frequently collapsed and often the engines could not "take much more of this."

Transporters were used to quickly disassemble crewmen in one place and reassemble them elsewhere. This useful special effect was employed regularly, precluding the necessity for bulky space suits and awkward, expensive scenes of crew members floating in space.

Three alien races made more than casual appearances on the show — Vulcans, Klingons, and Romulans. Vulcans were part of the United Federation of Planets; Klingons and Romulans were the Federation's major adversaries. Vulcans were pointy-eared "humanoids" with greater intellectual and physical prowess than humans. They were capable of reading thoughts and incapacitating opponents with a nerve-pinch. Vulcans also resisted emotions at all cost in favor of cold, hard logic. Mr. Spock, the most famous Vulcan, was a half-breed — the result of a mixed marriage between a Vulcan man and a human woman. Spock's ancestry could be considered suspect since Mark Lenard, who played his father Sarek, first appeared in the series as a Romulan captain in "Balance of Terror."

Klingons and Romulans shared a common goal, cosmic empire ... galactic domination. Klingons were brutish arch-foes of the Federation, plying the space lanes in battle cruisers while looking for chances to either board or destroy passing starships. This disagreeable, warlike race was introduced in "Errand of Mercy." The Klingons were the Soviet Union to the Federation's United States. Warfare between the two was held

Sarek (Spock's father, played by Mark Lenard) & Captain Kirk. *Courtesy of the Collection of Jeff Maynard — New Eye Studio*

Kirk, McCoy, Chekov, & a security guard meet the Klingons by Star Trek Galore, 1976. Guess which crew member is least likely to survive this encounter. *Courtesy of the Collection of Jeff Maynard — New Eye Studio*

The Romulans were introduced in the "Balance of Terror" television episode, now available on video tape. *Courtesy of the Collection of Jeff Maynard — New Eye Studio*

in check by a powerful but pacifistic civilization inhabiting the neutral world Organia rather than by the mutually-assured destruction of Cold War nuclear weaponry. In the movies and later series, Klingons have come into an uneasy alliance with the Federation. They have also become far uglier and more flamboyant with improved special effects and increased budgets.

Romulans are another matter. They are the evil, emotional, distant relations of the Vulcans. As such, they appear to be more refined than the Klingons. Romulans have, however, remained constantly belligerent in their dealings with the Federation and have been involved in innumerable border skirmishes. During the original series the Romulans apparently were in a technology swap with the Klingons and were frequently seen flying battle cruisers of Klingon design. Unlike the Klingons, Romulans were stealth fighters who employed a cloaking device which rendered them invisible to Federation ship's sensors. Romulans were first introduced in the episode "Balance of Terror." On Paramount's budget, the Romulans now fly warships of their own design.

Behind the scenes, Star Trek went through changes throughout its three season run. For the first twelve episodes, Gene Roddenberry was directly involved as the producer. Gene L. Coon took over the reins at that point for the rest of the first season. Gene Roddenberry took on the role of executive producer, never again to have direct involvement in the original series. For the second season, John Meredyth Lucas replace Coon and for the third season, Fred Freiberger took over from Lucas as producer of the show. Many feel the first two seasons produced Star Trek's best episodes. William Shatner felt Gene Roddenberry was turning his attentions elsewhere by the third season, letting the show slide.[2]

Animation, 1972-1974

One of the fears fans of the original series had while the show was being produced was that it would be rewritten in a children's format. After all, in the 1960s science fiction on television had always been for younger viewers. This fear was never realized. However, after Star Trek went into syndication a Saturday morning cartoon version of the show was produced from 1972 to 1974. Twenty-two episodes were created with limited animation by Filmation. The voices were those of original cast members William Shatner, Leonard Nimoy, DeForest Kelly, James Doohan, and Nichelle Nichols. Crew members not appearing on the animated series were left out to keep down expenses. D.C. Fontana, who wrote a number of the original live-action episodes, selected the stories produced for this series.[3]

Gene Roddenberry instructed Paramount, in later years, not to consider these animated episodes part of the "official" Star Trek chronicles. The single exception to the rule is an episode entitled "Yesteryear," written by D.C. Fontana and dealing with Spock's youth. However, while older brothers and sisters were off attending the first Star Trek conventions, a new and younger generation of fans was introduced to Star Trek through this cartoon series.[4]

mand of Federation Commander Benjamin Sisko. Together, the inhabitants preside over the wormhole, a stable rift in space offering speedy access to a distant part of the galaxy.

The major players in the cast include: Commander Benjamin Sisko (Avery Brooks), Major Kira Nerys — representative of Bejor and Sisko's second in command (Nana Visitor), Odo — shape shifting alien Chief of Security (Rene Auberjonois), Lieutenant Jadzia Dax — Science Officer, an alien within an alien (Terry Farrell), Dr. Julian Bashir — Chief Medical Officer (Siddig El Fadil), Chief Miles O'Brien — the station's handyman (Colm Meaney), and Quark — Ferengi owner of the stations bar and casino (Armin Shimerman).[13]

Secondary roles include Jake Sisko (Cirroc Lofton), the commander's son and Keiko O'Brien (Rosalind Chao), a botanist & wife of Miles. The irrepressible Lwaxana Troi (Majel Barrett) appears from time-to-time to bedevil Odo.

At the end of the 1994 season, Benjamin Sisko was promoted to Captain. For the 1995 season, Worf (Michael Dorn of The Next Generation cast) joins the crew as an advisor to Captain Sisko; peaceful relations between the Federation and the Klingon Empire crumble to enliven the series and draw in fans of the cancelled Next Generation series.

The largest sets in the show include "Ops" (the command center or the station's equivalent of the bridge), Sisko's office, various living quarters, the sick bay, Odo's office, the promenade, and Quark's bar. In the show's early incarnation, the only craft the crew had to explore their surroundings with were a couple of "runabouts" — bulked up shuttlecraft of sorts. In the 1994-95 season, the Defiant, the Federation's first ship designed strictly for warfare, was added to spice up the action. Gene Roddenberry had preferred to avoid space battles where he could, so this may be seen as a clear departure from his line of thinking by Rick Berman (to say nothing about that crumbling Klingon/Federation relationship).

Villains making life difficult for the station's personnel on a fairly regular basis include the previously mentioned Cardassians (who would like to get the station back), the Romulans, and a ruthless organization from the other side of the wormhole known as the "Founders." The Founders are shape shifters, the race Odo came from but has no memory of, dedicated to enforcing a peace over other species (non-shape shifting "solids") who had persecuted them in the past. As the story stands, the Founders are making inroads into Federation, Cardassian, and Romulan space as well in preparation for a hostile take over on this side of the galaxy.

The Maquis, a group of rebel humans and Bajorans dissatisfied with a precarious peace treaty between the Federation and the Cardassians, add to the troubles facing DS9. Members of this group also ship out in Star Trek: Voyager.

Star Trek: Voyager

Voyager is the newest offering in the Star Trek line. It is the mainstay of the new United/Paramount Network and the first Star Trek series to feature a woman as captain. It is also the first to be set far from Federation home turf, some seventy thousand light years across the galaxy. The basic premise for the show is that the Federation starship USS Voyager, and a rebel Maquis ship it is pursuing, have been instantly yanked across those thousands of light years by an alien force seeking to save a world it had damaged. The Maquis ship is destroyed and the combined Voyager and Maquis crews struggle to shave time off the seventy years required for the Voyager to make the return trip home. The crew must also manage to keep their ship together without any chance for dry dock refits along the way.

Nine crew members form the core of the show, including: Captain Kathryn Janeway (Kate Mulgrew), Commander Chakotay — tatooed Native American, former Maquis Captain

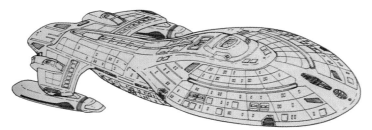

An early look at the U.S.S. Voyager, from the newest of the Star Trek series. *Courtesy of the author's collection*

and now Janeway's First Officer (Robert Beltran), Tom Paris — Voyager pilot, a former Federation officer turned Maquis (Robert Duncan McNeill), Tuvok — Tactical/Security Officer, captain's confidant, and the first Vulcan to serve as a series regular since Spock (Tim Russ), Harry Kim — recent Star Fleet graduate working as Ops/Communications officer (Garrett Wang), B'Elanna Torres — half human, half Klingon former Maquis and current Chief of Engineering (Roxann Biggs-Dawson), Neelix — a Talaxian picked up on the trip working as cook, guide, and handy man (Ethan Phillips), Kes — Neelix's Ocampa lady love interest with a nine year life span who works with the ship's doctor (Jennifer Lien), and the emotionless, holographic emergency doctor (Robert Picardo), devoid of bedside manner, who remained nameless in the first season and is forced to stand in permanently for his human counterpart, killed in the first episode.[14]

The Voyager is the smallest Federation ship to ply the small screen yet, carrying a crew of roughly 140 to 150. All the familiar sets are present from the bridge, to engineering, to a holodeck. The character of the show is a decided departure from the shows under Gene Roddenberry's control. Roddenberry was decidely against friction among Federation crew members. Rick Berman felt this limited dramatic potential and possible story lines. Therefore, he threw the two cultures, Federation and Maquis, together and let them get into trouble from time to time. This is a darker view of the twenty-fourth century than seen in the past.[15]

Two seasons into the series, Voyager had yet to find many villains presenting recurring threats to the crew. The most familiar foes remained 70,000 light years out of reach and John de Lancie (Q) was, for a time, a regular in another series. What empires will rise to the occasion to take the place of the Klingons and Romulans remains to be seen.

Up to date with all the shows and movies, it is time to move on to the ever expanding world of Star Trek collectibles.

Endnotes

1. Zoglin. "Trekking Onward."
2. David Gerrold. *The World of Star Trek.* (New York: Ballantine Books, 1973), 32-33; Sue Cornwell & Mike Kott. *The Official Price Guide: Star Trek And Star Wars Collectibles.* (New York: House of Collectibles, 1991), 3-4.
3. Wright. *The Science Fiction Image.* 287.
4. Michael Okuda & Denise Okuda. *Star Trek Chronology. The History of the Future.* (New York: Pocket Books, 1993), vi.
5. Cornwell & Kott. *The Official Price Guide: Star Trek And Star Wars Collectibles.* 5.
6. ibid. 5-6.
7. ibid. 6-7; Hardy. *Science Fiction.* 377.
8. Cornwell & Kott. *The Official Price Guide: Star Trek And Star Wars Collectibles.* 8; Variety Staff Writers, et al. *Variety Movie Guide.* (New York: Prentise Hall General Reference, 1992).
9. ibid. 10; ibid.
10. LeGuin. "My Appointment with the Enterprise. An Appreciation." 32.
11. Michael Walsh. "The Torch Has Passed Off-Camera, Too." *Time, Inc.* (transmitted to America On Line, November 20, 1994); Cornwell & Kott. *The Official Price Guide: Star Trek And Star Wars Collectibles.* 11; Michael Logan. "The Magnificent Seven." *TV Guide* 42(20) #2146, May 14-20, 1994, 12-13.
12. Logan. "The Magnificent Seven." 20.
13. Zoglin. "Trekking Onward."
14. Michael Logan. "A 'Star Trek' is Born. Voyager." *TV Guide* 42(41) 2167, October 8-14, 1994, 19.
15. ibid. 19.

Chapter III. Star Trek-
The Collectibles

Presented here is a survey of the ever increasing and extremely popular range of Star Trek collectibles available today. These objects and artifacts range from the model kits, comic books, and action figures produced in the late sixties and the mid-seventies to the almost endless array of materials currently available. A comprehensive listing would be next to impossible as new materials are being regularly produced.

When considering where in the Star Trek universe to begin collecting, first narrow your scope. The very best advice is to collect items which you will enjoy most and leave their future value as collectibles up to fate. Here is a listing of the general categories of collectibles available on the market today.

Categories of Collectibles:

Action & Collectors' Figures
Badges & Buttons
Banks
Blueprints
Books
Bumper Stickers & Auto Accessories
Calendars
Cels & Storyboards
Ceramics
Certificates & Diplomas
Christmas Ornaments
Clothing & Accessories
Coins & Medallions
Comics
Convention Program Books
Costumes, Patterns, & Makeup Kits
Decals & Stickers
Fanzines
Film & Video
Games & Accessories
Glasswares & Tankards
Greeting Cards
Household Wares
Jewelry
Lunch Boxes
Magazines
Models & Model Rocket Kits
Music (Sheet)
Patches
Pewter Figurines
Postage Stamps
Postcards
Posters
Props & Prop Reproductions
Promotional Items
Puzzles
Records, Tapes, & Compact Discs
School & Office Supplies
Scripts
Stills, Slides, & Photographs
Toys & Crafts
Trading Cards & Stickers[1]

When working within a limited budget, decide which category or categories of collectibles interest you most and specialize in those. Part of that decision will be determined by whether you are a fan of only one of the Star Trek series or of many.

If unsure which of several collectibles lines most appeals to you, here are some helpful hints as to what makes a

Four of the many, many books available about Star Trek. *Courtesy of the Collection of John E. Balbach*

really good collectible. To many collectors today, collectibles are seen as more than artifacts and souvenirs to be gathered for personal satisfaction alone, they are considered investments. As such, the best investments interest more than a single group of collectors. Action figures fall into this category. Star Trek action figures are of interest to Trekkers, science fiction collectors, television toy collectors, and others. The greater the numbers of collectors interested in a limited number of items, the greater the value of those items is likely to be.

A good collectible is also one that has been (or is being) produced only in limited numbers. Plastic toys make for safe investments. They are produced by skilled technicians working with expensive molds in a very competitive field. Toy manufacturers are required to change their product lines often to keep up with their competitors.[2]

Toy manufacturers such as Playmates are well aware of the fact that collectors are looking for limited runs of toys to collect. All of Playmates' Star Trek toys are now numbered editions with new items to any given line added regularly as older items are discontinued.

Many collectors speculate on toys readily available in the stores today. It can be great sport predicting which of today's toys will become tomorrow's hot collectibles.

In the past thirty years, a number of items officially licensed by Paramount have come to be recognized as top Star Trek collectibles. A sampling from each decade will give you an idea of what categories of collectibles you might like to aim for.

In the 1960s, while Star Trek was airing on NBC, very few items were manufactured. Those few are now among the most valued and sought after by today's collectors. By year, they include:

1966: AMT's model kit of the U.S.S. Enterprise, the first Star Trek collectible produced.

1967: Remco's Astrocruiser, a generic space toy with a Star Trek sticker added which is now very rare (never mind that there never was an astrocruiser on the series).

1967: Leaf Star Trek trading cards — black and white cards, the originals are among the most valued trading cards ever produced (watch out for the later reprints).

1967: Gold Key Star Trek #1, the first Star Trek comic which launched the Enterprise crew nonstop across thirty years in this format.

In the 1970s, merchandisers realized the depth of interest among fans in the syndicated series and began producing items in earnest. The speed with which fans purchased this merchandise helped encourage Paramount to produce a Star Trek film. The majority of these items were produced in 1975 and 1976 and include:

1975: Ballantine's Star Trek Blueprints. Created by the late Franz Joseph, these were the first "official" designs of the Enterprise released by Paramount. They inspired quite a few to pick up drafting equipment.

1975: Mego action figures, the first in the Star Trek action figure line and the favorites of many collectors.

1975: Mego U.S.S. Enterprise Action Playset, the bridge and transporter became the perfect backdrop for their figures.

1976: Mego's Star Trek Mission to Gamma VI playset, another set for their figures. This one sat on the store shelves then but can not be easily found today.

1976: Ballantine's Star Trek Concordance by Bjo Trimble. Written for fans, this book preceded the Pocket Books' volumes describing the Star Trek universe today.

1976: Topps Star Trek trading cards, the first color series for Star Trek, an 88-card set considered very valuable today.

1978: Dr. Pepper Star Trek set of four glasses, not to be confused with their more easily found 1976 set which featured art of the animated series. The 1978 set was well drawn and quite rare.

1979: Star Trek: The Motion Picture one-sheet poster. Being the first and colorful, this one is the most valuable of the movie posters.

1979: South Bend Star Trek Electronic U.S.S. Enterprise — while one of many toys produced for the first film, this one is modular, allowing for the creation of several starship configurations.

In the 1980s, Star Trek movies continued and Star Trek: The Next Generation first aired. This gave fans more collectibles than ever before.

1980: Mego's Star Trek: The Motion Picture aliens. This is a rare set of aliens released almost entirely overseas. They are based on aliens briefly seen throughout the film. Aliens in action figures tend to become better collectibles than the main characters, fewer of them are produced.

1980: Bantam Book's *Star Trek Maps,* a technical guide and poster set including an "Introduction to Navigation."

1987: Hamilton's Star Trek original episode plates. A second series of plates for Hamilton and by far the favorites among collectors as they display choice scenes from the best original television episodes.

1987: General Mills' U.S.S. Enterprise-D premium. A cereal premium and the first Next Generation collectible produced.

1988: Galoob's Star Trek: The Next Generation action figures. Galoob was the first licensee to produce Next Generation action figures; their second series of aliens are now very valuable.

In the 1990s, Star Trek is now a licensing super power.

1991: Franklin Mint's die cast U.S.S. Enterprise. Produced for Star Trek's 25th Anniversary, this is considered one of the finest representations available of the classic starship.

1991: Hallmark's U.S.S. Enterprise Christmas tree ornament, produced for the 25th Anniversary year, this is a wildly popular collectible.

1993: Pfaltzgraff's U.S.S. Enterprise bone china table settings designed as replicas of those seen in Star Trek VI have quadrupled in value since their release.

1993: Playmates classic Star Trek Collector's Figure set. Playmates produces popular, detailed toys.

1994: Masterpiece Replicas U.S.S. Enterprise-D. This brass, fiber-optically lit, two foot long model of the starship (with its limited run of 5000 and a hefty $2000 dollar price tag) was collectible the moment it was first produced.[3]

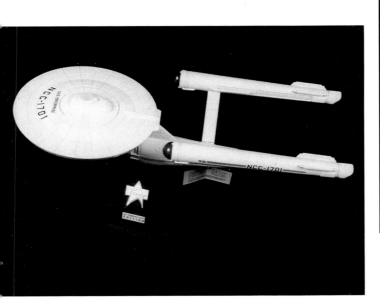

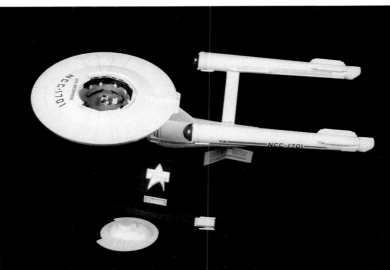

Star Trek U.S.S. Enterprise NCC-1701 25th anniversary model with detailed bridge by Franklin Mint, 1991. *Courtesy of the Collection of Jeff Maynard — New Eye Studio*

Conversely, items which may be easily manufactured and cheaply reproduced in abundance are unlikely to become highly valued collectibles. Buttons, blue prints, costume jewelry, patches, posters, scripts, stills, and tee shirts all tend to fall into this category.

Fan produced art is everywhere, painted coconuts w/images of Spock & Kirk from Hawaii. *Courtesy of the Collection of Jeff Maynard — New Eye Studio*

Original artwork, largely fan produced, makes for interesting collecting. As seen at conventions, it comes in a wide variety of forms including paintings, jewelry, leatherwork, and miniature figures. Some nationally known science fiction artists have produced pieces for Star Trek which command high prices. The works of "unknowns" are much more reasonable.[4]

It is best to steer clear of objects advertised as original movie props. The actual props were and are still the property of Paramount (whose legal department takes a dim view of theft), are next to impossible to come by, and would be just as difficult to authenticate. Actually, an original prop probably would not have a great deal of visual appeal on close inspection either. These things were not designed to be scrutinized.[5]

Once you have decided what to collect, there are a number of outlets available to you. Modern items currently on the market may be purchased at stores or through advertisements in magazines. However, if you wish to see a large cross-section of what is available in the collectibles marketplace firsthand, or if you are looking for older and rarer items, either seek out dealers or go to Star Trek conventions. Dealers may be easily located through advertisements in fan magazines. Dealers whose ads appear consistently in the magazines are the most likely to be reputable. Some dealers provide detailed catalogs of their inventory, others take want lists from clients. Make sure dealers you work with are willing to refund your money if their product does not live up to the descriptions provided.

Star Trek conventions are a little more difficult to find. They have been held in large cities since 1972. In 1974 there was a split between professionally run and fan run conventions. The professionally run conventions are larger and draw more dealers. Advertisements in the papers and on television usually precede large conventions. Official fan club magazines and science fiction magazines run advertisements for the conventions

Another consideration in today's collecting marketplace involves the changing relationship between Star Trek's producers and the fans. When Gene Roddenberry was alive, it was possible for an enthusiastic fan to reach an agreement with him personally (for a relatively small fee) to produce a limited number of prop or costume reproductions based on those seen on the television shows. Fan produced schematics of Federation vessels were also permitted and produced. Now, however, Trekkers find themselves facing a very different attitude about these items in the "post-Roddenberry" era. It has been reported to this author that attempts to reach similar agreements with Paramount are most often doomed to failure. Reports on the internet

state that Paramount representatives at Star Trek conventions have ordered fans wearing unlicensed uniforms or carrying props of their own design to remove them immediately or suffer the consequences.

Michael Dorn (Lt. Worf on The Next Generation) speaks of the changing attitudes in Star Trek's post-Roddenberry years from an actor's viewpoint, "There was a different feeling when we first came on board. If there was an answer you needed, you could always go right to Gene-and the answer made sense. It was well thought out because it was his vision. And we're kind of a conglomerate now. We're lost in the machinery."[6]

Classic Tricorder toy by Playmates (left) next to a full-sized fan created Tricorder from the original series. Both have working lights and sound effects. *Courtesy of the Collection of Jeff Maynard — New Eye Studio*

as well. Also, with access to the internet, convention schedules for the next few months can be found posted within fan club bulletin boards. There are no guarantees the conventions will stick to the posted schedules, but the internet bulletin boards do give you the means for some advanced planning.

Dealer rooms are large attractions at conventions. Shop around, often several dealers will carry the items you desire and prices do vary. While deciding what to buy, consider the condition of the individual items as you find them. Today, collectors have become as interested in the packaging of a collectible as in the object itself. When considering the condition of the collectible, the package it comes in plays an integral role. An unopened blister packed action figure is considered far more valuable than the figure alone.

Once you have purchased an item, resist all temptation to remove the price sticker from the packaging. This sticker does not affect the value of a collectible unless it damages the box when it is removed.[7]

As you begin to purchase the pieces you enjoy, take care to protect your collection. Keep your collection out of direct sunlight to avoid fading and discoloration. Extra care must be taken when collecting paper products. Not only should areas of direct sunlight be avoided, but damp areas where paper products will be exposed to moisture or musty places where they will accrue excessive dust build up should be shunned as well. Do not use adhesives when hanging paper products. Posters, when displayed, should be framed or at least backed with cardboard and encased in shrink wrap. When posters are not displayed, they are best stored loosely rolled up in cardboard tubes.

Books, comics, and trading cards should be stored in plastic holders available through comic book shops and mail-order companies. Never wrap rubber bands around trading cards. The rubber bands will dent the cards and, as the bands age, they will both stain and adhere to card surfaces.

The collectibles illustrated and listed in this book are divided between the shows as follows:

Star Trek — The Original Series & The First Six Films (covering all items, old and new, based on the original series)
Star Trek: The Next Generation & Star Trek: Generations
Star Trek: Deep Space Nine
Star Trek: Voyager
Crossover Products (collectibles combining two or more of the Star Trek television series or films)

Within these divisions, the collectibles are organized around the categories of collectibles previously listed in this chapter.

The pricing is in United States dollars. Values vary immensely according to the condition of each piece, the location of the market, the overall quality of the design and manufacture, and the enthusiasms of the collecting audience at a particular time. Prices in the Midwest differ from those in the West or East, and those at Star Trek conventions will vary from those in dealer's catalogues, specialty shops, and toy or hobby stores.

All these factors make it impossible to create absolutely accurate price listings, but we can offer a guide to realistic pricing (for items in their original packaging when appropriate). Good luck!

This interest in packaging dates back to 1928, when Richard B. Franken and Carroll B. Larrabee published *Packages That Sell.* They stated that one of the most important things a package could do was to sell the product within it.[8] This led to all sorts of colorful packaging. Today, the detailed, colorful boxes and blister packs are so impressive, it can be difficult to tell where the packaging ends and the product begins. This is well illustrated with Playmates Classic Star Trek Collectors' Figures Set. The inside of the box is designed to look like the bridge of the original Enterprise with the crew standing around it. Now, exactly where does that package end and the product begin?

Playmates Classic Star Trek, Classic Collector Figure Set, Collector's Edition No. 032546 of 150000. Where does the box end and the product begin? *Courtesy of the Collection of Bob Hoag*

Mego Star Trek first series action figures (the first to blaze this TV series action figure trail in 1975), 8" high: top: Capt. Kirk; Mr. Spock; Dr. McCoy; bottom: Mr. Scott; Lt. Uhura; Klingon. *Courtesy of the Collection of Jeff Maynard — New Eye Studio*

ACTION FIGURES, COLLECTORS' FIGURES, & DOLLS

Action Figures From The Original Series

First Star Trek Action Figures—Mego

Mego was the industry leader in action figures when they introduced the first Star Trek action figures in 1975. Their early Star Trek 8" plastic figures had rivet-fastened bodies. These were quickly replaced with more detailed bodies made entirely of plastic. All the figures are costumed, have accessories, and were packaged in blister packs. They were produced in three series. The second and third series are all aliens. The third series is the most difficult to find. The Andorian and Romulan from this final series are especially fine.

First Series

- ❑ Captain Kirk: with belt, communicator, & phaser. $50-55
- ❑ Mr. Spock: with belt, communicator, tricorder, & phaser. $50-55
- ❑ Dr. McCoy: with tricorder. $150-165
- ❑ Mr. Scott: with belt, communicator, & phaser. $185-200
- ❑ Lt. Uhura: with tricorder. $95-105
- ❑ Klingon: with belt, communicator & phaser. Brown costume from animated series. $50-55

Captain Kirk action figure by Mego. *Courtesy of the Collection of Jeff Maynard — New Eye Studio*

Mr. Spock action figure by Mego. This blister pack is signed by Leonard Nimoy. *Courtesy of the Collection of Jeff Maynard — New Eye Studio*

Dr. McCoy action figure by Mego. *Courtesy of the Collection of Jeff Maynard — New Eye Studio*

Mr. Scott action figure by Mego. *Courtesy of the Collection of Jeff Maynard — New Eye Studio*

Klingon action figure by Mego. *Courtesy of the Collection of Jeff Maynard — New Eye Studio*

Lt. Uhura action figure by Mego. *Courtesy of the Collection of Jeff Maynard — New Eye Studio*

Second Series

- ❑ Cheron: black & white alien. Chemicals coloring the body are unstable and stain the clothing over time. This will not devalue the figure. $135-150
- ❑ Gorn: reptilian with phaser. $300-330
- ❑ The Keeper: barefoot, blue, light colored robes, with head reminiscent of false Balok in "The Corbomite Maneuver." $145-160
- ❑ Neptunian: green amphibian, webbed hands and feet, never seen in Star Trek series. $125-140

Mego Aliens second series action figures, 8" high. Mego provided the first Star Trek action figures. Top: The Keeper; The Gorn; Cheron; bottom: Talos; Andorian; Mugato.

Cheron action figure by Mego. *Courtesy of the Collection of Jeff Maynard — New Eye Studio*

The Gorn action figure by Mego. *Courtesy of the Collection of Jeff Maynard — New Eye Studio*

The Keeper action figure by Mego. *Courtesy of the Collection of Jeff Maynard — New Eye Studio*

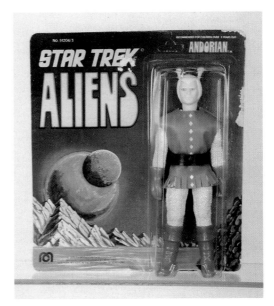

Mego Aliens out of their blister packs: top: Romulan with metallic helmet, red phaser, & communicator - $200-1000; Neptunian, a green lizard monster which never appeared on Star Trek - one of two figures never appeared on show but are valuable none the less - $200-500; Keeper - the other figure never appearing on the series - $200-300; Klingon, shown without the red phaser & communicator belt (same accessories as the Romulan's) - $15-50; bottom: Andorian - Romulan, Andorian, & Mugatos are the three most valued figures in that order - ranging from $200-900; Charon, white & black faced; Talosian - value $200-500. *Courtesy of the Collection of Jeff Maynard — New Eye Studio*

Andorian action figure by Mego. *Courtesy of the Collection of Jeff Maynard — New Eye Studio*

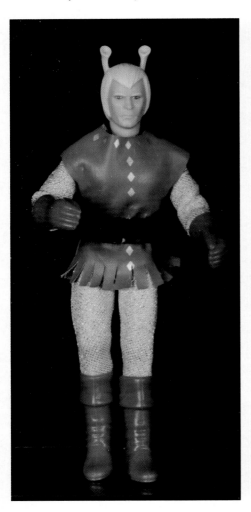

Talos action figure by Mego. *Courtesy of the Collection of Jeff Maynard — New Eye Studio*

Mego paid a lot of attention to details in their 8" tall action figures, as may be seen here with the Andorian figure. *Courtesy of the Collection of Jeff Maynard — New Eye Studio*

Mugato action figure by Mego. *Courtesy of the Collection of Jeff Maynard — New Eye Studio*

Imposter Figures
Cleverly crafted one-of-a-kind imposters made to look like the Mego Aliens. Note on the back the inclusion of Khan as appearing in Star Trek II which was designed to give away these clever fakes.

❏ Harry Mudd   market value
❏ Orion Slave Girl   market value

Recent Figures

PLAYMATES, Classic Star Trek Collector's Figure Set
Playmates entered the action figures line in 1992, beginning with Next Generation figures. Their line of small action figures measure approximately 4 1/2" tall. To this line they added a cleverly boxed collector's set of the "classic" original crew. The box is an integral part of the set, as its interior (viewed through a front window) is modeled as the Enterprise bridge.

❏ Classic Star Trek Collector's Figure Set: includes figures
of Kirk, Spock, McCoy, Chekov, Scott, Sulu, and Uhura $60-70

PLAYMATES, Star Trek Collectors Series
Playmates extended its line of small Star Trek action figures (see below beginning in The Next Generation) with 9 1/2" high Command and Starfleet Collectors Series "classic" Captain Kirk figures (Next Generation & Deep Space Nine figures were also produced as part of this series - see appropriate sections). This may drive up demand for the earlier Mego figures

Command Edition 1994

❏ Kirk: in classic uniform with Type II phaser, communicator,
tricorder, base, & collector card. $25-50

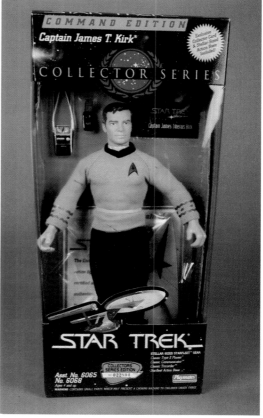

Star Trek Collector Series, Command Edition Captain James T. Kirk by Playmates, 1994. *Courtesy of the Collection of Jeff Maynard — New Eye Studio*

Clever Harry Mudd and the Orion Slave Girl imposter figures made to look like the Aliens Collection by Mego, from the mid-1970s. One-of-a-kind figures with the movie Khan in gray hair on the back rather than his younger TV image. *Courtesy of the Collection of Jeff Maynard — New Eye Studio*

Star Trek Collector Series, Starfleet Edition Captain James T. Kirk in original series dress uniform by Playmates, 1995. *Courtesy of the Collection of Jeff Maynard — New Eye Studio*

Large Porcelain figures, (14" high average), by R.J. Ernst (in business from 1966-1988). Includes basic cast, Kirk, Spock, McCoy, Uhura, Sulu, Checkov, & Scotty. Figures included detailed, authentic cloth uniforms, porcelain faces, hands, feet, & porcelain upper torso. *Courtesy of the Collection of Jeff Maynard — New Eye Studio*

Starfleet Edition 1995
- ❑ Kirk: in dress uniform with phaser, communicator, tricorder, base, & "space cap." $25-50

HAMILTON GIFTS PVC Figures
Hamilton Gifts produced series of 3 1/2" tall PVC figurines for the crews of the original series, The Next Generation, Generations, and Deep Space Nine. These are simple, molded, unarticulated figures in full color.

Star Trek Crew
❑	Kirk	$4-5
❑	Spock	$4-5
❑	McCoy	$4-5
❑	Scott	$4-5
❑	Chekov	$4-5
❑	Sulu	$4-5
❑	Uhura	$4-5

Star Trek Aliens
❑	Andorian	$4-5
❑	Gorn	$4-5
❑	Mugato	$4-5
❑	Talosian	$4-5
❑	Telerite	$4-5

Star Trek Dolls

ERNST, Star Trek Doll Collection
Large figures, averaging 14", produced by the R.J. Ernst in 1988 (the firm was in business from 1966-1988). The heads, upper torsos, hands, and feet are porcelain. Soft bodied with cloth uniforms. These dolls (packaged in white cardboard boxes sporting an drawing of the blue logo and original Enterprise) were accompanied with accessories and metal stands.
- ❑ Capt. Kirk: with silver phaser. $150-200

❑	Mr. Spock: with black & gold communicator.	$150-200
❑	Dr. McCoy: with beaker	$150-200
❑	Scott: with communicator & phaser	$150-200
❑	Sulu: with communicator & phaser	$150-200
❑	Chekov: with communicator & phaser	$150-200
❑	Uhura: no accessories	$150-200

HAMILTON GIFTS, Vinyl Dolls
By 1994, Hamilton Gifts was manufacturing a line of 9" - 12" vinyl dolls of characters from Star Trek, The Next Generations, Star Trek: Generations, and Deep Space Nine.

Star Trek — original series characters
❑	Kirk	$10-11
❑	Spock	$10-11
❑	McCoy	$10-11
❑	Scotty	$10-11
❑	Chekov	$10-11
❑	Uhura	$10-11
❑	Sulu	$10-11
❑	Andorian	$10-11
❑	Telosian	$10-11

Star Trek: The Motion Picture Figures

Mego 12" figures
Produced in 1979 for the movie. Poseable figures in costume with equipment.
❑	Kirk: with belt buckle and phaser	$50-55
❑	Spock: with belt buckle and phaser	$50-55
❑	Decker: with belt buckle and phaser	$150-165
❑	Ilia: with necklace and white shoes	$50-55
❑	Arcturian: beige uniform, heavy folds in face	$50-55
❑	Klingon: with movie facial features and uniform	$95-105

Star Trek: The Motion Picture Capt. Kirk by Mego, 1979. *Courtesy of the Collection of Jeff Maynard — New Eye Studio*

Star Trek: The Motion Picture Ilia by Mego, 1979. *Courtesy of the Collection of Jeff Maynard — New Eye Studio*

Star Trek: The Motion Picture Mr. Spock by Mego, 1979. *Courtesy of the Collection of Jeff Maynard — New Eye Studio*

Star Trek: The Motion Picture Arcturian by Mego, 1979. *Courtesy of the Collection of Jeff Maynard — New Eye Studio*

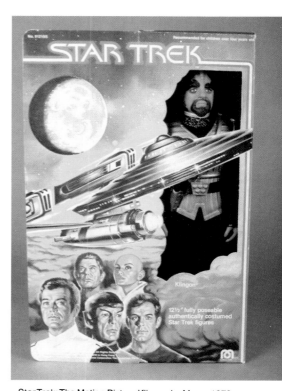

Star Trek: The Motion Picture Klingon by Mego, 1979. *Courtesy of the Collection of Jeff Maynard — New Eye Studio*

Star Trek: The Motion Picture figures by Mego, 1979: top: Kirk, Decker, Ilia; bottom: McCoy, & Kirk. Kirk figure is reversed. *Courtesy of the Collection of Jeff Maynard — New Eye Studio*

Mego 3 3/4" high figures
Also produced for the movie in 1979, packed in blister packs.
First Series

❏	Kirk	$40-45
❏	Spock	$40-45
❏	McCoy	$50-55
❏	Scott	$35-40
❏	Decker	$35-40
❏	Ilia	$20-25

Second Series
Aliens sold mostly overseas although available in the U.S. through Sears mail order.

❏	Arcturian: wrinkled face	$95-105
❏	Betelgeusian: black headpiece, dark skin	$125-150
❏	Klingon: movie features	$115-140
❏	Megarite: black costume, multiple lips	$125-150
❏	Rigellian: white costume, purple skin	$95-105
❏	Zaranite: gray costume, silver mask	$95-105

Knickerbocker Soft Poseable Figures
Plastic heads, soft bodies with Star Trek: The Motion Picture uniforms, 13" high.

❏	Kirk	$35-50
❏	Spock	$35-50

Star Trek III: The Search for Spock

ERTL figures from 1984 with accessories: 3 3/4" high, fully poseable and blister packed.

❏	Kirk: with communicator	$20-22
❏	Spock: with phaser	$20-22
❏	Scott: with phaser	$20-22
❏	Klingon: with "dog"	$20-22

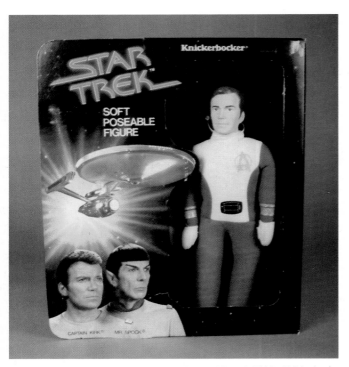

Star Trek: The Motion Picture soft poseable figure of Captain Kirk by Knickerbocker, 1979. *Courtesy of the Collection of Jeff Maynard — New Eye Studio*

Star Trek: The Motion Picture soft poseable figure of Mr. Spock by Knickerbocker, 1979. *Courtesy of the Collection of Jeff Maynard — New Eye Studio*

Star Trek III: The Search for Spock action figures by ERTL, 1984: left to right: Captain Kirk, Mr. Spock, Scotty, Klingon Leader (Kruge) & his "dog." *Courtesy of the Collection of Jeff Maynard — New Eye Studio*

The Best of Trek

❑ Editors Walter Irwin and G.B. Love, working for Signet, have published a recent series based on a quality fan-published magazine active in the 1970s. Each book is a series of articles discussing Star Trek topics including actors, characters, and fan activities. These do not stay in print very long and began in 1978. In 1990 this group published a trade paperback (large sized paperback) entitled the *Best of Best of Trek.* $8-9

First Professional Star Trek Novel

❑ Mission to Horatius by Mack Reynolds, hardback by Western, 1968 $25-50

Pocket Books Original Star Trek Novels

Pocket Books reissues these books regularly. The first printing is offered with raised title lettering. Subsequent printings do not have the raised letters. Each of these books are organized by number from the first to the most recent release rather than by alphabetical title listing. Issue #1 was released in 1977.

❑ #1 *Star Trek The Motion Picture*	$6-8
❑ #2 *The Entrophy Effect*	$25-30
❑ #3 *The Klingon Gambit*	$12-14
❑ #4 *The Covenant of the Crown*	$35-40
❑ #5 *The Prometheus Design*	$6-7
❑ #6 *The Abode of Life*	$8-9
❑ #7 *Star Trek II: The Wrath of Khan*	$6-8
❑ #8 *Black Fire*	$6-7
❑ #9 *Triangle*	$6-8
❑ #10 *Web of the Romulans*	$35-40
❑ #11 *Yesterday's Son*	$35-40
❑ #12 *Mutiny on the Enterprise*	$6-7
❑ #13 *The Wounded Sky*	$12-14
❑ #14 *The Trellisane Confrontation*	$6-8
❑ #15 *Corona*	$35-40
❑ #16 *The Final Reflection*	$6-7
❑ #17 *Star Trek III: The Search for Spock*	$12-14
❑ #18 *My Enemy, My Ally*	$12-14
❑ #19 *The Tears of the Singer*	$12-14
❑ #20 *Vulcan Academy Murders*	$35-40
❑ #21 *Uhura's Song*	$12-14
❑ #22 *Shadow Lord*	$12-14
❑ #23 *Ishmael*	$12-14
❑ #24 *Killing Time*	$12-14
❑ #25 *Dwellers in the Crucible*	$25-28
❑ #26 *Pawns & Symbols*	$6-7
❑ #27 *Mindshadow*	$12-14
❑ #28 *Crisis on Centaurus*	$35-40
❑ #29 *Dreadnought*	$25-28
❑ #30 *Demons*	$25-28
❑ #31 *Battlestations*	$8-9
❑ #32 *Chain of Attack*	$35-40
❑ #33 *Deep Domain*	$25-28
❑ #34 *Dreams of the Raven*	$25-28
❑ #35 *Romulan Way*	$12-14
❑ #36 *How Much for Just the Planet?*	$12-14
❑ #37 *Bloodthirst*	$35-40
❑ #38 *The Idic Epidemic*	$12-14
❑ #39 *Time for Yesterday*	$6-8
❑ #40 *Time Trap*	$6-8
❑ #41 *The Three Minute Universe*	$6-8
❑ #42 *Memory Prime*	$12-14
❑ #43 *The Final Nexus*	$12-14
❑ #44 *Vulcan's Glory*	$12-14
❑ #45 *Double, Double*	$25-28
❑ #46 *Cry of the Only's*	$35-40
❑ #47 *Kobayashi Maru*	$12-14
❑ #48 *Rules of Engagement*	$12-14
❑ #49 *Pandora Principle*	$35-40
❑ #50 *Doctor's Orders*	$6-7
❑ #51 *Enemy Unseen*	$25-28
❑ #52 *Home is of the Hunter*	$12-14
❑ #53 *Ghost-Walker*	$12-14
❑ #54 *A Flag Full of Stars*	$12-14
❑ #55 *Renegade*	$12-14
❑ #56 *Legacy*	$12-14
❑ #57 *The Rift*	$12-14

Original Star Trek novels by Pocket Books, regularly reissued. *Courtesy of the Collection of Jeff Maynard — New Eye Studio*

❑ #58 *Faces of Fire*	$25-28
❑ #59 *The Disinherited*	$25-28
❑ #60 *Ice Trap*	$12-14
❑ #61 *Sanctuary*	$12-14
❑ #62 *Death Count*	$25-28
❑ #63 *Shell Game*	$6-7
❑ #64 *Starship Trap*	$6-7
❑ #65 *Windows of a Lost World*	$6-7
❑ #66 *From the Depths*	$6-7
❑ #67 *Great Starship Race*	$6-7
❑ #68 *Firestorm*	$6-7
❑ #69 *Patrian Transgression*	$6-7
❑ #70 *Traitor Winds*	$6-7
❑ #71 *Crossroad*	$6-7
❑ #72 *The Better Man*	$6-7
❑ #73 *Recovery*	$6-7
❑ #74 *The Fearful Summons*	$6-7
❑ #75 *First Frontier*	$6-7

Pocket Books Movie Novelizations

❑ *Star Trek: The Motion Picture*	$6-8
❑ *Star Trek II: The Wrath of Khan*	$6-8
❑ *Star Trek III: The Search for Spock*	$6-8
❑ *Star Trek IV: The Voyage Home*	$6-8
❑ *Star Trek V: The Final Frontier*	$6-8
❑ *Star Trek VI: The Undiscovered Country*	$6-8

Star Trek movie novelizations, published by Pocket Books. *Courtesy of the Collection of Jeff Maynard — New Eye Studio*

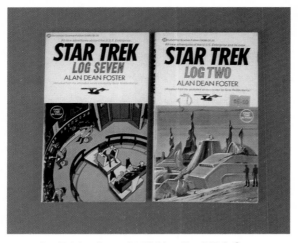

Star Trek Log Seven (1976) & Log Two (1974). *Courtesy of the Collection of Jeff Maynard — New Eye Studio*

For years Leonard Nimoy struggled to free himself of the Spock image...prior to Star Trek: The Motion Picture. After the death of Spock in Star Trek II, Nimoy stated that the death scene had been a difficult emotional moment and that he regretted Spock's passing. Times do change. *Courtesy of the Collection of Jeff Maynard — New Eye Studio*

Star Trek. The Klingon Dictionary, 1992. Speak the language with feeling! *Courtesy of the Collection of Jeff Maynard — New Eye Studio*

Pocket Giant Classic Paperback Novels
The first was released in 1986.

❑	*Enterprise The First Adventure*	$7-8
❑	*Final Frontier*	$12-14
❑	*Lost Years*	$7-8
❑	*Metamorphosis*	$12-14
❑	*Spock's World*	$6-8
❑	*Star Trek IV: The Voyage Home*	$7-8
❑	*Star Trek V: The Final Frontier*	$7-8
❑	*Strangers From the Sky*	$6-8
❑	*Tek War*	$6-8
❑	*Prime Directive*	$7-8
❑	*Probe*	$7-8

Star Trek Log Books
These were novelizations of the animated Star Trek series aired from 1972-1974. These paperbacks were imaginatively titled Log One through Log Ten. They were written by Alan Dean Foster and published by Ballantine. The first six logs contain several episodes apiece and are still in print. Logs seven through ten contain only one story each and are out of print.

❑	*Log One, 1974*	$5-7
❑	*Log Two, 1974*	$5-7
❑	*Log Three, 1975*	$5-7
❑	*Log Four, 1975*	$5-7
❑	*Log Five, 1975*	$5-7
❑	*Log Six, 1976*	$5-7
❑	*Log Seven, 1976*	$5-7
❑	*Log Eight, 1977*	$5-7
❑	*Log Nine, 1977*	$5-7
❑	*Log Ten, 1978*	$5-7

Star Trek Readers
Hardback compilations of James Blish adaptations of the original episodes. Published by Dutton.

❑	Volume I: 21 episodes, 1970	$20-30
❑	Volume II: 19 episodes, 1972	$20-30
❑	Volume III: 19 episodes, 1973	$25-35
❑	Volume IV: 12 episodes & *Spock Must Die*	$25-35

Novels By The Stars

William Shatner
❑ *Star Trek: The Ashes of Eden.* Hardbound. 1995 $22-24
(When William Shatner introduced the Tek series in 1989 he once remarked that he expected these novels to be picked up at the airport, read on the plane, and thrown away.)

❑	*Tek War,* Ace (Putnam), paperbacks, 1989	$6-7
❑	*Tek Lords*	$6-7
❑	*Tek Lab*	$6-7
❑	*Tek Vengeance*	$6-7
❑	*Tek Secret*	$6-7
❑	*Tek Power*	$6-7

George Takei
❑ *Mirror Friend, Mirror Foe,* with R. Aspirin, Playboy Press, 1979 $12-14

References, Manuals, & Memoirs

❑ *Beyond Uhura. Star Trek & Other Memories* by Nichelle Nichols $23-25
❑ *Captain's Log: Star Trek V, The Final Frontier* by Lisabeth Shatner, Pocket, 1989 $15-20
❑ *The Classic Trek Crew Book* $15-17
❑ *Encyclopedia of Trekkie Memorabilia* by Chris Gentry & Sally Gibson Downs, Books Americana, 1988 $15-17
❑ *Enterprise Officers' Manual* (& revised edition) by Geoffrey Mandel, self-published $13-15
❑ *Gene Roddenberry. The Myth and The Man Behind Star Trek* by Joel Engel $23-25
❑ *I Am Not Spock* by Leonard Nimoy, Celestial Arts, 1975
(Other books of poetry and photography by Leonard Nimoy during the years he struggled to separate himself from Spock have become very popular with collectors and include: *Come Be with Me* (Blue Mountain), Thank You for Your Love (Blue Mountain), *These Words are for You* (Blue Mountain), *Warmed by Love* (Blue Mountain) $16-18,

We are All Children Searching for Love (Blue Mountain),
Will I Think of You (Celestial Arts, first edition & Dell reissue),
and You and I (Celestial Arts, first editions & Avon)) $35

❑ Klingon Dictionary by Mark Okrand, Pocket, 1985. Complete
with English/Klingon translations. I know one reporter who
has met a national security expert who speaks fluent
Klingon. $10-11

❑ Letters to Star Trek by Susan Sackett, Ballantine, 1977 $14-24

❑ Line Officers Requirements produced by fans in 1978. Later
editions were divided into three volumes in 1987. $25-30

❑ Make-Your-Own Costume Book by Lynn Edelman
Schnurnberger, Wallaby, 1979 $15-18

❑ The Making of Star Trek by Stephen Whitfield & Gene
Roddenberry, Ballantine, 1968 (later editions by Del Rey,
a Ballantine division) $25-30

❑ The Making of Star Trek: The Motion Picture by
Susan Sackett with Gene Roddenberry, Wallaby, 1980 $20-25

❑ The Making of Star Trek II: The Wrath of Khan by Allan
Asherman, Pocket, 1982 $15-18

❑ The Making of the Trek Conventions by Joan Winston,
hardcover by Doubleday, 1977 $30-40

❑ paperback by Playboy Press, 1979 $20-30

❑ The Man Between the Ears. Star Trek's Leonard Nimoy by
James Van Hise $15-17

❑ The Man Who Created Star Trek. Gene Roddenberry by
James Van Hise $15-17

❑ Meaning in Star Trek by Karen Blair, hardcover by Anima,
1977, paperback by Warner Books, 1977. $12-14

❑ The Monsters of Star Trek by D. Cohen, Pocket, 1980 $12-14

❑ Mr. Scott's Guide to the Enterprise by Shane Johnson,
Simon and Schuster, 1987 $11-13

❑ The Nitpickers Guide for Trekkers by Phil Farrand $13-15

❑ The Official Star Trek Cooking Manual by Ann Piccard,
Bantam, 1978 $35-40

❑ The Official Star Trek Quiz Book by Mitchell Magilo,
Pocket, 1985 $15-17

❑ The Official Star Trek Trivia Book by Rafe Needleman,
Pocket, 1980 $12-14

❑ On the Good Ship Enterprise by Bjo Trimble, Donning, 1982 $14-16

❑ Starfleet Dynamics, 1991 $20-22

❑ Star Fleet Medical Reference, edited by Eileen Palestine,
1977 Trade paperback. Fan produced with a white cover.
A Ballantine edition was produced with a blue cover.
(white cover) $20-25

❑ Starfleet Officer's Requirements. Volume 1. $15-17

❑ Star Fleet Technical Manual by Franz Joseph, Ballantine,
1975 trade paperback (20th anniversary reprint produced). $12-14

❑ Star Fleet Uniform Recognition Manual by Shane Johnson,
fan published, 1985 $12-14

❑ Starlog Science Fiction Trivia, Signet, 1986 $6-12

❑ Star Trek Catalog by Gerry Turnball, Grosset & Dunlap, 1979.
In trade & regular paperback sizes $10-11

❑ Star Trek Concordance by Bjo Trimble, Ballantine, 1976 $85-90

❑ Star Trek: Good News in Modern Image by Sheed,
Andrews, & McNeel, Betsy Caprio, 1976. Both hard &
paperback. $30-70

❑ Star Trek Intergalactic Puzzles by James Razzi, 1977.
Trade paperback. $10-20

❑ Star Trek Interview Book by Allan Asherman, Pocket, 1988.
Trade paperback. $8-10

❑ Star Trek Maps, Bantam, 1980. $250-275

❑ Star Trek Memories by William Shatner with Chris Kreski,
Harper, 1993 $22-24

❑ Star Trek Movie Memories by William Shatner et al., Harper $25-28

❑ Star Trek Puzzle Manual by J. Razzi, Bantam, 1976
(trade paperback). Paperback 1977. $10-20

❑ Star Trek Quiz Book by B. Andrew with B. Dunning,
Signet, 1977 $12-14

❑ Star Trek, TV & Movie Tie-ins by James A. Lely, Creative
Education & Publishing, 1979 $20-30

❑ Star Trek: The Motion Picture by Gene Roddenberry,
Pocket, 1979 $10-15

❑ Star Trek: The Motion Picture Peel-Off Graphics Book by
Lee Cole, Wallaby, 1979 $40-50

❑ Star Trek II: Short Stories by William Rotsler $4-5

❑ Star Trek 25th Anniversary Celebration Book by
James Van Hise $15-17

❑ To The Stars by George Takei $22-24

❑ Trouble With Tribbles by David Gerrold, Ballantine, 1973.
(Making of the episode) $6-8

❑ USS Khai Tam Technical Orientation Manual by Kevin
McNulty, Intergalactic Press $13-15

❑ World of Star Trek by David Gerrold, 1973, Ballantine (later
editions by Del Rey) $35-40

❑ Writer's Guide, Lincoln Enterprises pamphlet used as
guidelines for potential writers. Lincoln Enterprises
was operated by Gene Roddenberry's lawyer. $12-18

Four of the many Star Trek references, manuals, and
memoirs. *Courtesy of the Collection of Jeff Maynard
— New Eye Studio*

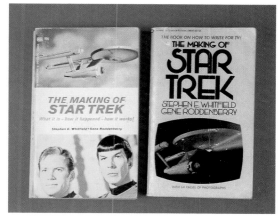

The Making of Star Trek and its reprint. *Courtesy of
the Collection of Jeff Maynard — New Eye Studio*

The Making of Star Trek: The Motion
Picture, 1980. *Courtesy of the Collec-
tion of Jeff Maynard — New Eye
Studio*

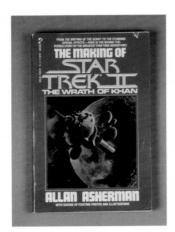

The Making of Star Trek II: The Wrath of Khan, 1982. *Courtesy of the Collection of Jeff Maynard — New Eye Studio*

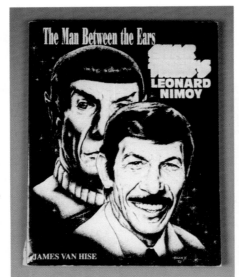

The Man Between the Ears, 1992. *Courtesy of the Collection of Jeff Maynard — New Eye Studio*

The Man Who Created Star Trek, 1992. *Courtesy of the Collection of Jeff Maynard — New Eye Studio*

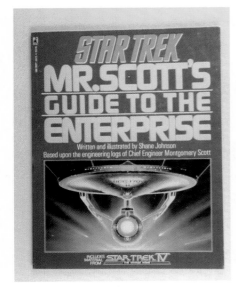

Mr. Scott's Guide to the Enterprise, 1987. *Courtesy of the Collection of Jeff Maynard — New Eye Studio*

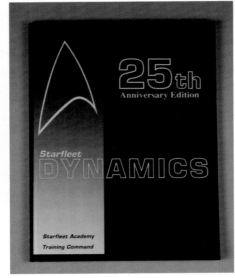

Original series, 25th Anniversary Edition Starfleet Dynamics, 1991. *Courtesy of the Collection of Jeff Maynard — New Eye Studio*

Starfleet Officer Requirements, 1988. *Courtesy of the Collection of Jeff Maynard — New Eye Studio*

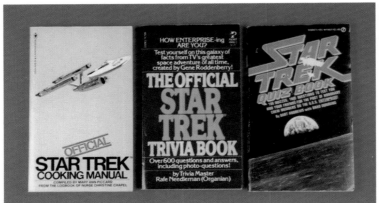

Manuals and trivia books for Star Trek abound. *Courtesy of the Collection of Jeff Maynard — New Eye Studio*

Star Trek Concordance, 1976. *Courtesy of the Collection of Jeff Maynard — New Eye Studio*

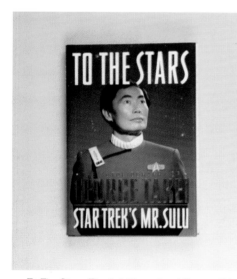

To The Stars. The Autobiography of George Takei, 1994. Cast members are writing their views of the long-lived saga now. *Courtesy of the Collection of Jeff Maynard — New Eye Studio*

U.S.S. Enterprise Officer's Manual, Revised. *Courtesy of the Collection of Jeff Maynard — New Eye Studio*

USS Khai Tam Technical Orientation Manual by Intergalactic Press, 1994. *Courtesy of the Collection of Jeff Maynard — New Eye Studio*

William Shatner has become a prolific author. Harper Spotlight Publisher edition, 1993. Watch for collectibles by the various Enterprise crews as they expand their careers in new directions. *Courtesy of the author's collection*

Star Trek II Short Stories, 1982. Note the upside-down Enterprise image. *Courtesy of the Collection of Jeff Maynard — New Eye Studio*

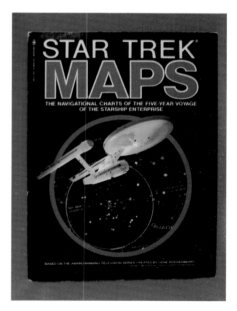

Star Trek Maps by Bantam Books, 1980. Displayed at the Smithsonian Air and Space Museum in Washington, D.C. for their Star Trek exhibit. Four color space charts of the original series five year mission of the Enterprise. *Courtesy of the Collection of Jeff Maynard — New Eye Studio*

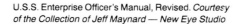

Star Trek Starfleet Technical Manual, 25th Anniversary Edition, 1991. *Courtesy of the Collection of Jeff Maynard — New Eye Studio*

Star Trek Star Fleet Technical Manual, original hard cover, 1975. *Courtesy of the Collection of Jeff Maynard — New Eye Studio*

BUTTONS

Buttons with words or pictures are easily produced by anyone who purchases an inexpensive button machine. There is no copyright hazard involved in cutting out photos from a magazine and making buttons of them, even less so with simple word buttons. Buttons noted here are mass produced and/or licensed. There is no room to add more.

Avia
From Star Trek: The Motion Picture, 1979. 2 1/4" color
    licensed with logo added to picture. $3-5 per button
- ❑ Enterprise Crew: on the bridge
- ❑ Kirk: movie uniform
- ❑ Kirk: standing
- ❑ Kirk, Spock, & McCoy
- ❑ Spock: movie uniform
- ❑ Spock: Vulcan costume

Button-Up
Original TV series, 1984, 1 1/2" licensed color. $2-3 per button
- ❑ Kirk: head shot
- ❑ Kirk & McCoy
- ❑ Kirk & Spock
- ❑ Kirk, McCoy & Spock
- ❑ McCoy, Uhura, & Chekov
- ❑ Sulu
- ❑ Enterprise
- ❑ Enterprise & Constellation

Star Trek III: The Search for Spock, 1 1/2" diameter,
    licensed, color, 1984, with logo and photo $2-3 per button
- ❑ Kirk: head shot
- ❑ Kirk: head & shoulders
- ❑ McCoy
- ❑ Spock: Vulcan costume
- ❑ Chekov: head shot
- ❑ Sulu: head shot
- ❑ Uhura: holding phaser
- ❑ David Marcus: head & shoulders
- ❑ Saavik: head shot
- ❑ Kruge: head shot
- ❑ Star Trek III logo

Image Products
Star Trek II: The Wrath of Khan, 1982, licensed, color,
    3" diameter, photo & logo. $3-4 per button

- ❑ Kirk
- ❑ Spock
- ❑ Khan
- ❑ Enterprise Crew
- ❑ Enterprise

Langley & Associates
Out of business, licensed early, 1976, color, 2 1/4"
diameter. $2-3 per button
- ❑ Kirk: head shot
  - ❑ dress uniform
  - ❑ on transporter pad
  - ❑ behind bars
  - ❑ with communicator
  - ❑ with tribbles
- ❑ Spock: profile head shot
  - ❑ head shot
  - ❑ arched eyebrow
  - ❑ smiling
  - ❑ laughing
  - ❑ bearded
- ❑ McCoy: head shot
  - ❑ speaking
  - ❑ quizzical
- ❑ Sulu: at the helm
  - ❑ head shot
  - ❑ looking up
- ❑ Chekov: with crew
  - ❑ on bridge
  - ❑ smiling
  - ❑ frowning
- ❑ Uhura: at her station
  - ❑ with earpiece
- ❑ Scott: head shot
- ❑ Nurse Chapel: close-up
- ❑ Yeoman Rand: plaited hair
- ❑ Captain Pike: Jeffrey Hunter, the original, from the Cage & the Menagerie
- ❑ Khan: Ricardo Montalban in the original episode
- ❑ Enterprise: with "Star Trek"
  - ❑ in orbit above planets (2 buttons)
  - ❑ firing phasers
  - ❑ flying away
- ❑ Klingon Battle Cruiser: overhead view

Paramount
- ❏ Star Trek V: The Final Frontier: promotional, blue, rectangular with logo, 1989 $3-4

Pocket Books
- ❏ Spock: promotional button, reads — "Star Trek: The Only Logical Books to Read" $2-3

Star Trek Galore
- ❏ Unlicensed manufacturer of 2 1/4", 2 1/2" & 3" color buttons, 1976. Out of business. $2-3 per button
- ❏ Kirk: dress uniform
  - ❏ chin in hand
  - ❏ Troubles with Tribbles
  - ❏ glitter button with black background
- ❏ Kirk, Spock & McCoy: on the bridge
- ❏ Spock: Vulcan greeting
  - ❏ pointing phaser
  - ❏ emotional
  - ❏ with 3-D chess set
  - ❏ with Vulcan child
  - ❏ with harp
  - ❏ with beard
  - ❏ from animated series
- ❏ McCoy: glittering button with black background
- ❏ Chekov & Sulu: on bridge
- ❏ Uhura
- ❏ Scott: portrait
  - ❏ worried
- ❏ Enterprise Crew: on bridge
- ❏ Enterprise: firing phasers
- ❏ Shuttlecraft Galileo

Taco Bell
- ❏ Star Trek III: The Search for Spock, 3" blue & yellow promotional buttons $3-4 per button
- ❏ Beam Home with the Enterprise Crew
- ❏ Beam Home with Kruge
- ❏ Beam Home with Spock
- ❏ Beam Home with T'Lar

Universal Studios
- ❏ 1989 Promotional Button: Color Enterprise photo emblazoned with "Paramount Pictures Star Trek Adventure." $4-6

CALENDARS

Star Trek calendars continue to be produced and are to be found for each of the new series produced. When collecting, look for calendars which have not been written in as such markings devalue these items. The first Pocket calendar and Ballantine calendars were sold boxed.
- ❏ 1973 Lincoln Enterprises: color television stills $18-20
- ❏ 1974 Lincoln Enterprises: animated series $18-20
- ❏ 1976, 77 & 78 Lincoln Enterprises: three year calendar using color TV stills $18-20 each
- ❏ 1976 Ballantine Books: Kirk & Spock on cover with TV color stills within $45-50

Star Trek original series calendar, 1976. *Courtesy of the Collection of Jeff Maynard — New Eye Studio*

Star Trek: The Wrath of Khan Calendar, 1983 by Pocket Books. *Courtesy of the Collection of Jeff Maynard — New Eye Studio*

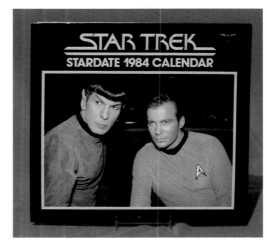

Star Trek 1984 Calendar. *Courtesy of the Collection of Jeff Maynard — New Eye Studio*

Star Trek (movie series) 1986 Calendar. *Courtesy of the Collection of Jeff Maynard — New Eye Studio*

45

- ❏ 1977 Ballantine Books: Kirk & Spock on black bordered cover, with TV color stills within — $15-17
- ❏ 1977 Franco: hanging cloth calendar — $35-55
- ❏ 1978 Ballantine Books: Kirk, Spock & McCoy on cover with blue border — $15-17
- ❏ 1979 Ballantine Books: Spock with silver border on cover — $15-17
- ❏ 1980 Pocket Books: Star Trek: The Motion Picture Enterprise & original cast on cover. — $25-30
- ❏ 1980 Wallaby: "The Official U.S.S. Enterprise Officer's Date Book. 5 1/2" x 8" spiral bound desk calendar — $18-20
- ❏ 1980 Blue Mountain Press: Leonard Nimoy on cover, Nimoy's Spock distancing poetry & nature art within — $18-20
- ❏ 1981 Pocket Books: Star Trek: The Motion Picture. Space docked Enterprise on cover. — $15-17
- ❏ 1981 Blue Mountain Press: Leonard Nimoy Calendar. Spiral bound with poetry & art. Very un-Vulcan. — $18-20
- ❏ 1982 Pocket Books: Star Trek: The Motion Picture with Kirk, Spock & the ship on the cover. — $15-17
- ❏ 1983 Pocket Books: Star Trek II: The Wrath of Khan. Enterprise's arrival at Regula 1 science station on cover. — $20-22
- ❏ 1984 Pocket Book: Kirk & Spock on cover, classic series TV stills within. — $15-17
- ❏ 1985 Pocket Books: Star Trek III: The Search for Spock. Enterprise nears space dock on cover. — $15-17
- ❏ 1985 onward Datazine: produces a series of Hysterical Calendars with Star Trek cartoons and dates significant in the shows. Added the new series to their repertoire beginning with The Next Generation in 1989 — $12-14 each
- ❏ 1986 Pocket Books: movie cast on cover, casts of the movies within. — $15-17
- ❏ 1987 Pocket Books: Kirk, Spock, McCoy & Uhura on cover. — $20-22
- ❏ 1988 Pocket Books: color stills from first four movies & classic TV show — $15-17
- ❏ 1989 Pocket Books: Star Trek Celebration Calendar, Kirk, Spock & McCoy on cover, color stills of original series within — $20-22
- ❏ 1990 Pocket Books: Star Trek V: The Final Frontier Calendar. Group shot cover — $10-11
- ❏ 1991 Pocket Books: Star Trek Classic Calendar, color stills from all five films — $15-17
- ❏ 1993 Pocket Books: Star Trek VI: The Undiscovered Country Calendar, color stills from film within. — $10-11
- ❏ 1994 Pocket Books: Star Trek Classic Calendar — $10-11
- ❏ 1995 Pocket Books: Star Trek Classic Calendar — $11-12
- ❏ 1996 Pocket Books: Star Trek 30th Anniversary Calendar with Kirk & Spock looking upward on the cover — $12-14

CELS& STORYBOARDS

From 1972 to 1974 the animated Star Trek series produced hundreds of storyboards (preliminary artists' sketches of the animated episode) and thousands of color cels (the individual transparencies which make up each frame of each story's action). Cels which are sought after contain complete character figures of the main characters (or groups thereof) and are well centered in the frame. Since backgrounds were reused for many action sequences, backgrounds are not usually part of authentic cels. Cels were originally offered from Filmation, the company which created the series, in 1977. Lincoln Enterprises and Paramount both offered cels in 1983 and 1989 respectively. Paramount's offerings were reproductions of the originals.

Filmation — 1977
Offered fourteen cels in 14" x 18" mats with authenticity seals. $45-85 each
- ❏ Cel 00 Star Trek Title Scene
- ❏ 1A The Enterprise Crew
- ❏ 5 Yesteryear
- ❏ 6 More Tribbles, More Troubles
- ❏ 9 The Ambergris Element
- ❏ 11 Jihad (aliens composite)
- ❏ 12 Spock (as a boy riding L'Chaya)
- ❏ 14 The Time Trap
- ❏ 15 The Enterprise & Aqua Shuttle
- ❏ 16 Beyond the Farthest Star
- ❏ 20 Kulkukan & Enterprise
- ❏ 22 Time Warp
- ❏ 23 Ready to Battle a Klingon
- ❏ 25 The Counter Clock Incident

Lincoln Enterprises — 1983
Offered 4" x 8" acetate character cel copies. $4-6 each
- ❏ The Enterprise
- ❏ Captain Kirk
- ❏ Mr. Spock
- ❏ Dr. McCoy
- ❏ Nurse Chapel
- ❏ Mr. Scott
- ❏ Lt. Sulu
- ❏ Lt. Uhura
- ❏ Lt. Arex
- ❏ Lt. M'Hress

Paramount — 1989
- ❏ Kirk & Spock: on bridge — $350-400 each
- ❏ Kirk & Spock: on transporter pads
- ❏ Kirk & Spock: on planet
- ❏ Kirk & Spock: waist up
- ❏ Kirk & McCoy: McCoy carrying hypo
- ❏ Kirk & Nurse Chapel
- ❏ Kirk: full figure
- ❏ Kirk: waist up in action
- ❏ Kirk: with communicator
- ❏ Spock: waist up in action
- ❏ Spock: waist up
- ❏ Spock: amidst machinery
- ❏ Spock: detained by 2 aliens
- ❏ McCoy: on planet, waist up
- ❏ McCoy: behind window
- ❏ Scott: holding tricorder
- ❏ Scott: waist up
- ❏ Scott: on the bridge
- ❏ Scott & Arex
- ❏ Sulu: waist up
- ❏ Sulu: amidst machinery
- ❏ Crew member & Alien
- ❏ Limited Edition Crew on the Bridge, only 400 produced — $1000-1100

CERAMICS — Commemoratives, Drinking & Dining Wares

Collector's Plates, Dining & Serving Wares

HAMILTON/ERNST
Working together Hamilton and Ernst produced three series of an intended eight between c. 1983 and 1989. The third series was incomplete as the license was lost before the run was completed. Hamilton, with artist Susie Morton, provided the artwork and design. Ernst Company produced the plates. The plates were all numbered on the back. These plates have become popular items. Hamilton has gone on to produce additional plates under their name alone in both the original series and The Next Generation.

First Series
Character plates of the original crew. These blue bordered plates measuring 8 1/2" in diameter. Within the blue border were the inscriptions "The Voyages of the Starship Enterprise" and "To Boldly Go Where No Man Has Gone Before." Licensed in 1983, these plates were released from 1985 to 1989. In 1986 these plates were released with larger platinum decorated rims carrying the inscriptions: "Star Trek," "NCC 1701," and "Twentieth Year Anniversary Collection."
- ❏ Beam Us Down Scotty, group portrait on transporter — $50-55
- ❏ Chekov — $50-55
- ❏ Kirk — $50-55
- ❏ McCoy — $50-55
- ❏ Scotty — $40-50
- ❏ Spock — $50-55
- ❏ Sulu — $50-55
- ❏ Uhura — $75-85

Enterprise Collector's Plate
- ❏ Between 1987 and 1989, the Hamilton/Ernst partnership produced a 10 1/4" diameter plated featuring the Enterprise firing her phasers while suspended over the heads of the seven main characters from the original series. Gold trim encircles the edge bearing the inscription "U.S.S. Enterprise NCC 1701" above and the names of each character below. Two versions were produced. The first was unsigned, the second had copied signatures of the seven cast members, the artist — Susie Morton, and Gene Roddenberry around the back rim. Both signed and unsigned plates are numbered. — $85-135

The Hamilton/Ernst First Series Collector's Plate, Mr. Spock, released from 1985-1989. *Courtesy of the Collection of John E. Balbach*

Original series blue rim Captain Kirk plate (this plate is signed by William Shatner) by Ernst, 1985. *Courtesy of the Collection of Jeff Maynard — New Eye Studio*

Original series blue rimmed Mr. Scott plate by Ernst, 1984. *Courtesy of the Collection of Jeff Maynard — New Eye Studio*

Original series blue rimmed Sulu plate by Ernst, 1983. *Courtesy of the Collection of Jeff Maynard — New Eye Studio*

Original series blue rimmed Uhura plate by Ernst, 1983. *Courtesy of the Collection of Jeff Maynard — New Eye Studio*

Original series blue rimmed McCoy plate by Ernst, 1983. *Courtesy of the Collection of Jeff Maynard — New Eye Studio*

Original series 20th anniversary Platinum rimmed Kirk plate by Ernst, 1986. *Courtesy of the Collection of Jeff Maynard — New Eye Studio*

Original series 20th anniversary Platinum rimmed Spock plate by Ernst, 1986. *Courtesy of the Collection of Jeff Maynard — New Eye Studio*

Second Series

Produced from 1987-1989, these depicted scenes for favorite episodes of the original television series. This series plates measure 8 1/2" in diameter, are trimmed with gold, and the gold is decorated with small renderings of the Enterprise and the inscriptions, "Star Trek" and "The Commemorative Collection." Each plate is numbered on the back.

❑ Amok Time: Battle between Kirk & Spock, armed with Lirpas $100-160
❑ City on the Edge of Forever: Kirk, Spock & McCoy outside
    Mission $300-330
❑ Devil in the Dark: Spock mind-melds with the Horta $100-160
❑ Journey to Babel: Kirk, Sarek & Telerite $100-160
❑ Menagerie: Pike & Vina in front of castle on Rigel $100-160
❑ Mirror, Mirror: Kirk confronts his crew's opposite numbers
    in an alternate universe $175-195
❑ Piece of the Action: Kirk & Spock in 1920s period garb cut
    a deal $75-160
❑ Trouble with Tribbles: Kirk up to his elbows in Tribbles $75-80

Original series episode "Mirror, Mirror" plate, signed by the artist Susie Morton, by Ernst, 1986. *Courtesy of the Collection of Jeff Maynard — New Eye Studio*

Original series 20th anniversary "The Menagerie" plate by Ernst, 1987. *Courtesy of the Collection of Jeff Maynard — New Eye Studio*

Original series episode "A Piece of the Action" plate by Ernst, 1986. *Courtesy of the Collection of Jeff Maynard — New Eye Studio*

Original series episode "The Trouble With Tribbles" plate by Ernst, 1986. *Courtesy of the Collection of Jeff Maynard — New Eye Studio*

Third Series

The partnership began to produce plates for Star Trek: The Next Generation. These were numbered and never finished. The edges were decorated in silver and carried the title, "Star Trek: The Next Generation." (see Star Trek: The Next Generation for photographs of later Hamilton plates featuring the crew of this series).

❑ Picard $300-400
❑ Data $200-300

HAMILTON

Hamilton would release the above plates in 1991. They went on to produce Commemorative series of plates of their own.

Miniature Collector's Series

In 1991, Hamilton released the first series of plates as miniatures measuring 4 1/4" diameter. They came boxed with small plastic display stands.

❑ Beam Us Down Scotty, group portrait on transporter $8-9
❑ Chekov $8-9
❑ Kirk $8-9
❑ McCoy $8-9
❑ Scotty $8-9
❑ Spock $8-9
❑ Sulu $8-9
❑ Uhura $8-9

A series of 4 1/4" diameter plates by Hamilton Gifts, 1991. Miniatures of their larger plates, sold in boxes with small plastic easels. *Courtesy of the Collection of Jeff Maynard — New Eye Studio*

Star Trek 25th Anniversary Series
Hamilton offering illustrated by Thomas Blackshear II and decorated with a 23K gold border.
- ❏ Kirk $35-40
- ❏ Spock $35-40
- ❏ McCoy $35-40
- ❏ Chekov $35-40
- ❏ Scott $35-40
- ❏ Sulu $35-40
- ❏ Uhura $35-40

Star Trek: The Movies Commemorative Series
Hamilton plates featuring a montage of scenes from several of the first six movies. Edged borders.
- ❏ ST II: The Wrath of Khan $35-40
- ❏ ST IV: The Voyage Home $35-40
- ❏ ST VI: The Undiscovered Country $35-40

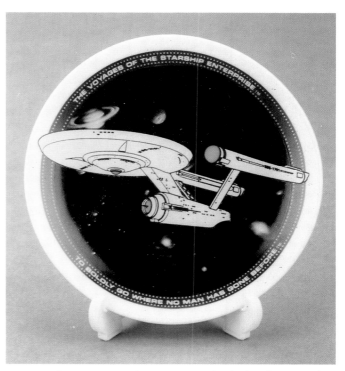

The original Enterprise on a 4 1/4" diameter plate, by Hamilton Gifts, 1991. Come complete with small plastic stand. "THE VOYAGES OF THE STARSHIP ENTERPRISE. TO BOLDLY GO WHERE NO MAN HAS GONE BEFORE." *Courtesy of the Collection of John E. Balbach*

Original series 25th anniversary Chekov plate by Hamilton, 1993. *Courtesy of the Collection of Jeff Maynard — New Eye Studio*

Original series 25th anniversary Spock plate by Hamilton, 1991. *Courtesy of the Collection of Jeff Maynard — New Eye Studio*

Original series 25th anniversary Kirk plate by Hamilton, 1991. *Courtesy of the Collection of Jeff Maynard — New Eye Studio*

Original series 25th anniversary Scotty plate by Hamilton, 1991. *Courtesy of the Collection of Jeff Maynard — New Eye Studio*

Original series 25th anniversary Sulu plate by Hamilton, 1991. *Courtesy of the Collection of Jeff Maynard — New Eye Studio*

Original series 25th anniversary Uhura plate by Hamilton, 1991. *Courtesy of the Collection of Jeff Maynard — New Eye Studio*

The Hamilton Collection Plate, Star Trek Voyagers Commemorative Series, U.S.S. Enterprise NCC-1701, 8 1/2" in diameter. *Courtesy of the Collection of John E. Balbach*

Star Trek Voyages Commemorative Series
Hamilton's 1994 plates largely dealing with Star Trek: The Next Generation, but beginning with the starship that started it all. Gold gilt edged plates.

- ❏ #1 U.S.S. Enterprise NCC-1701 — $35-40
- ❏ #2 U.S.S. Enterprise NCC-1701-D — $35-40
- ❏ #3 Klingon Battle Cruiser — $35-40
- ❏ #4 Romulan Warbird — $35-40

ENESCO
- ❏ Enesco produced a single Star Trek commemorative plate featuring portraits of the crew as seen in the original television series along with the original Enterprise flying through space. — $25-28

PFALTZGRAFF
Pfaltzgraff has contributed a line of both stoneware and bone china dining ware sets. These are the dining wares bearing the emblems of the U.S.S. Enterprise NCC-1701-A and the U.S.S. Excelsior, as seen in Star Trek VI: The Undiscovered Country.

U.S.S. Enterprise NCC-1701-A Stoneware Buffet Set
Each is a three piece set.

- ❏ Dinner plate
- ❏ Mug
- ❏ Saucer — (set of three) $26-28

Star Trek VI: The Undiscovered Country stoneware buffet set: cup, saucer, & plate by Pfaltzgraff, 1993. *Courtesy of the Collection of Jeff Maynard — New Eye Studio*

Star Trek VI: The Undiscovered Country stoneware ceramics cookie jar and tankard with the Great Seal of the Enterprise NCC-1701-A by Pfaltzgraff, 1993. *Courtesy of the Collection of Jeff Maynard — New Eye Studio*

Star Trek VI: The Undiscovered Country stoneware candy dish by Pfaltzgraff, 1994. *Courtesy of the Collection of Jeff Maynard — New Eye Studio*

U.S.S. Enterprise NCC-1701-A Stoneware Set
- ❏ Cookie Jar $35-40
- ❏ Mug $9-11
- ❏ Tankard $24-26

U.S.S. Enterprise NCC-1701-A Stoneware Serving Dishes
- ❏ Candy Dish $22-24
- ❏ Coasters (4) $26-28
- ❏ Chip 'n Dip Set $35-37

U.S.S. Enterprise NCC-1701-A Limited Edition Bone China Set
Do not confuse these with the stoneware sets above. These were sold in sets with three pieces each. Limited edition sets include repeating three dot patterns just inside the blue border. If your eyes are sharp you will find this pattern in the dinner ware portrayed in Star Trek VI.
- ❏ 1 Dinner Plate
- ❏ 1 Cup
- ❏ 1 Saucer   (set of three) $400-440

Star Trek VI: The Undiscovered Country bone china buffet set with cup, saucer, & plate. The set includes a photo of George Takei (Sulu) using it. Decorated with the seal of the U.S.S. Excelsior NCC-2000 and dot-edged by Pfaltzgraff, 1993. *Courtesy of the Collection of Jeff Maynard — New Eye Studio*

Star Trek VI: The Undiscovered Country stoneware chip and dip set by Pfaltzgraff, 1994. *Courtesy of the Collection of Jeff Maynard — New Eye Studio*

Star Trek VI: The Undiscovered Country bone china plate (no dot rim) by Pfaltzgraff, 1992. *Courtesy of the Collection of Jeff Maynard — New Eye Studio*

U.S.S. Enterprise NCC-1701-A Bone China Set
The three dot pattern is absent in this set.
- ❑ Dinner Plate — $50-55
- ❑ Coffee Cup — $35-40

U.S.S. Excelsior NCC-2000 Bone China Buffet Dinner Set
Once again, the three dot pattern is present here below the rim. This three piece set is sold with a photo of George Takei in the captain's seat using his tea cup of this pattern.
- ❑ Dinner Plate
- ❑ Cup
- ❑ Saucer — (set of three) $110-120

Decanters
GRENADIER
- ❑ 1979 Golden metallic glazed Spock figure liquor decanter by **Grenadier,** 13 1/2" high. The head is removable. These rare items occasionally were packaged in dark blue satin display boxes. — $800-1000
- ❑ 1979 Spock bust liquor decanter by **Grenadier.** Packaged in a window display box with a movie still of Spock from Star Trek: The Motion Picture displayed on the side. The insignia patch circles vary between orange and white colored. Neither is more prevalent but the orange is correct for Spock's character. 10" high. — $75-85

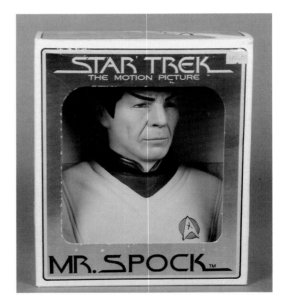

Star Trek: The Motion Picture Spock gold plated decanter, the figure measures 13 1/2" high and the head is removable. Manufactured by Grenadier, 1979. *Courtesy of the Collection of Jeff Maynard — New Eye Studio*

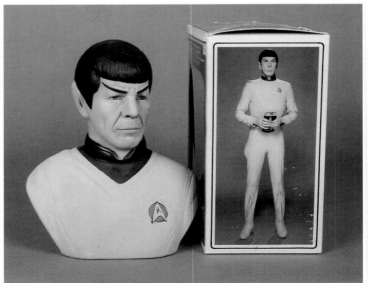

Star Trek: The Motion Picture Mr. Spock Decanter (Cielo Liqueur) by Grenadier, 1979. *Courtesy of the Collection of Jeff Maynard — New Eye Studio*

Mugs

HAMILTON/ERNST

Hamilton and Ernst produced mugs jointly from 1986-1989 bore the same design as the first series plates and were originally sold as a set of eight. They were reissued by Hamilton in 1991.

- [ ] Beam Us Down Scotty. Group portrait on transporter $10-15
- [ ] Chekov $10-15
- [ ] Kirk $10-15
- [ ] McCoy $10-15
- [ ] Scotty $10-15
- [ ] Spock $10-15
- [ ] Sulu $10-15
- [ ] Uhura $10-15

BEE INTERNATIONAL — 1993

Movie poster mugs of the first six Star Trek films. These were sold filled with candy.

- [ ] Star Trek: The Motion Picture $10-11
- [ ] Star Trek II: The Wrath of Khan $10-11
- [ ] Star Trek III: The Search for Spock $10-11
- [ ] Star Trek IV: The Voyage Home $10-11
- [ ] Star Trek V: The Final Frontier $10-11
- [ ] Star Trek VI: The Undiscovered Country $10-11
- [ ]   (set of six) $60-65

CENTRIC — 1993

- [ ] Centric produced a set of mugs with two images printed on opposite sides for both Star Trek and The Next Generation.

Two-sided Mugs

- [ ] Enterprise & Klingon Bird Of Prey $10-11
- [ ] Kirk & Spock $10-11

IMAGE DESIGN CONCEPTS, INC.

Image Design produced a series of Star Trek "Magic Mugs" with designs produced from heat sensitive materials which disappeared when hot beverages were added to the mugs. The mugs measure roughly 3 1/4" in diameter and 3 5/8" high. They produced mugs for both the original series and The Next Generation.

Magic Mugs, Original Series 1989-1990

- [ ] Kirk, Spock & McCoy on the transporter pad $13-15
- [ ] Klingon Bird of Prey uncloaks before starship Enterprise when the mug is heated $13-15

IMAGE PRODUCTS

Image Products created three six inch high character mugs for the Wrath of Khan movie. The film logo is on the back and the mugs have blue glazed linings. Faces are prominently molded on the front and glazed.

Star Trek II: The Wrath of Khan

- [ ] Khan
- [ ] Kirk $175-190
- [ ] Spock $175-190

Star Trek pyramid of movie poster mugs (which came filled with candy). Star Trek: The Motion Picture is at the top. Moves down through the films to Star Trek VI: The Undiscovered Country at the lower right. Manufactured by Bee International, 1993. *Courtesy of the Collection of Jeff Maynard — New Eye Studio*

Star Trek II: The Wrath of Khan ceramic Mr. Spock mug. *Courtesy of the Collection of Jeff Maynard — New Eye Studio*

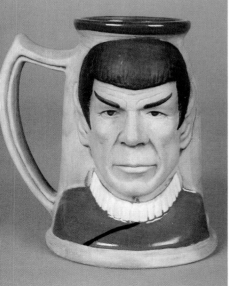

Add hot liquid to the mug and the original crew beam out until the cup cools. 3 1/4" diameter and 3 5/8" high Magic Mug by Image Design Concepts, Inc. 1989. *Courtesy of the author's collection*

❑ **Official Star Trek Fan Club Mug:** emblazoned with fan
club logos and 20th Anniversary. $12-16

Star Trek Figural Mugs
Sculpted three dimensional busts of characters from Star Trek, ST:TNG, & DS9.
The entire bust is hollow and open at the top of the head, forming the mug.
   ❑ Kirk $15-17
   ❑ Spock $15-17

UFP Mugs: several manufacturers produced black or gray mugs featuring silver or
blue United Federation of Planets emblems. (see Crossover Products for three
examples)

Tankards & Steins — Ceramics

ERNST
Produced sepia toned 6 1/4" high steins in 1986.
   ❑ Kirk $30-45
   ❑ Spock $30-45

CHRISTMAS ORNAMENTS

HALLMARK
Hallmark first produced Christmas tree ornaments in 1991 for Star Trek's 25th
anniversary. The first two of this "Keepsake Magic Ornament" line are from the
original series. The 1993 through 1995 contributions may be found in The Next
Generation section. In 1995 an additional boxed set was added to the line, titled
"The Ships of Star Trek." (see Crossover Products)
   ❑ U.S.S. Enterprise NCC-1701: 1991 ornament, very popular collectible to-
day $350-390
   ❑ Shuttlecraft Galileo: 1992 $40-45

Hallmark store display (without its background) for the Shuttlecraft Galileo Keepsake Magic Ornament, 1992. *Courtesy of the Collection of Jeff Maynard — New
Eye Studio*

CLOTHING & ACCESSORIES

Belts
   ❑ Star Trek: The Motion Picture, Star Trek emblem in stretch
cloth $15-20
   ❑ Rarities Mint black and brown reversible belt with silver
classic Enterprise on a gold-plated buckle, 1989. $50-55

Belt Pouches
Produced by T-K Graphics, these are 6" x 9" vinyl pouches with snap closures and
silkscreened designs. The designs include:
   ❑ Enterprise $10-15 each
   ❑ Imperial Klingon Fleet
   ❑ Star Fleet Academy (UFP design with Janus Head)
   ❑ Star Fleet Headquarters Tactical Operation Center
   ❑ U.S.S. Enterprise/NCC 1701
   ❑ UFP Diplomatic Service
   ❑ Vulcan Science Academy

Caps
Baseball caps are popular for Star Trek applications. Most carry embroidered
patches.
   ❑ Star Fleet Academy: academy emblem on cap. $12-14
   ❑ Star Trek II: silkscreened cap by Thinking Cap Co. $15-20
   ❑ Star Trek III: embroidered patch by Lincoln Enterprises $15-20
   ❑ Star Trek IV corduroy cap: embroidered logo by Official Star
Trek Fan Club, 1986 $15-20
   ❑ Star Trek V black & white cap: silver & red embroidered logo,
1989. $15-25
   ❑ Star Trek 20th Anniversary: embroidered patch by Lincoln
Enterprises, 1986 $15-20
   ❑ Star Trek 25th Anniversary: silkscreened anniversary logo
patch, 1991. $10-15
   ❑ Star Trek 25th Anniversary: painters caps with a variety of
25th anniversary designs. $10-15
   ❑ Star Trek Crew black cap: featuring original TV logo & white
embroidered "Crew" by Paramount Special Effects, 1989. $10-15
   ❑ U.S.S. Enterprise: embroidered patch featuring command star
by Thinking Cap Co. $10-15
   ❑ U.S.S. Enterprise: movie ship & Star Trek logo. $10-15
   ❑ "U.S.S. Enterprise NCC-1701": printed ship designation on
mesh back cap. $10-15
   ❑ United Federation of Planets (UFP): embroidered movie patch
by Thinking Cap Co. $10-15
   ❑ Vulcan Ear Cap: with rubber pointed ears and at times
embroidered "Spock Lives" patch by Thinking Cap Co. $10-15

Jackets

D.D. Bean & Sons
   ❑ Star Trek: The Motion Picture: lightweight with silver first
movie insignia, 1979. $85-110
   ❑ Star Trek: The Motion Picture: UFP patch on front, movie
logo over Enterprise with red flashing L.E.D.s on back,
1979. $110-130

Hallmark Keepsake Magic Ornaments, Christmas tree
ornaments: left to right: U.S.S. Enterprise NCC-1701
25th Anniversary Edition, 1991; original series
Shuttlecraft Galileo, 1992; Star Trek: The Next Gen-
eration U.S.S. Enterprise NCC-1701-D, 1993; Star
Trek: The Next Generation Klingon Bird of Prey, 1994.
*Courtesy of the Collection of Jeff Maynard — New Eye
Studio*

Great Lakes
- ❑ Original TV series science emblem: jacket light blue with black cuffs & collar. Two white stripes on arms. — $45-60
- ❑ UFP design from original series: silver jacket, 1974. — $45-60

Lincoln Enterprises
- ❑ Star Trek III: The Search for Spock: embroidered movie patch on front with "U.S.S. Enterprise" on back of a black light weight jacket with white trim. — $30-35
- ❑ Star Trek III: The Search for Spock: same jacket above in white or blue satinique. — $60-70
- ❑ Star Trek IV: The Voyage Home: embroidered movie logo on back with Enterprise, Golden Gate Bridge & whales on a white crew jacket with navy trim. — $135-160
- ❑ Star Trek IV: The Voyage Home: patch showing Bird of Prey over Golden Gate Bridge and whales on front, Enterprise on back. White, black, navy blue, red satinique, or gray windbreaker. — $35-40
- ❑ 20th Anniversary: patch with Enterprise & "U.S.S. Enterprise," "Star Trek—20th Anniversary" on a white, black or navy blue windbreaker. — $60-70

Official Star Trek Fan Club
- ❑ Star Trek IV: The Voyage Home: two-color Star Trek IV logo on back of a silver satin jacket, 1986. — $50-60

Paramount Special Effects
- ❑ Star Trek V: The Final Frontier: embroidered strip logo over front pocket of a denim jacket, 1989 — $80-85

Star Trek 25th Anniversary Jackets
- ❑ Official 25th Anniversary Logo: leather university jacket with embroidered logo on back & original series embroidered command insignia on front. — $225-250
- ❑ Official 25th Anniversary Logo: blue or black denim jacket with embroidered logo on back. — $90-100
- ❑ Official 25th Anniversary Logo: red, black or blue satin jacket with embroidered logo on back & command insignia on front. — $90-100

Silk Ties

Colorful silk ties have been recently offered for both Star Trek and The Next Generation.
- ❑ Original Crew — $20-22
- ❑ Kirk — $14-16
- ❑ Spock — $14-16
- ❑ Enterprise Blueprint: movie ship — $25-28
- ❑ Enterprise/Klingon Ship Standoff — $25-28
- ❑ Original Enterprise: at warp speed — $25-28
- ❑ Mirror, Mirror: scenes from the original show — $14-16
- ❑ Combination Ships: outlines of the original, movie, and Next Generation Enterprise overlaid over each other. — $20-22

Tee Shirts

Tee shirts are produced quickly, cheaply, and in large quantities. Licensed and unlicensed Star Trek tee shirts abound. Silkscreening allows small runs of many different designs. With this situation there has been an eye-popping proliferation of tee shirts over the past thirty years of Star Trek. By in large, tee shirts will never become great collectibles and, as such, they will not be covered here.

COINS & MEDALLIONS

HANOVER MINT
Star Trek Medallions, First Series — 1974
Coins minted with detachable necklace chain rims measuring 1 1/2" in diameter. Kirk & Spock shown in front before an alien background, the back shows the original Enterprise. Serial numbers are stamped around the edges.
- ❑ Gold plating over silver — $500-550
- ❑ Silver — $400-440
- ❑ Bronze — $95-115

Star Trek Medallions, Second Series
The same coins as above without the serial numbers.
- ❑ Bronze — $85-105

Star Trek Medallions, Third Series
Lesser quality minting with a chain ring cast as part of the coin. Serial numbers are on the rims.
- ❑ Bronze — $95-105

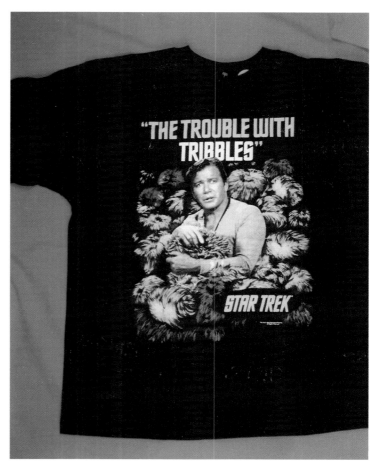

Star Trek tee shirt. *Courtesy of the Collection of Jeff Maynard — New Eye Studio*

Star Trek Commemorative Medallions by Hanover Mint. *Courtesy of the Collection of Jeff Maynard — New Eye Studio*

LINCOLN ENTERPRISES

Tenth Anniversary Commemorative Medallion

Medallion front depicts Kirk, Spock, McCoy, & Scott in right profile with 1966-1976 dating. On the back the Enterprise orbits a planet. Medallion measures 1 1/2" in diameter.

- ❏ Copper colored $8-10

Twentieth Anniversary Commemorative Medallion

- ❏ A 1 1/2" diameter medallion featuring Kirk & Spock on the front and the Enterprise with the 1966-1986 dates on the back. $15-20

Star Trek III: The Search for Spock Commemorative Medallion

- ❏ Kirk & Spock are found on the front with the movie title around their heads. On the back is the Enterprise and a planet. These are 1 1/2" diameter lightweight metal coins with rims and chains. $15-20

Star Trek IV: The Voyage Home/Challenger Commemorative Medallion

On front the Enterprise is over the Golden Gate Bridge and whales; on the reverse is the space shuttle Challenger commemorating the tragic explosion which cost the astronauts their lives and destroyed their vessel. These are numbered coins, 2 1/2" in diameter, numbered at the bottom, dated from 1986, with molded ring for a ribbon. A neck ribbon came with the coin.

- ❏ Gold plated $70-80
- ❏ Gold & silver plated $90-100
- ❏ Bronze $25-30
- ❏ Pewter $25-30

HUCKLEBERRY DESIGN

Vulcan Nickel

A large wooden nickel featuring Spock's face on the front and the phrases "In Spock We Trust" and "Leonard Nimoy Wouldn't Lie" on the back. 1972 issue & 1975 reissue $10-15

RARITIES MINT

Star Trek Coins — 1989

Coin fronts show original characters in frosted relief on mirrored background. The backs all show the original Enterprise over the Star Trek logo and metal content. Number appears around the edge of the coin. Unsold coins were melted, meaning your numbers may be higher than actual numbers of coins in circulation.

One ounce silver coins: packaged in a plastic holder inside a velveteen box

- ❏ Kirk $50-55
- ❏ Spock $55-60
- ❏ McCoy $55-60
- ❏ Scott $55-60
- ❏ Sulu $50-55
- ❏ Chekov $50-55
- ❏ Uhura $50-55
- ❏ Set of seven

Gold-plated silver, 1/4 ounce coin: keychain or necklace format in velveteen box

- ❏ Spock $40-50

Silver 1/10 ounce coin: necklace in velveteen box

- ❏ Kirk $20-25
- ❏ Spock $20-25
- ❏ McCoy $20-25

Gold 1/4 ounce coin: packaged in plastic container in velveteen box

- ❏ Kirk $350-450
- ❏ Spock $350-450
- ❏ McCoy $350-450
- ❏ Scott $350-450
- ❏ Sulu $350-450
- ❏ Chekov $350-450
- ❏ Uhura $350-450
- ❏ Set of seven

Gold one ounce coin: special order item made only in sets, packaged in embossed leather display books. Very few produced.

- ❏ Individual coin $2000-3500
- ❏ Set of seven $15500-25500

Star Trek 25th Anniversary Coin Set

Three silver coins proof coins, each numbered and packaged in a coin holder. Backs of the coins feature the 25th anniversary logo. The three fronts feature Kirk, Spock, and the original Enterprise.

- ❏ Kirk $175-200
- ❏ Spock $175-200
- ❏ Enterprise $175-200

One ounce silver coins by Rarities Mint. *Courtesy of the Collection of Jeff Maynard — New Eye Studio*

Gold-plated silver 1/4 ounce coins in necklace format. *Courtesy of the Collection of Jeff Maynard — New Eye Studio*

COMICS

Star Trek was brought into the comic universe in 1967 by Gold Key and continues to travel there today. Comic listings are chronological, by publishers. See the sections on The Next Generation, Deep Space Nine, and Crossover products for additional listings.

GOLD KEY COMICS — July 1967 - March 1979

Comics based on the 1966-1968 television series, featuring the characters in original stories. Issues Number 1-9 feature covers with photographs from the original series.

❑ Issue #1	$125-150
❑ #2	$100-125
❑ #3-5	$60-100
❑ #6-9	$50-70
❑ #10-20	$30-50
❑ #21-40	$20-30
❑ #42-59	$20-30
❑ #60-61	$20-30

DAN CURTIS GIVEAWAYS — 1974

Twenty four page reprints of the Gold Key stories in full color, measuring 3" x 6".

❑ #2 Star Trek, Enterprise Mutiny	$10-20
❑ #6 Star Trek, Dark Traveler	$10-20

THE ENTERPRISE LOGS — 1976-1977

Each of the four volumes, published by Golden Press, reprinted eight of the Gold Key comics.

❑ #1 (reprints comic issues 1-8)	$25-45
❑ #2 (reprints comic issues 9-17)	$25-45
❑ #3 (reprints comic issues 18-26)	$25-45
❑ #4 (reprints comic issues #27-28, 30-34, 36, & 38)	$25-45

DYNABRITE COMICS — 1978-1979

Cardboard covered reprints of Gold Key stories in full cover, 48 pages.

❑ No. 11357 Star Trek: # 33 & 44	$10-20
❑ No. 11358 Star Trek: #34 & 36	$10-20

MARVEL COMICS — 1980-1982

❑ Based on the 1979 film *Star Trek: The Motion Picture* and moves forward with original stories of their own. Eighteen issues were produced.	$6-15
❑ Marvel Super Special No. 15: relates the entire movie in a magazine format. This issue came in a $1.50 & a more rare $2.00 cover price.	$10-30

DC COMICS

DC Comics — 1984-1988

❑ Published 56 issues based on Star Trek characters from the series and movies from February 1984 to November 1988. Original stories with reference and flashbacks to characters from the TV episodes. Issue No. 33 celebrated the 20th anniversary of the TV show. A Star Trek Annual was published in 1985, 1986, and 1988 and Who's Who in Star Trek issued No. 1 and 2. Tom Sutton provided artwork for issues No. 1-6, 8-18, 20-27, 29, 31-34, 39-52, and 55. Gray Morrow was the artist for issues No. 28, 35-36, and 56. Dan Spiegle (issue No. 19) and Dave Cockrum also contributed. Issue No. 19 was written by Walter Koenig. (depending on issue & condition) $2-20

Star Trek Movie Specials — 1984-1994

DC Comics adaptations of Star Trek movies III-VI. (see The Next Generation for Generations)

❑ No. 1. *Star Trek III: The Search for Spock*, June 1984	$8-12
❑ No. 2. *Star Trek IV: The Voyage Home*, 1987	$6-8
❑ No. 3. *Star Trek V: The Final Frontier*, 1989	$6-8
❑ No. 4. *Star Trek VI: The Undiscovered Country*, 1991	$6-8

Star Trek Graphic Novels

In recent years, graphic novels have become very popular. DC comics has produced two for Star Trek.

❑ *Tests of Courage*	$18-20
❑ *Who Killed Captain Kirk*	$17-19

Star Trek — 1989 - present

An ongoing DC Comics series with original stories based on the Star Trek movie series. Over 70 issues to date.$1.75 for a current issue. $2.50-4 for older issues.

❑ No. 1	$6-10

Star Trek Gold Key comic, 1968. *Courtesy of the Collection of Jeff Maynard — New Eye Studio*

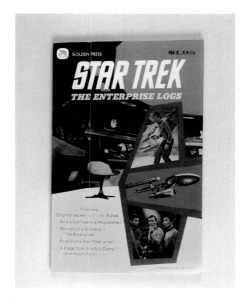

Star Trek. The Enterprise Logs comic, 1976. *Courtesy of the Collection of Jeff Maynard — New Eye Studio*

COSTUMES, PATTERNS, & MAKEUP KITS

Costumes and patterns have been produced from the early 1970s onward. Fans enjoy wearing them to conventions. In the "post-Roddenberry" era, Paramount frowns on conventioneers wearing unlicensed patterns to public events. Paramount also keeps tight control of all original uniforms from the movies and television series that followed the original Star Trek series. It is unlikely there are many original uniforms to be found on the market. Makeup kits have begun to appear, based on the exotic features of The Next Generation Klingons and Ferengi. See both the sections of on The Next Generation and Deep Space Nine for additional costumes, patterns, and for the makeup kits

Original Star Trek Television Show Costumes

Star Fleet Uniforms

A company, which sold almost exclusively to fans, produced uniforms under limited license during the 1970s. Star Fleet Uniforms produced authentic reproduction adult sized shirts in knit materials.

❑ Gold	$30-33
❑ Blue	$30-33
❑ Red	$30-33

Star Trek, original series men's uniform shirt. *Courtesy of the Collection of Jeff Maynard — New Eye Studio*

COLLEGEVILLE Halloween Costumes

Children's lightweight costumes with tie-on jump suits decorated with the Enterprise and the words "Star Trek" in felt with sparkles on the front. Plastic character masks were part of these costumes produced in 1967 and packaged in window boxes.

❑ Kirk	$30-50
❑ Spock	$30-50

BEN COOPER

This company produced children's costumes in 1973 and 1975.

❑ 1973: single-piece jump suit with a plastic mask and pictures of Spock and the Enterprise. Packaged as a "Super Hero" costume. $20-40

❑ 1975: single-piece jump suits picturing characters & Enterprise with plastic masks. Character masks included:

❑ Kirk	$20-30
❑ Spock	$20-30
❑ Klingon	$20-30

RUBIES

Costumes produced for adults and children in 1990 based on the original television series from the same firm that produced the Klingon and Ferengi makeup kits. Silkscreened insignias. Produced in gold, blue, and red.

❑ Men's shirt	$28-30
❑ Women's dress	$33-35

FRANCO

❑ Vulcan Ears: produced in 1974 and packaged in a bag with a header featuring a Spock line drawing. $10-12

Original Star Trek Television Series Patterns

LINCOLN ENTERPRISES

In 1976, this firm produced men's and women's uniform patterns.

❑ Men's uniform shirt pattern (several sizes)	$6-7
❑ Women's uniform pattern (several sizes)	$6-7

SIMPLICITY Star Trek Classic Uniform Pattern

Patterns produced in 1989 for the original series and packaged together in the same envelope.

❑ Men's shirt and trousers (various sizes)	$7-8
❑ Women's dress (various sizes)	$7-8

Star Trek: The Motion Picture

AVIA

❑ Spock Ears: produced in children's sizes in 1979 packaged in a blister pack with a color photo of Spock. $15-25

COLLEGEVILLE

In 1979, Collegeville produced one-piece children's costumes decorated with characters and the series logo. Packaged in a window box.

❑ Kirk	$20-35
❑ Spock	$20-35
❑ Ilia $20-35	
❑ Klingon	$20-35

Star Trek II: The Wrath of Khan — Costumes & Patterns

BALLANTINE BOOKS

❑ 20th Anniversary Vulcan Ears: promotional giveaways bagged with a 20th anniversary sticker. $10-16

COLLEGEVILLE

Halloween one-piece costume from 1982 featuring characters, the Enterprise, and the Star Trek II logo. Produced for children and sold in window boxes.

❑ Kirk	$20-30
❑ Spock	$20-30

DON POST

❑ Spock Ears: bagged ears sold in 1982 with a header with a color Star Trek II logo. $9-14

LINCOLN ENTERPRISES

1983 patterns in several sizes each.

❑ Men's jacket	$9-12
❑ Women's jacket	$9-12
❑ Recreational jump suit	$9-12
❑ Pants	$7-10
❑ Turtleneck undershirt	$7-10

DECALS & STICKERS

LINCOLN ENTERPRISES — Decals

❑ Sheet No. 1. three different insignia designs, water mount, two color	$2-4
❑ Sheet No. 2. Enterprise, Klingon Fighter, & Galileo	$2-4
❑ Sheet No. 3. Communicator, Phaser, & 3-D Chess Game	$2-4
❑ Sheet No. 4. NCC-1701 decal in several sizes	$2-4
❑ Sheet No. 5. eight Star Trek monsters	$2-4
❑ Sheet No. 6. - 7. four different original series stars on each	$2-4

❑ **Star Fleet Academy Decal:** fan produced words	$2-3

❑ **Star Trek V: The Final Frontier Decal:** promotional, red & silver logo, Enterprise on star field	$4-6

LINCOLN ENTERPRISES — Stickers

❑ Federation Star Fleet Academy sticker	$2-3
❑ Command insignia, black on gold foil	$2-3

AVIA

❑ Star Trek: The Motion Picture puffy stickers, three sets depicting characters and the ship, 1979 $6-16

❑ Star Trek: The Motion Picture instant stained glass stickers of 1979, including:

❑ Admiral Kirk	$2-8
❑ Spock	$2-8
❑ Spock giving Vulcan salute	$2-8
❑ Spock with Federation science symbol	$2-8
❑ The Vulcan Salute	$2-8
❑ The Enterprise	$2-8

Celebrity Stamps — 1979

Set included an album and six different stamp packets.

❑ Set No. 1. U.S.S. Enterprise	$65-75
❑ Set No. 2. Captain Kirk	$65-75
❑ Set No. 3. Mr. Spock	$65-75
❑ Set No. 4. Klingons & Romulans	$65-75
❑ Set No. 5. Aliens of the Galaxy	$65-75
❑ Set No. 6. Creatures of the Galaxy	$65-75

PARAMOUNT

Vending Machine Decals: McDonald's promotional peel-back set of four, color stickers from 1979 of:

- ❑   Kirk
- ❑   Spock
- ❑   Kirk & Spock
- ❑   Enterprise $10-12/set
- ❑ Twentieth Anniversary Sticker: promotional, 1986 $1-2

POCKET BOOKS

- ❑ "Star Trek 20th Anniversary, the only logical books to read!" promotional sticker, yellow & blue, 1986. $2-3

A.H. PRISMATIC

- ❑ Star Trek Hologram Stickers: original series nine scenes in cartoon format. $6-8

Sticker Books: "The Seige" story and stickers, Canadian from 1975. $15-17

T-K GRAPHICS Stickers

- ❑ Company with a large line of offset-printed, pressure sensitive labels from Star Trek. $1-2

WALLABY

- ❑ Star Trek: The Motion Picture Peel-Off Graphics Book by Lee Cole. $40-45

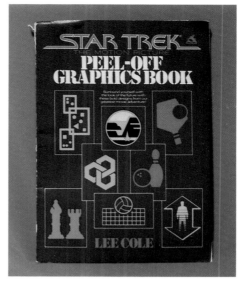

Star Trek: The Motion Picture Peel-Off Graphics Book by Lee Cole, published by Wallaby. *Courtesy of the Collection of Jeff Maynard — New Eye Studio*

FANZINES

This is one heading under which no attempt will be made to separate the items between the various series. Fanzines are fan written and produced magazines which have been in distribution since 1967. In that year the very first fanzine, "Spockinalia," hit the streets. It was intended to be a one issue release. However, it proved very popular and four additional issues were printed before this first Star Trek fanzine folded. Fanzines are created at irregular intervals and are circulated through subscriptions or through private channels. The length of the magazine depends on the wear-withal of the editor, varying from several pages to over one hundred. More than a few successful science fiction writers began their careers in the pages of fanzines when professional magazines would not have them. These include Ray Bradbury, Frederik Pohl, James Blish, Harlan Ellison, and David Gerrold. Harlan Ellison wrote the Hugo Award winning Star Trek episode "City on the Edge of Forever" and David Gerrold penned the immensely popular "The Trouble With Tribbles." Early fanzines may be purchased through Star Trek conventions or at fanzine auctions listed in Datazine (a subscription only publication out of Denver, Colorado listing fanzines in print and their prices).

Star Trek fanzines fall into five basic categories, Action/Adventure, Mixed Media, Adult, Love/Romance, and Informational. Material falling into the informational category is now also available through on-line services on the internet. Listed below are all of the fanzines and their publishers. No attempt has been made here to separate currently in print from out of print fanzines. Some come and go very quickly, making any in print listing dubious at best.

Some of the more popular or are fanzines are priced below. However, depending upon the popularity of the fanzine, they range from:

$8-30 for in-print 'zines
$10-80 for out-of-prints.

One Way Mirror fanzine, 1980. *Courtesy of the Collection of Jeff Maynard — New Eye Studio*

- ❑ Abode of Strife, Bill Hupe
- ❑ Accumulated Leave, Yeoman Press
- ❑ Act Five, MKASHEF Ent
- ❑ Alexi, MKASHEF Ent
- ❑ All Our Yesterdays No. 4, Dolly Weissberg
- ❑ Alternate Universe, No. 1-2, Shirley Maiewski
- ❑ Alternates, Bill Hupe
- ❑ Archives, Yeoman Press
- ❑ As I Do Thee, A. Gelfand
- ❑ As I Do Thee, MKASHEF Ent
- ❑ Azimuth to Zenith, Mary Case
- ❑ Babel, Laura & Margaret Basta
- ❑ Before the Glory, Kathleen Resch
- ❑ Beneath an Angry Star
- ❑ Berengaria, V. Kirlin

Night of the Twin Moons Collection Volume 2 fanzine collected works, 1979. *Courtesy of the Collection of Jeff Maynard — New Eye Studio*

Off The Beaten Trek fanzine, Vol. 1, No. 3. *Courtesy of the Collection of Jeff Maynard — New Eye Studio*

- Beside Myself, Merry Men Press
- Beyond Antaries, Bill Hupe
- Beyond the Farthest Star, Bill Hupe
- Bloodstone, C. Frisbie
- Broken Images, V. Clark
- The Castaways, V. Kirlin
- Cheap Thrills, Carol Hunterton
- Companion, Carol Hunterton
- Complete Kershu Fighter, Poison Pen
- Contact, No. 1-6, Bev Volker & Nancy Kippax
- Courts of Honor, Syn Ferguson
- Crucible for Courage, Bill Hupe
- Daring Attempt, W. Rathbone
- Day of Vengeance, Kathleen Resch
- Daystrom Project, Bill Hupe
- Delta Triad, Melinda Reynolds
- Diamonds and Rust, Cheryl Rice
- Displaced, L. Welling
- Don't Tell It to the Captain, M. Lamski
- Duet, D. Dabinett (ed.)
- Echoes of the Empire, J. Thompson
- Elysia, Bill Hupe
- Empire Books, Empire Books
- The Enterprise Review, Dolly Weissberg
- Epilogue, Jean Lorrah (Lorrah's novels proved so popular, she has been published by Pocketbooks-see Vulcan Academy Murders)
- Epilogue #2, Jean Lorrah
- Eridani, Bill Hupe
- Eridani Triad No. 1-5, Judith Brownlee
- Fesarius Series, T.J. Burnside
- Fetish, Merry Men
- Final Frontier, Sandra Gent
- First Time, Merry Men
- Formazine, A Light Stimulant, Linda Channack
- Full Moon Rising, Jean Lorrah
- Furaha, Virginia Walker
- Games of Love and Duty, Poison Pen
- The Garden Spot, Bill Hupe
- A Gathering of Blacque, MKASHEF
- Genesis Aftermath, Bill Hupe
- Grup, Carrie Brennan
- Hailing Frequencies, Natash Mohr
- Handful of Snowflakes, Steve Barnes
- Hellguard Social Register, Bill Hupe
- The Hive, Roberta Debono
- Honorable Sacrifice, Bev Zuk
- Hostages to Fortune, Roberta Debono
- Idylls, Bill Hupe
- In a Different Reality, Bill Hupe
- In a Different Reality, M. Krause
- In the Wilderness, Rosemary Wild
- Interlude, Bill Hupe
- In Triplicate, MKASHEF

- It Takes Time on Impulse, H. Stallings
- Interphase!, Connie Faddis
- Just This Once, Bill Hupe
- Kefrendar, Bill Hupe
- Kraith Collected Series, Carol Lynn
- Laff Trek, Bill Hupe
- Lifeboat, Bev Zuk
- Lore, Bill Hupe
- The Marriage, Dolly Weissberg
- Masiform D, Devra Langsam
- Masiform D, Poison Pen
- Matter/Antimatter, Sandra Gent
- McCoy Gets the Last Word, Nancy Borden
- Menagerie, Sharon Ferraro & Paula Smith
- Mindset, Roberta Debono
- Mirrors of Mind and Flesh, Gayle Feyrer
- Mixed Metaphors, D. Barry
- More Missions-More Myths
- Naked Times, Pon Farr Press
- NCC-1701D, Natasha Mohr
- The Neofan's Guide to Fandom, Joan Verba
- A Next Generation Compendium, FOTP
- Night of the Twin Moons, Jean Lorrah (possibly the most popular fanzine)
- Night of the Twin Moons Collected, Vol. 1 & 2
- No Peaceful Roads Lead Home, Poison Pen
- Nome Series, V. Clark & B. Storey
- Nu Ormenel, F. Marder
- Nu Ormenel Collected No. 5, Poison Pen
- Nuage, K. Bates
- Obsession 2-3, M. Lowe & K. Scarrett
- Odyssey, Ingrid Cross
- One Way Mirror, Poison Pen (251 page novel)
- One Way Mirror, Barbara Wenk
- Orion, Bill Hupe
- OSC'Zine, T'Kuhtian
- Out of Bounds, P. Rose & L. Shell
- Penumbra, M. Arvizu
- Perchance to Dream, Roberta Debono
- Perfect Object, Yeoman Press
- Pit of Archeron, Bill Hupe
- Pledge, C. Davis
- Portraits, Merry Men
- Precessional, Laurie Huff
- Price and the Prize, Gayle Feyrer
- The Price of Freedom, Kathleen Resch
- R & R No. 1-5, Yeoman Press
- Rendezvous, Mary Case
- Renegades, Mary Case
- Revenge of the Wind Rider, Roberta Debono
- Ring of Deceit, Empire Books
- Sahaj, Leslie Lilker
- Scattered Stars, Merry Men
- The Search for Patrick Stewart-The Bibliography, Helen Bookman
- The Search for Patrick Stewart-The Collection, Helen Bookman
- Sensor Readings, Bill Hupe
- Sensuous Vulcan, D.T. Steiner
- Shades of Grey, MKASHEF
- Ship's Log, Lee Pennell
- Spinerisms-Annotated Bibliography of Brent (Data) Spiner's career
- Spock, Bill Hupe
- Spock Enslaved
- Spockanalia No. 1-5, Devra Langsam (the first fanzine)
- Spockanalia, Poison Pen
- Spunk, Bill Hupe
- Squired Again, Mary Case
- Star Art, Dolly Weissberg
- Starbound 2, FONN
- Stardate Unknown No. 1-5, Gerry Downes
- Starlines, Bill Hupe
- Sun and Shadow, C. Frisbie
- T-Negative, Ruth Berman
- Tales of Feldman, Mindy Glazer
- Third Verdict, Bev Zuk
- Thoroughbreds, Rowena Warner
- T'HY'LA, Kathleen Resch
- Thrust, C. Frisbie
- Timeshift, Florence Butler
- Touchstone, Robyn Berkley
- Transwarp, Bill Hupe

- ❑ Trojan Angel, Bill Hupe
- ❑ The Uhura Papers, Jan Walker
- ❑ Ultimate Mary Sue, Bill Hupe
- ❑ Vaeya, Lee Pennell
- ❑ Vault of Tomorrow, Marion McChesney
- ❑ A Very Special Shore Leave, Dolly Weissberg
- ❑ The Voice, Rosemary Wild
- ❑ Vulcan's Lyre, Kelly Cline
- ❑ Warped Space, T'Kuthian Press
- ❑ The Weight, Leslie Fish
- ❑ Where Do We Go From Here?, Lee Pennell

FILM & VIDEO

Prior to the advent of video tape, serious film collectors devoted large portions of their homes to libraries of delicate 16 mm films. The original episodes of Star Trek were produced in this format and some have made it into the market place despite the studio's best attempts to prevent it. If you should happen across one, be aware that these aging color films will turn red if not properly cared for.

Star Trek movies have been, and continue to be, produced in 35 or 70 mm film formats. This make them very difficult for home viewing. These projectors are simply too large. Star Trek: The Next Generation, Deep Space Nine, and Voyager are all produced on high quality video tape, leaving the age of reel to reel in the dust.

RCA Laser Discs

Several of the original television episodes exist in this format. Each laser disc holds two episodes. The first four films also were released on laser disc.

❑ Original Star Trek TV episodes	$20-40
❑ Star Trek: The Motion Picture	$40-50
❑ Star Trek II: The Wrath of Khan	$40-50
❑ Star Trek III: The Search for Spock	$40-50
❑ Star Trek IV: The Voyage Home	$40-50

Video Tape

PARAMOUNT HOME VIDEO

Paramount released the original episodes in VHS and Beta formats. Those Betas should now be difficult for collectors to find.

Original Star Trek Episodes

❑ Individual episode: all original series episodes have been available in single episode tape format	$13-15
❑ Double episode tapes: 1982, several of these were produced	$26-30
❑ The Cage, No. 1: (original pilot turned down by NBC)	$13-15
❑ The Cage, No. 99: all color video	$13-15
❑ Menagerie: two-part episode which salvaged much of The Cage	$13-15

The original series television episodes are now available on video tape. *Courtesy of the Collection of Jeff Maynard — New Eye Studio*

When The Cage was turned down by NBC as Star Trek's premier, much of the footage was salvaged for use in this two part episode, "The Menagerie." *Courtesy of the Collection of Jeff Maynard — New Eye Studio*

"The Trouble With Tribbles," one of the best-loved episodes. *Courtesy of the Collection of Jeff Maynard — New Eye Studio*

"Mirror, Mirror" on video tape. *Courtesy of the Collection of Jeff Maynard — New Eye Studio*

All of the first seven Star Trek movies are currently available on video. *Courtesy of the Collection of Jeff Maynard — New Eye Studio*

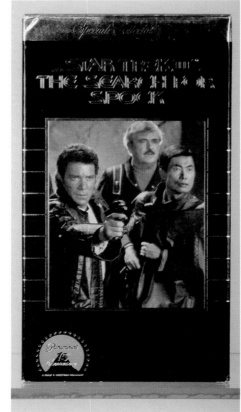

Star Trek Animated Series
❑ 11 tapes: two episodes per tape covering all 22 episodes aired. $13-15

Star Trek Movies
❑ Star Trek: The Motion Picture $20-30 each
❑ Star Trek II: The Wrath of Khan
❑ Star Trek III: The Search for Spock
❑ Star Trek IV: The Voyage Home
❑ Star Trek V: The Final Frontier
❑ Star Trek VI: The Undiscovered Country
❑ **Star Trek Gift Set-The Movies-25th Anniversary Collection:**
Hosted by William Shatner & Leonard Nimoy, included films I-V in widescreen format on four cassettes, 3 enamel pins, & a commemorative certificate from Gene Roddenberry. $50-80
❑ **Star Trek-The Starfleet Collection-1993:** includes films I-VI, Starfleet timepiece, trading cards, official hologram, & a case only opened by a Starfleet Access Card included in set. Limited to 5000 copies. $50-80
❑ **Star Trek-The Screen Voyages:** boxed set including films I-VI. $50-80

Star Trek Game, Action & Adventure in Outer Space, board game by Hasbro, 1974. *Courtesy of the Collection of Jeff Maynard — New Eye Studio*

GAMES & ACCESSORIES

Games are listed by general categories from arcade to role playing and trivia games. Within each category, the games are listed by manufacturer whenever possible.

Arcade Game
SEGA
❑ Star Trek Strategic Operations Simulator, based on Star Trek: The Motion Picture: standing or sitting versions for commercial use, 1980. $2000-3000

Board Games
BMI
❑ Star Trek The Final Frontier: board game with Kirk, Spock & scenes from the original series on the cover. $20-50

HASBRO
❑ Star Trek Game: includes fold-out board game with plastic pieces & spinners. 1974 $100-110

IDEAL
❑ Star Trek Game: includes board, 4 game cards, & many playing pieces. 1966 $125-150

Star Trek Game, a board game by Ideal, 1967. *Courtesy of the Collection of Jeff Maynard — New Eye Studio*

Star Trek The Final Frontier board game by BMI, 1992. *Courtesy of the Collection of Jeff Maynard — New Eye Studio*

StarTrek (The Motion Picture) Game, a board game by Milton Bradley, 1979. *Courtesy of the Collection of Jeff Maynard — New Eye Studio*

MILTON BRADLEY
- ❑ Star Trek Game: based on Star Trek: The Motion Picture, included board, playing cards, markers, & playing pieces. 1979 $100-110

PALITOY (BRITISH)
- ❑ Star Trek Game: Kirk & Spock on the blue cover. $75-100

Cartridge & CD Games
Games for home game systems (see The Next Generation listings for more)

GENERAL CONSUMER ELECTRONICS
- ❑ Star Trek: The Motion Picture game from 1982 for Vectrex system $30-40

MICROVISION (Milton Bradley)
- ❑ Star Trek Phaser Strike: hand-held cartridge game $30-40

SEGA
- ❑ Star Trek Strategic Operations Simulator: home version of their commercial arcade game, 1983. $30-40

Computer Games
BERKELEY SYSTEMS
- ❑ Star Trek: Images from the Motion Pictures: screen posters, 1994 $50-75

MACPLAY
- ❑ Star Trek 25th Anniversary Voice Activated CD ROM: features the voices of Kirk, Spock, & McCoy, 1991 $50-75

SIMON AND SCHUSTER (licensed games)
- ❑ First Contact $40-50
- ❑ The Kobayashi Alternative $50-60
- ❑ The Promethean Prophecy $40-50
- ❑ The Rebel Universe $50-60
- ❑ Transinium Challenge $60-70

Crossword Puzzles
RUNNING PRESS
- ❑ A large color poster puzzle shaped like the starship Enterprise. $25-30

Darts
- ❑ **Star Trek Regulation Dart Board:** closed cover decorated with classic Enterprise in flight over a planet. Includes six darts with Star Trek flights (the "feathers") showing either the Enterprise or a Klingon battle cruiser. $80-90

- ❑ **Star Trek Dart Game Cabinet:** closed covered decorated with Klingon bridge, Klingons, & the

---

classic Enterprise on the screen. Includes 14" diameter dart board, 6 brass darts, score boards, chalk, eraser, & rules booklet. $50-55

LINCOLN ENTERPRISES
- ❑ Photon Balls: styrofoam balls stick to a cloth dart board. Targets are drawn ships. $30-40

Pinball Games
AZRAK-HAMWAY
- ❑ Plastic toy pinball game, 12". Decorated with art based on original TV series. Two version produced, with either Kirk or Spock. $65-100

BALLY
- ❑ Star Trek: The Motion Picture: commercial pinball machine with electronic L.E.D. scoring. Crew members and ship decorated the back display. Two different playing surfaces were produced. $800-1000

Playing Cards
AVIVA
- ❑ Star Trek: The Motion Picture. Drawings of Enterprise on back of a standard card set. 1979. $25-30

MOVIE PLAYERS
Star Trek II: The Wrath of Khan: each character card features a character's face. Boxed with color movie logo on cover. 1982.
- ❑ First printing, accidental misprint, omitted "II" in logo. $30-40
- ❑ Second printing. $20-25

Role Playing & War Games

CITITEL MINIATURES
Produced a series of pewter 25 mm gaming pieces based on Star Trek: The Motion Picture in 1979.
- ❑ Pewter sets include: Chapel, Chekov, Decker, Ilia, McCoy, Janice Rand, Scott, Spock, Sulu, Uhura, Andoreans, Deltans, & the Enterprise Crew. $20-30

FASA
- ❑ FASA has made an industry out of their game **Star Trek Role-Playing Game** with different sets, game supplements, and accessories. $65-75
- ❑ Star Trek: The Role-Playing Game 2001 (Deluxe Limited Edition): includes Star Trek Basic Set (2004) & Star Trek III Combat Game (2006), a set of 3 adventures & deck plans for Constitution cruiser & Klingon D-7 battle cruiser. $80-100
  - ❑ Special autographed edition: signed by James Doohan or Walter Koenig $100-150
  - ❑ Enterprise deck plans, to game 2001 $40-50
  - ❑ Klingon deck plans, to game 2001 $30-40
- ❑ Star Trek: The Role-Playing Game, Second Deluxe Edition: no deck plans. $65-80
- ❑ Star Trek: The Role-Playing Game, 2004 (Basic Set): complete rules in 3 books. $20-22

Star Trek Role-Playing Game Supplements:
- ❑ The Klingons: A Sourcebook & Character Generation Supplement, 2002: in book or boxed set form. $30-50
- ❑ Ship Construction Manual, 2204: build your own starship. Sold in two editions. $20-30
- ❑ The Romulans: A Sourcebook & Character Generation Supplement, 2005 $15-17
- ❑ The Romulan Intelligence Manual: An Expansion Sourcebook, 2005A $4-5
- ❑ The Romulan Operations Manual: An Expansion Sourcebook, 2005B $2-3
- ❑ The Orions: A Sourcebook & Character Generation Supplement, 2008 $15-17
- ❑ Trader Captains and Merchant Princes, 2203: two versions of supplement allowing creation of traders, merchants, and riff-raff. $15-17
- ❑ Star Trek II: Starship Combat Game, 2003: short release time preceding ST III, brings game up to movie time frame. $20-30
- ❑ Starship Combat Game, 2003: generic version of movie update. $20-30

- ❏ Star Trek III: Movie Update and Sourcebook, 2214: brings the game up into the movie's time frame. $15-20
- ❏ The Triangle, 2007 $15-17
- ❏ The Federation, 2011 $15-17
- ❏ Star Fleet Intelligence Manual, 2014: details spies and covert operatives. $15-17
- ❏ Star Fleet Intelligence Agent Orientation Manual, 2014A $4-5
- ❏ Star Fleet Intelligence Operations Manual, 2014B $2-3
- ❏ **Star Trek Adventure Books:** add new scenarios to the extensive Role-Playing Game. Ranges from $8-10.
  - ❏ Witness for the Defense, 2202
  - ❏ Denial of Destiny, 2205
  - ❏ Termination, 1456-2206
  - ❏ Demand of Honor, 2207
  - ❏ The Orion Ruse, 2208
  - ❏ Margin of Profit, 2209
  - ❏ The Outcasts, 2210
  - ❏ A Matter of Priorities, 2211
  - ❏ A Doomsday Like Any Other, 2212
  - ❏ The Mines of Selka, 2213
  - ❏ Triangle Campaign, 2215
  - ❏ Graduation Exercise, 2216
  - ❏ Where Has All the Glory Gone? 2217
  - ❏ Return to Axanar, 2218
  - ❏ Decision at Midnight, 2219
  - ❏ Imbalance of Power, 2220
  - ❏ Old Soldiers Never Die/The Romulan War, 2221
  - ❏ A Conflict of Interest/Klingon Intelligence Briefing, 2222
  - ❏ Dixie Gambit, 2223
  - ❏ The White Flame, 2225: starship combat scenario pack
  - ❏ The Strider Incident/Regula I deck plans, 2226 (or deck plans alone)
- ❏ **Ship Recognition Manuals:** game statistics

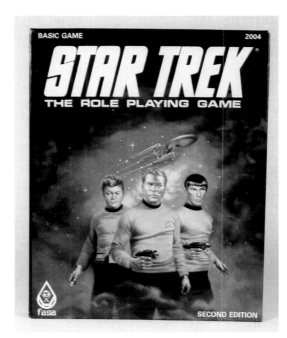

Star Trek The Role Playing Game, Second Edition, by Fasa, #2004. *Courtesy of the Collection of Jeff Maynard — New Eye Studio*

The Mines of Selka by FASA, 1986. *Courtesy of the Collection of Jeff Maynard — New Eye Studio*

The White Flame Starship Combat Scenario Pack by FASA, 1988. *Courtesy of the Collection of Jeff Maynard — New Eye Studio*

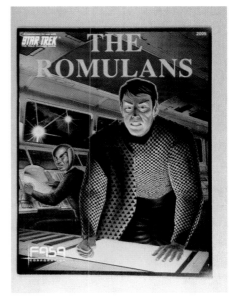

The Romulans by FASA, 1984. *Courtesy of the Collection of Jeff Maynard — New Eye Studio*

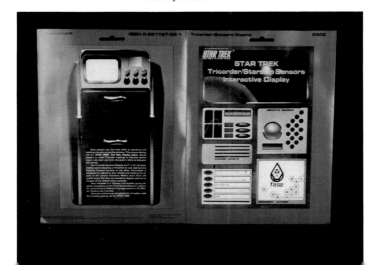

Tricorder/Starship Sensors Interactive Display by FASA, 1984. *Courtesy of the Collection of Jeff Maynard — New Eye Studio*

for 40 ships and their variants. Ranges from $10-12.
- ☐ The Klingons, 2301
- ☐ The Federation, 2302
- ☐ The Romulans, 2303
- ☐ **Playing Aids:** additional items not required to play.
  - ☐ Starship Combat Hex Grid, 2801: 3 22" x 33"
    star field maps $5-7
  - ☐ Gamemaster's Kit, 2802: 3 screens with tables
    & charts. $10-12
  - ☐ Tricorder/Sensors Interactive Display, 2803: use
    a tricorder in play. $15-17

Starship Miniatures: 1/3900 scale lead miniatures needing
assembly, blister packed. Ranges from $5-15.
- ☐ U.S.S. Enterprise, 2501
- ☐ U.S.S. Reliant, 2502
- ☐ Klingon D-7, 2503
- ☐ Romulan Bird of Prey, 2504
- ☐ U.S.S. Enterprise, 2505
- ☐ Regula I Space Laboratory, 2506
- ☐ U.S.S. Larson, 2507
- ☐ Klingon D-10, 2508
- ☐ Klingon D-18, 1509
- ☐ Gorn MA-12, 2511
- ☐ Orion Blockade Runner, 2512
- ☐ Klingon L-9, 2513
- ☐ U.S.S. Loknar, 2514
- ☐ Romulan Winged Defender, 2515
- ☐ U.S.S. Chandley, 2516
- ☐ U.S.S. Excelsior, 2517
- ☐ Klingon L-42 Bird of Prey, 2518
- ☐ U.S.S. Grissom, 2519
- ☐ Deep Space Freighter, 2520
- ☐ Romulan Graceful Flyer, 2521
- ☐ Orion Wanderer, 2522
- ☐ Kobayashi Maru, 2523
- ☐ Romulan Gallant Wing, 2524
- ☐ Gorn BH-2, 2525
- ☐ U.S.S. Baker, 2526
- ☐ Romulan Nova, 2527
- ☐ Romulan Bright One, 2528
- ☐ Klingon L-24, 2529
- ☐ Klingon D-2, 2530
- ☐ Romulan Whitewind, 2531
- ☐ U.S.S. Northampton, 2532
- ☐ U.S.S. Remora, 2533
- ☐ U.S.S. Andor, 2534

Star Trek II: The Wrath of Khan: 25mm lead miniature figures,
blister packed. $5-7 each
- ☐ James T. Kirk, 2601
- ☐ 1st Officer Spock, 2602
- ☐ Dr. McCoy, 2603
- ☐ Lt. Saavik, 2604
- ☐ Scotty, 2605
- ☐ Lt. Uhura, 2606
- ☐ Sulu, 2607
- ☐ Chekov, 2608
- ☐ Khan, 2609
- ☐ David Marcus, 2610
- ☐ Joachim, 2611
- ☐ Carol Marcus, 2612
- ☐ Captain Terrell, 2613
- ☐ Khan (Ceti Alpha V), 2614
- ☐ Klingon Officer, 2615
- ☐ Klingon Soldier 1, 2616
- ☐ Klingon Soldier 2, 2617
- ☐ Boxed Sets: each includes a ship & 8 crew figures $30-35
  - ☐ Enterprise & crew, 3001
  - ☐ Reliant & Khan's crew, 3002
  - ☐ Regula I & scientists, 3003
  - ☐ Klingon D-7 & crew, 3004

Star Trek Microadventure Games: small boxed games, short
playing times, simple rules $15-20 each
- ☐ Star Trek III: The Search for Spock, 5001
- ☐ Star Trek III: Starship Duel 1, 5002
- ☐ Star Trek III: Struggle for the Throne, 5004
- ☐ Star Trek III: Starship Duel 2, 5005

TASK FORCE GAMES
War games, combat between ships or fleets. Every item listed here is used in the
game **Star Fleet Battles:**
- ☐ Introduction to Star Fleet Battles, 3000 $8-10
- ☐ Star Fleet Battles, 5001: starting set for game includes
  108 page Vol. I Commander's Rulebook, 32 page SSD
  & chart booklet, 216 die-cut counters & a large map.
  Boxed set. $30-50
- ☐ Star Fleet Battles Volume II, 5008 $30-40
- ☐ Star Fleet Battles Volume III, 5009 $30-40
- ☐ Star Fleet Battles Supplements: game expansions with rules
  and playing pieces: $10-15
  - ☐ No. 1 Fighters & Shuttles, 3003
  - ☐ No. 2 X-Ships, 3013
  - ☐ No. 3 Fast Patrol Ships
- ☐ Star Fleet Battles Reinforcements, 3014: more playing pieces $8-10
- ☐ Star Fleet Battles Rules Update 1, 3015 $7-9
- ☐ Federation & Empire, 5006 $50-70
- ☐ Federation & Empire Deluxe, 5006 $60-80
- ☐ Federation & Empire Deluxe Fleet Pack, 3203 $30-40
- ☐ Federation & Empire Deluxe Folio Pack, 3204 $8-10
- ☐ **Captain's Log:** each includes a story, over 20 scenarios, & new rules for
  playing Star Fleet Battles $8-10
  - ☐ No. 1, 3004
  - ☐ No. 2, 3008
  - ☐ No. 3, 3010
  - ☐ No. 4, 3012
- ☐ Commander's SSD Books: each contains 48 SSDs per book $8-10
  - ☐ No. 1, 3005, Federation, Andromedan, Orions, & Kzinti
  - ☐ No. 2, 3006, Klingons, Lyran, Hydran, & Wyn
  - ☐ No. 3, 3007, Romulan, Tholian, & Gorn
  - ☐ No. 4, 3009, Tugs, Star Bases, Battle Stations, &
    Freighters
  - ☐ No. 5, 3016, Q-ships, Booms & Saucers, Special &
    Variant Ships
  - ☐ No. 6, 3018, Police Ships, Light Tugs, Survey Cruisers,
    & Space Control Ships
  - ☐ No. 7, 3020, Tholian, Gorn, Federation, Kzinti, & Hydran
    Ships
  - ☐ No. 8, 3021, Klingon, Lyran, Orion, & Romulan Ships
  - ☐ No. 9, 3023, New Commander's SSD for all races

Starline 2200 Miniatures: 1/3900 scale lead or plastic miniatures
- ☐ Federation: $8-15 each
  - ☐ Federation Dreadnought, 7010
  - ☐ Federation Heavy Cruiser, 7011
  - ☐ Federation New Light Cruiser, 7012
  - ☐ Federation Light Cruiser, 7013
  - ☐ Federation Destroyer, 7014
  - ☐ Federation Scout, 7015
  - ☐ Federation Tug, 7016
  - ☐ Federation Frigate (2), 7017
  - ☐ Federation Carrier, 7020
  - ☐ Federation Starbase, 7025
- ☐ Klingons: $8-15 each
  - ☐ Klingon B-10 Battleship, 7040
  - ☐ Klingon C-8 Dreadnought, 7042
  - ☐ Klingon D-7 Battlecruiser, 7043
  - ☐ Klingon D-5 Cruiser, 7044
  - ☐ Klingon F-5 Frigate (2), 7046
  - ☐ Klingon Tug (carrier), 7051
  - ☐ Klingon PFs (6), 7053
- ☐ Romulans: $8-10 each
  - ☐ Romulan Condor, 7060
  - ☐ Romulan Warbird (2), 7064
  - ☐ Romulan Sparrowhawk, 7071
  - ☐ Romulan Skyhawk & Seahawk, 7073
- ☐ Gorns: $8-10 each
  - ☐ Gorn Dreadnought, 7080
  - ☐ Gorn Heavy Cruiser, 7081
  - ☐ Gorn Light Cruiser, 7082
  - ☐ Gorn Destroyer (2), 7084
- ☐ Kzintis: $8-10 each
  - ☐ Kzinti Space Control Ship, 7100
  - ☐ Kzinti Carrier, 7101
  - ☐ Kzinti Escort Carrier, 7103
  - ☐ Kzinti Strike Cruiser, 7104
  - ☐ Kzinti Frigate (2), 7107
  - ☐ Kzinti Tug, 7108
  - ☐ Kzinti PFs (6), 7110

- ❏ Lyrans: $8-10 each
  - ❏ Lyran Lion Dreadnought, 7120
  - ❏ Lyran Cruiser, 7122
  - ❏ Lyran War Cruiser, 7123
  - ❏ Lyran Destroyer (2), 7124
  - ❏ Lyran PFs (6), 7126
- ❏ Hydrans: $8-10 each
  - ❏ Hydran Paladin DN, 7140
  - ❏ Hydran Ranger, 7141
  - ❏ Hydran Horseman, 7142
  - ❏ Hydran Lancer (2), 7143
  - ❏ Hydran Hunter/Scout (2), 7144
  - ❏ Hydran PFs (6), 7147
- ❏ Tholians: $8-10 each
  - ❏ Tholian Dreadnought, 7160
  - ❏ Tholian Cruiser (2), 7161
  - ❏ Tholian Patrol Cruiser (2), 7164
  - ❏ Neo-Tholian Dreadnought, 7172
  - ❏ Neo-Tholian Cruiser (2), 7174
- ❏ Orions: $8-10 each
  - ❏ Orion Heavy Cruiser, 7181
  - ❏ Orion Salvage Cruiser, 7182
  - ❏ Orion Raider (2), 7183
  - ❏ Orion Slaver (2), 7184
- ❏ Andromedans: $8-10 each
  - ❏ Andromedan Intruder, 7221
  - ❏ Andromedan Satellite Ships (3), 7222
  - ❏ Andromedan Conquistador & Python, 7223
- ❏ Interstellar Concordium: $7-9 each
  - ❏ ISC Dreadnought, 7250
  - ❏ ISC Star Cruiser, 7252
  - ❏ ISC Destroyer & Frigate, 7256
- ❏ All Races: $6-8 each
  - ❏ Small Freighters (2), 7200

-     ❏ Battle Station, 7211
- ❏ Starline 2220 Starships, 7300: boxed set including one each of Federation Heavy Cruiser, Klingon D-7 Battlecruiser, Klingon F-5 Frigate, Gorn Destroyer, & Romulan Warbird $15-20
- ❏ Starline 2200 Hex Sheets, 7000: four 18" x 24" maps $20-25

GAMESCIENCE
This company produced their own Star Trek war game, complete with ships.
- ❏ Star Fleet Battle Manual: combat game with starships.
  - ❏ Booklet $15-20
  - ❏ Deluxe boxed set including 8 plastic ships $40-50
- ❏ Ships: 1/3788 scale plastic game pieces with stands. Ships all provided in white, clear, phosphorescent green, & phosphorescent blue, representing different game states.$6-8 each
  - ❏ Cruiser, 10504
  - ❏ Destroyer, 10505
  - ❏ Scout, 10506
  - ❏ Dreadnought, 10507
  - ❏ Tug, 10508

Trivia Games

CLASSIC
- ❏ Star Trek: The Game: included board game, dice, trivia cards, & playing pieces. Box art has artist renderings of classic Enterprise, Kirk & Spock. Boxes included collector's numbers. 1992. $50-55

WESTERN PUBLISHING
Golden Trivia Game, Star Trek Edition: complete version includes game board, trivia cards, & dice. Second version sold as cards only. Boxed with color photo of Enterprise and small inset photos from the original TV episodes.
- ❏ Complete game $100-110
- ❏ Cards only $35-40

Star Trek: The Game, a trivia game based on the original series by Classic Co., 1992. *Courtesy of the Collection of Jeff Maynard — New Eye Studio*

Star Trek: The Motion Picture glasses: left to right: Spock, Kirk, & McCoy; U.S.S. Enterprise & Kirk; Ilia & Decker by Coca-Cola. *Courtesy of the Collection of Jeff Maynard — New Eye Studio*

GLASSWARES & TANKARDS

COCA-COLA
Star Trek: The Motion Picture set: a franchise to carry these was never found, few stores carried them, 5 1/2" high, 1979. Three glasses with descriptions on the back and the following pictures on front: $50-75/set
- ❏ Kirk, Spock, & McCoy
- ❏ Decker & Ilia
- ❏ Enterprise

Dr. Pepper animated series glasses, 4 to a set (Spock not present here), 1976. *Courtesy of the Collection of Jeff Maynard — New Eye Studio*

One of a set of four 1978 Dr. Pepper Star Trek Collectors Series 6 1/4" high drinking glasses. Original series U.S.S. Enterprise. *Courtesy of the author's collection*

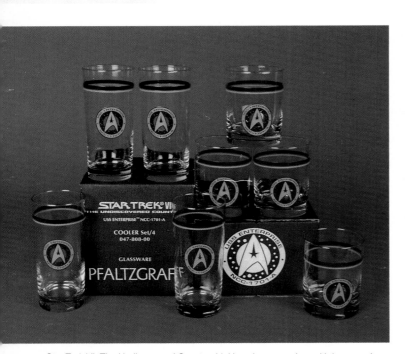

Star Trek VI: The Undiscovered Country drinking glass grouping, with large cooler glasses and small Double Old Fashion glasses by Pfaltzgraff, 1994. *Courtesy of the Collection of Jeff Maynard — New Eye Studio*

DR. PEPPER

1976 set of 4 drinking glasses measuring 6 1/4" high, with information on back and color illustrations on front:

❑ Captain James T. Kirk		$45-50
❑ Dr. Leonard McCoy		$75-85
❑ Mr. Spock		$75-100
❑ U.S.S. Enterprise		$85-95

1978 set of 4 drinking glasses, 6 1/4" high, with somewhat different artwork but the same subject matter. Less common set. $250-300/set

- ❑ Captain James T. Kirk
- ❑ Dr. Leonard McCoy
- ❑ Mr. Spock
- ❑ U.S.S. Enterprise

OFFICIAL STAR TREK FAN CLUB

❑ Porcelain 20th anniversary mug with fan club logos	$20-30

PFALTZGRAFF

Large Cooler sized and smaller Double Old Fashion sized glasses with U.S.S. Enterprise NCC-1701-A insignia from the film Star Trek VI: The Undiscovered Country:

❑ Cooler glasses	$22-24
❑ Double Old Fashion glasses	$22-24

TACO BELL

1984, 4 glasses based on the movie Star Trek III emblazoned with:

- ❑ "Spock Lives"
- ❑ "Enterprise Destroyed"
- ❑ "Lord Kruge"
- ❑ "Fal-tor-pan"   (set of 4) $45-50

FRANKLIN MINT

- ❑ **Twenty-fifth Anniversary Pewter Tankard:** features three paneled renderings from the original series, 1991. $125-140

GREETING CARDS

CALIFORNIA DREAMERS
Color photos taken from the original series on 5" x 7" cards with envelopes. Three series were produced, dating from 1985-1987.

First Series — 1985 $2-4 each
Birthday Cards:
- ❑ Kirk Talking Into Communicator: "The landing party is expendable. The ship is not. If we're not back by 0500, contact Star Fleet Command, get the Enterprise out of here, & whatever you do...Have a good time on your Birthday!
- ❑ Kirk in Romulan Disguise, Speaking into Communicator: "This is Captain James T. Kirk of the Starship Enterprise. Our mission is a peaceful one. We mean no harm...Sure the check's in the mail & you're 29. Happy Birthday."
- ❑ Kirk & Spock: "Fire all phasers...Fire all photon torpedoes...What the heck. It's your Birthday!
- ❑ Spock: "Readings indicate an unparalleled cosmic phenomena occurred on this day. It was in a time so ancient, the year cannot be ascertained by ship's computers...I guess we'll just have to look at the cake & count all those candles! Happy Birthday."
- ❑ Spock in Vulcan Salute: "You were born on this day. It is therefore quite logical to wish you a Happy Birthday...Live long & prosper."
- ❑ Spock in Environment Suit: "The heat here is extreme. Fra beyond normal ranges...How many candles were on that cake, anyway? Happy Birthday."
- ❑ Spock Wearing Visor: "Just because on is logical...does not mean one cannot be cool. You're cool. Happy Birthday."
- ❑ Spock Regards Bridge Instruments: "History Banks indicate that inhabitants of 20th century Earth would oftentimes undergo a strange suicidelike ritual on many of their post-30th birthdays...Death by chocolate. Happy Birthday."
- ❑ Spock Plays Harp: "I fail to understand the inexplicable human need to so primitively celebrate the anniversary of one's birth. Nevertheless, I offer you the words of Surak, the most revered of all Vulcan philosophers. 'Krut Toba Grig-Toba Grig.' If you party, party BIG!! Happy Birthday."
- ❑ Spock Holds Cat: "There are 3 billion worlds in the known universe, with a combined population of approximately 6,307,000,000,000 composed of carbon- and noncarbon-based life forms...But there's only 1 of you. Happy Birthday."
- ❑ McCoy Checking Medical Equipment: "I've run every test, checked every medical reference in the galaxy, and damn it, I can't find a cure for what you've got...Old Age...Happy Birthday."

- ❑ McCoy Injured: "Listen to me. I'm a doctor. I know...Birthdays are hell!"
- ❑ Scott: "Three dilithium crystals, a tablespoon of kironide, a pinch of anti-matter, and just a dash of phaser...I'm going to make you a birthday cake that will light up the universe...Happy Birthday."
- ❑ Chekov Screams: "Inhuman Cossacks! Pigs! They've destroyed everything. You'll never be 29 again. Happy Birthday."

Other First Series Cards:
- ❑ Kirk with Bow & Arrow: "I was going to shoot you with a phaser...But it seemed so unromantic."
- ❑ Disgusted Kirk: "Sometimes I just want to say to hell with Star Fleet, to hell with regulations and responsibility, to hell with everything...Except you!"
- ❑ Kirk, Arms Folded: "There's an amusing little custom we have on Earth...Report to my quarters and I'll explain!"
- ❑ Kirk with "Gamesters of Triskelion" Providers: "Who am I? Where am I? Why do I have on these strange clothes...Why do I have such strange friends?"
- ❑ Kirk Attacked by Gorn: "Beam me up Scotty...It's been one of those days."
- ❑ Kirk, Spock, & McCoy in Suits from "Piece of the Action": "You've got to dress for success!"
- ❑ Kirk, McCoy, & Uhura: "Phasers charged and ready. Photon torpedoes fully armed...Here comes Monday!"
- ❑ Smiling Spock: "You make me smile!"
- ❑ Seated Spock: "It is not logical. It makes no sense...It must be Love!"
- ❑ Bridge Screen, Planet in View: "To boldly go where no man has gone before...or woman either. Congratulations."
- ❑ Enterprise: "Space is not the final frontier...You are!"

Second Series — 1986
Birthday Cards: $2-4 each
- ❑ Kirk & Spock: "You are correct, Captain, I see them. On our right as well as our left...Gray hair. Happy Birthday."
- ❑ Kirk & Spock in Force Field: "Time is a dimension, like height, width or depth, therefore we're getting shorter, fatter, denser, and older! Happy Birthday!"
- ❑ Kirk, Spock, & McCoy in Bushes: "Analysis concludes that this is both the correct time and correct place...Throw down the blanket and let's party...Happy Birthday."
- ❑ Smiling Crew: "A group of us got together to do something special for your birthday...We're having you sent into space. Happy Birthday."
- ❑ Spock: "Regrettably, the laws of gravity are absolute...Birthdays are a drag. Happy Birthday."
❑ Other Second Series Cards:
- ❑ Kirk: "The universe is a big place...How did two great people like us ever find each other?"
- ❑ Pained Kirk: "This syndrome is like that of the madness associated with severe cases of Rigelian fever. Actually, it's something quite different...Love."
- ❑ Kirk & Chekov on Bridge: "Damage control reports we've taken a direct hit. Power out on decks 1, 2, and 3. Life support systems functioning on auxiliary power...Has anybody got an asprin? Get well soon."
- ❑ Spock: "Forgive me if I'm lengthy, however, mathematics is an extremely precise science...You're a 9.99999999999999."
- ❑ Spock: "It is one of the most painful of all biological phenomena...I've got you under my skin."

Third Series — 1987
Birthday Cards: $2-4 each
- ❑ Kirk & Spock: " You are now and always shall be...My best friend. Happy Birthday."
- ❑ Kirk & Spock: "Captain, sensors indicate that subspace interference has prevented our transmission from arriving at the intended time...Sorry I was late! Happy Birthday."
- ❑ Kirk, Spock, & Uhura on Bridge: "Incoming message is extremely primitive...But very sincere. Happy birthday to you."
- ❑ Kirk in Sickbay with Crewman: "Twenty years in the fleet and I've never seen anything like it...45 pieces of double fudge chocolate birthday cake! Happy Birthday!"
- ❑ Spock: "Logic dictates that you recently had a birthday. Correctly applied, logic is seldom wrong...Sometimes late, but never wrong. Sorry I missed your birthday. Hope you had a good one."
- ❑ Spock: "It would be illogical to assume that this card is your birthday present...So much for logic! Happy Birthday."
- ❑ Spock: "These tools are extremely antiquated...Just like you! Happy Birthday."
- ❑ Spock: "My conclusion is that you are a magnificently superior being. My method of analysis was simple...It takes one to know one! Happy Birthday."
- ❑ Spock, Head in Hands: "The level of pain is quite extraordinary...I hate being so far away on your birthday."

Star Trek 25th Anniversary Edition pewter mug with three panels, 1991. *Courtesy of the Collection of Jeff Maynard — New Eye Studio*

Pop up "3-D" birthday card "Trouble with Tribbles" by PopShots. *Courtesy of the Collection of Jeff Maynard — New Eye Studio*

Star Trek pop up 3-D birthday card with McCoy, Kirk, & Spock by PopShots. *Courtesy of the Collection of Jeff Maynard — New Eye Studio*

Star Trek pop up 3-D birthday card, "No Escape" by PopShots. *Courtesy of the Collection of Jeff Maynard — New Eye Studio*

❑ Spock Reads Tricorder: "I must conclude that we are in a dimension where the laws of known physics do not apply...You're much too young to be that old! Happy Birthday."

❑ McCoy: "Don't quote regulations to me and don't give me any of that 'logic stuff'...Just go out there...And have a Happy Birthday."

❑ Chekov: Captain, there's an unidentified object appearing on the screen. It's blocking our path...Another Birthday!"

❑ Uhura: "What I'm picking up is barely understandable. Primitive music forms. Simplistic language patterns. Assorted and wildly off-key noises. I'm not sure what it is but it sounds as if they're trying to sing...Happy Birthday to you."

Other Third Series Cards: $2-4 each

❑ Kirk & Spock: "Thought about in a logical fashion, current circumstances are not as desperate as they seem...Of course, who can think logically at a time like this. Hang in there!"

❑ Kirk & Spock, Chained: Thought about in a logical fashion, current circumstances are not as desperate as they seem...Of course, who can think logically at a time like this. Hang in there!"

❑ Kirk, Spock, & McCoy at Party: "Star Fleet Command has created living conditions for us in space identical to those which we experience on Earth...Underpaid, Overworked, Underloved!"

❑ Kirk & Tellarite at Party: "Call me...We'll do lunch."

❑ Kirk Using Communicator: I've just ordered the ship's computer to provide me with your complete psychological profile...You're warped, factor-10. I like that in a person."

❑ Kirk at Swordpoint: "Keep your shields up!"

❑ Spock: "The thing most rare in the universe...A friend as good as you."

❑ Spock Wearing Headpiece: "Batteries may fail...But Rock and Roll will never die!"

CAMBRIDGE — 1979

❑ From Star Trek: The Motion Picture: $2-4 each
   ❑ Kirk & Spock with Enterprise Above
   ❑ Enterprise Above Crew
   ❑ Kirk with Wrist Communicator
   ❑ Kirk, Spock, & McCoy on Bridge
   ❑ Spock at Science Station
   ❑ Enterprise: forward view
   ❑ Enterprise: side view
   ❑ Enterprise: head on

HALLMARK

❑ Kirk, Spock, & McCoy as Cartoon Birds: "Your mission, Graduate, is to boldly go where no man has gone before...Bet you're proud as a peacock." $2-4

❑ Spock Gives Vulcan Salute: "Congratulations." $2-4

❑ Spock & Enterprise Cartoon for Halloween: "Trekker treat!" $2-4

POPSHOT POP UP BIRTHDAY CARDS

Three dimensional pop up cards featuring characters from the original series and The Next Generation (also see Next Generation section)

❑ Kirk with Tribbles: "The Tribble With Birthdays...They Keep Adding Up!" $5-7

❑ Kirk, Spock, & McCoy with Enterprise: "Birthday Greetings... From the Starship Enterprise." $5-7

❑ Kirk, Spock, Uhura, Chekov, & McCoy leaping though portal: "There Is No Going Back...There Is No Escape From Your Birthday." $5-7

RANDOM HOUSE — 1976

Several sizes of cards, largest were punch-out cards. $4-6 each

❑ Kirk: "This is your Captain speaking...Have a far-out Birthday!"

❑ Kirk: "Star light, star bright, first star I see tonight...I wished on a star for your birthday."

❑ Kirk Holding Rose: "The Captain and I both wish you a very Happy Birthday."

❑ Kirk & McCoy: "Happy Birthday from one big shot...to another." Includes 3 piece punch-out blue phaser.

❑ Kirk, Spock, McCoy, Uhura, & Scott, individual shots on cover: Happy Birthday to a great human being!"

❑ Kirk, Scott, Spock, McCoy, Uhura, & Chekov: "Happy Birthday From the Whole Spaced-Out Crew."

❑ Spock in Dress Uniform: "It is illogical not to wish a Happy Birthday to someone so charming."

❑ Spock Salutes (with eye shield): "Having a Birthday?"

❑ McCoy, Scott, Chekov, & Uhura: "Happy Birthday."

❑ Uhura: "I hear it's your Birthday...Open all hailing frequencies!"

❑ U.S.S. Enterprise: "For Your Birthday I'd Like to Take You on a Trip to Venus."

OTHER BUCKLES
- ❑ Enterprise painted, embossed, & lettered "Star Trek" — $15-25
- ❑ Enterprise (original) in center of a rectangular buckle with "Star Trek Lives," "U.S.S. Enterprise," & "To Boldly Go Where No Man Has Gone Before" around the ship, by Tiffany Studio — $15-25
- ❑ Kirk & Spock in center of oval-shaped brass buckle, "Star Trek" above, by Tiffany Studio — $20-25
- ❑ Kirk & Spock in relief in center circle of an oblong buckle, silver or gold finish — $15-20

Cloisonne, Enamel, and Polychrome Pins

AVIVA — 1979
- ❑ Kirk enamel — $15-20
- ❑ McCoy enamel — $15-20
- ❑ Kirk polychrome — $15-20
- ❑ Spock polychrome — $15-20
- ❑ Vulcan Greeting polychrome — $15-20
- ❑ McCoy polychrome — $5-10
- ❑ Enterprise polychrome — $15-20
- ❑ Uniform Insignia polychrome — $15-20
- Tie Clasps:
    - ❑ Circular, Mr. Spock with "Live Long & Prosper," gold & black — $5-7
    - ❑ Circular, Vulcan Greeting, gold, hand & black lettering — $5-7
    - ❑ Enterprise outlined in black, gold clasp — $5-7
    - ❑ Uniform insignia from original series in gold — $5-7

HOLLYWOOD COMMEMORATIVE PIN COMPANY
- ❑ Commendation Bars: set of four — $10-11
- ❑ Enterprise Cutout: 1985 — $6-7
- ❑ Enterprise & Logo: blue background, 1985 — $6-7
- ❑ Enterprise: large pin, red background, 1985 — $6-7
- ❑ Enterprise: small pin, red background, 1985 — $8-9
- Enterprise Crew: cutouts, 1986:
    - ❑ Kirk — $8-9
    - ❑ Spock — $8-9
    - ❑ Scotty — $8-9
    - ❑ McCoy — $8-9
    - ❑ Chekov — $8-9
    - ❑ Uhura — $8-9
    - ❑ Sulu — $8-9
- ❑ Insignia Cutout: movie design, small, in blue, burgundy, green, red, orange, yellow, or white — $6-7
- ❑ Insignia Cutout: large, 1986 — $8-9
- ❑ Insignia Cutout: original series, 1986 & 1991
    - ❑ Command: black, white, red, or blue on gold — $6-7
    - ❑ Science — $6-7
    - ❑ Engineering — $6-7
- ❑ Insignia & Logo: 1985:
    - ❑ Blue background — $6-10
    - ❑ White background — $6-10
- ❑ Klingon Admiral: 1985 — $6-7
- ❑ Klingon Captain: 1985 — $6-7
- ❑ Klingon Symbol: 1985 — $6-7
- ❑ Klingon Symbol: large, 1986 — $8-9
- ❑ Live Long and Prosper: phrase & Vulcan salute, blue background (also in red or burgundy background), 1985 — $8-12
    - ❑ Same as above, smaller with blue background — $6-10
- ❑ Mirror Mirror Pin: red Earth pierced with gold sword — $8-9
- ❑ Rank Insignias:
    - ❑ Admiral — $6-7
    - ❑ Cadet — $6-7
    - ❑ Captain — $6-7
    - ❑ Commander — $6-7
    - ❑ Commodore — $6-7
    - ❑ Fleet Admiral — $6-7
    - ❑ Lieutenant — $6-7
    - ❑ Lieutenant Commander — $6-7
- ❑ Romulan Symbol, 1985 — $8-9
- ❑ Romulan Symbol: cutout, 1985 — $10-11
- ❑ Star Fleet Division Insignias, 1986:
    - ❑ Colonial Operations — $8-9
    - ❑ Communications — $8-9
    - ❑ Engineering — $8-9
    - ❑ Headquarters — $8-9
    - ❑ Intelligence — $8-9

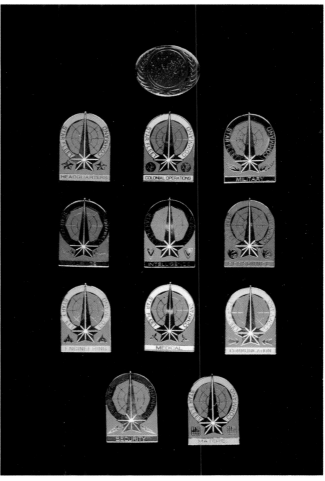

The Hollywood Commemorative Pins Company, enamel pins:
Left: Original Enterprise (1988); Center: Enterprise-D (1990); Right: Next Generation Romulan Warbird (1990). *Courtesy of the Collection of Jeff Maynard — New Eye Studio*

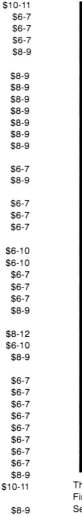

The Hollywood Commemorative Pins Company, enamel pins:
First Row: United Federation of Planets Insignia (1990)
Second Row: Headquarters (1985); Colonial Operations (1985); Military (1988).
Third Row: Marines (1985); Intelligence (1990); Personnel (1985).
Fourth Row: Engineering (1986); Medical (1985); Communications (1988).
Fifth Row: Security (1985); Materiel (1985). *Courtesy of the Collection of Jeff Maynard — New Eye Studio*

The Hollywood Commemorative Pins Company, enamel pin:
Insignia on uniform chests during the second through sixth Star Trek movie (1992).
Courtesy of the Collection of Jeff Maynard — New Eye Studio

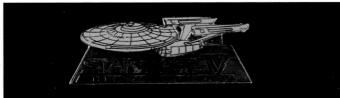

The Hollywood Commemorative Pins Company, enamel pin:
Star Trek V: The Final Frontier (1989). *Courtesy of the Collection of Jeff Maynard — New Eye Studio*

The Hollywood Commemorative Pins Company, The Cage (first pilot offering rejected by NBC) enamel pin, 1990. *Courtesy of the Collection of Jeff Maynard — New Eye Studio*

The Hollywood Commemorative Pins Company, enamel episode pins (featuring episodes from all three years of the original series - not in episode order in photos):
First Row: "The Man Trap" (1990); "Charlie X" (1990); "Where No Man Has Gone Before" (1990); The Naked Time (1990).
Second Row: The Enemy Within (1990); "Mudd's Women" (1990); What Are Little Girls Made Of? (1990); Miri (1990).
Third Row: Dagger Of The Mind (1990); "The Corbomite Maneuver" (1990); Menagerie (1991); "The Conscience of the King" (1991).
Fourth Row: Balance Of Terror (1990); Shore Leave (1990); The Galileo Seven (1990); The Squire of Gothos (1991).
Fifth Row: Arena (1991); Tomorrow Is Yesterday (1991); Court-Martial (1990); The Return Of The Archons (1991).
Sixth Row: A Taste Of Armageddon (1991); This Side Of Paradise (1991); The Devil in the Dark (1991); Errand Of Mercy (1991).
Seventh Row: The Alternative Factor (1991); The City On The Edge Of Forever (1991); Operation-Annihilate! (1991). *Courtesy of the Collection of Jeff Maynard — New Eye Studio*

☐ Marines	$8-9
☐ Materiel	$8-9
☐ Medical	$8-9
☐ Merchant Marines	$8-9
☐ Military	$8-9
☐ Personnel	$8-9
☐ Security	$8-9
☐ Star Fleet Chest Insignia: as seen in Star Trek films II-VI, in enamel, chrome, or gold-plate finish, 1992	$15-17
☐ UFP Symbol: large cutout, 1985	$8-9
☐ UFP Symbol: small cutout, 1985	$6-7
☐ Twentieth Anniversary Pin: red, white, & blue, blue & yellow, and white & blue versions, 1986	$10-12
☐ Twentieth Anniversary Pin: "To Boldly Go...," 1986	$10-15
☐ Twentieth Anniversary "WOW Pin": 1986	$15-17
☐ Twenty-fifth Anniversary Pin: red Delta Shield with gold lettering, 1991	$6-7
☐ Twenty-fifth Anniversary Pin: green Delta Shield with gold lettering, 1991	$6-7
☐ Star Trek Lives: red, 1988	$8-9
☐ Star Trek Forever: blue, 1988	$8-9
☐ Vulcan Salute: gold, 1988	$5-7
☐ Spock: Live Long and Prosper: 1988	$8-9
☐ Phaser: original TV design, 1989	$8-9
☐ Communicator: 1989	$8-9
☐ Communicator: "Beam Me Up Scotty"	$8-9
☐ Star Trek V: The Final Frontier Pins:	
☐ Star Fleet Insignia: red & white, 1989	$6-7
☐ Star Trek V logo over insignia, 1989	$6-7
☐ Star Trek V: small Enterprise, 1989	$8-9
☐ Star Trek V: large Enterprise, 1989	$10-11
☐ Star Trek V: small Galileo, 1989	$10-11
☐ Star Trek V: large Galileo, 1989	$10-11
☐ Star Trek V: Galileo logo, 1989	$6-7
☐ Star Trek V: The Final Frontier logo	$6-7
☐ Star Trek Episode Pins: 1990-onward manufacture:	
☐ Star Trek Episodes Title	$8-9
☐ The Cage	$8-9
☐ "Where No Man Has Gone Before": 1990 (pin manufacture dates)	$7-8

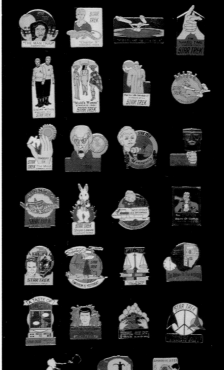

The Hollywood Commemorative Pins Company, enamel pins, (featuring episodes from all three years of the original series - not in episode order in photos):
First Row: Amok Time (1991); Who Mourns For Adonais? (1991); The Changeling (1991); Mirror, Mirror (1992).
Second Row: The Apple (1992); Catspaw (1991); Metamorphosis (1993); Journey To Babel (1992).
Third Row: The Deadly Years (1992); Wolf In The Fold (1991); The Troubles With Tribbles (1992); The Gamesters Of Triskelion (1992).
Fourth Row: A Private Little War (1992); Return To Tomorrow (1993); Patterns Of Force (1992); The Omega Glory (1993).
Fifth Row: The Ultimate Computer (1993); Bread And Circuses (1992); Friday's Child (1991); Assignment: Earth (1993). *Courtesy of the Collection of Jeff Maynard — New Eye Studio*

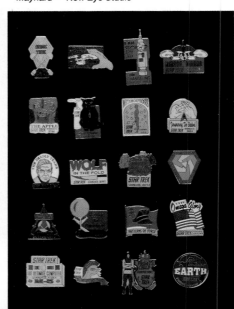

The Hollywood Commemorative Pins Company, enamel pins, (featuring episodes from all three years of the original series - not in episode order in photos):
First Row: Elaan Of Troyus (1993); The Empath (1993); Plato's Stepchildren (1994).
Second Row: Whom Gods Destroy (1993); The Way To Eden (1994). *Courtesy of the Collection of Jeff Maynard — New Eye Studio*

❏ "The Corbomite Maneuver": 1990	$8-9
❏ "Mudd's Women": 1990	$10-11
❏ The Enemy Within: 1990	$10-11
❏ The Man Trap: 1990	$8-9
❏ The Naked Time: 1990	$8-9
❏ "Charlie X": 1990	$6-7
❏ Balance Of Terror: 1990	$6-7
❏ What Are Little Girls Made Of?: 1990	$6-7
❏ Dagger Of The Mind: 1990	$6-7
❏ Miri: 1990	$6-7
❏ "The Conscience of the King": 1991	$6-7
❏ The Galileo Seven: 1990	$6-7
❏ Court-Martial: 1990	$8-9
❏ Menagerie: 1991	$8-9
❏ Shore Leave: 1990	$8-9
❏ The Squire of Gothos: 1991	$6-7
❏ Arena: 1991	$6-7
❏ The Alternative Factor: 1991	$8-9
❏ Tomorrow Is Yesterday: 1991	$8-9
❏ The Return Of The Archons: 1991	$8-9
❏ A Taste Of Armageddon: 1991	$8-9
❏ Space Seed: 1991	$8-9
❏ This Side Of Paradise: 1991	$8-9
❏ The Devil in the Dark: 1991	$8-9
❏ Errand Of Mercy: 1991	$8-9
❏ The City On The Edge Of Forever: 1991	$8-9
❏ Operation-Annihilate!: 1991	$8-9
❏ Catspaw: second season, 1991	$6-7
❏ Metamorphosis: 1993	$10-11
❏ Friday's Child: 1991	$8-9
❏ Who Mourns For Adonais?: 1991	$8-9
❏ Amok Time: 1991	$8-9
❏ Wolf In The Fold: 1991	$8-9
❏ The Changeling: 1991	$8-9
❏ The Apple: 1992	$8-9
❏ Mirror, Mirror: 1992	$8-9
❏ The Deadly Years: 1992	$8-9
❏ The Troubles With Tribbles: 1992	$8-9
❏ Bread And Circuses: 1992	$8-9
❏ Journey To Babel: 1992	$8-9
❏ A Private Little War: 1992	$8-9
❏ The Gamesters Of Triskelion: 1992	$8-9
❏ Obsession: 1992	$8-9
❏ The Immunity Syndrome	$8-9
❏ Return To Tomorrow: 1993	$8-9
❏ Patterns Of Force: 1992	$8-9
❏ The Ultimate Computer: 1993	$10-11
❏ Assignment: Earth: 1993	$8-9
❏ The Omega Glory: 1993	$10-11
❏ Spectre of the Gun: third season, 1993	$10-11
❏ Elaan Of Troyus: third season, 1993	$8-9
❏ The Enterprise Incident: 1993	$10-11
❏ And the Children Shall Lead: 1993	$10-11

❏ The Empath: 1993	$10-11
❏ Plato's Stepchildren: 1994	$10-11
❏ Whom Gods Destroy: 1993	$10-11
❏ The Mark of Gideon	$10-11
❏ The Cloud Minders	$10-11
❏ The Way To Eden: 1994	$10-11

LINCOLN ENTERPRISES — 1986-1990s

❏ Enterprise cutout	$8-9
❏ Enterprise & Statue of Liberty	$8-9
❏ Klingon Bird of Prey	$8-9
❏ Peace in Our Galaxy (IDIC)	$8-9
❏ Star Trek, Gateway to a New Beginning	$8-9
❏ Star Trek: The Final Frontier	$8-9
❏ Star Trek: The Motion Picture (from movie poster)	$8-9
❏ Star Trek III: The Search for Spock: commemorative	$8-9
❏ Star Trek III: from movie poster	$8-9
❏ Twentieth Century Pin	$8-9
❏ United Federation of Planets (UFP) Symbol: Star Trek IV	$6-7
❏ Whales	$8-9

Command Insignia Jewelry

❏ Command Insignia Necklace: Star Trek: The Motion Picture, gold plated or painted by Lincoln Enterprises (large or small necklace) $6-9

❏ Command Insignia Pin: by Lincoln Enterprises (large or small pin) $6-9

❏ Command Insignia Pin: brushed brass by Don Post Studios $7-8

❏ Command Insignia Pin: gold plated by Lincoln Enterprises $4-6

❏ Command Insignia Charm: original TV design, 18" chain by Lincoln Enterprise $4-6
in silver $30-35;
14K gold $90-95;
& 14K gold & diamonds $275-300

❏ Command Insignia Earrings: pierced, dangling or clip-on by Lincoln Enterprises $10-12
also in:
sterling silver $30-35;
gold $125-150;
or gold & diamonds $575-600

❏ Command Insignia Ring: adjustable by Lincoln Enterprises 22K gold plated $6-8
or sterling silver $7-10

❏ Insignia Wire Charm: with 18" chain by Lincoln Enterprises (also as pierced earrings or clip-ons) $5-12

Enterprise Ship Jewelry

A variety of manufacturers produce these popular items.
❏ Original Ship, 3/4" Charm: gold or silver plate ship, with or without chain $6-7

- ❑ Original Ship, 1 1/2" Charm: gold or silver plate, with or without chain $8-9
- ❑ Original Ship, 1 1/2" Charm: silver plate, adjustable ring $6-8
- ❑ Original Ship, 3/4" Earrings: gold or silver plate, pierced or clip-ons $11-12
- ❑ Original Ship: hologram surface, microscopically etched $8-9
- ❑ Original Ship: hologram printed on delta shield earrings $9-10
- ❑ Movie Ship, 1 3/4" Charm: gold or silver plate, with or without chain $8-9
- ❑ Movie Ship, 1" Charm: gold or silver plate, with or without chain $8-10
- ❑ Star Trek: The Motion Picture ID Bracelet: gold or silver children's, a General Mills premium $3-5

LINCOLN ENTERPRISES
Movie Enterprise in 14K Gold:
- ❑ Charm $125-150
- ❑ Charm with diamonds $300-330
- ❑ Earrings $250-280
- ❑ Earrings with diamonds $600-650

IDIC

Infinite Diversity in Infinite Combinations, a Vulcan symbol used in the third season (a bone of contention with the cast according to William Shatner), metal pieces with a gold circle with superimposed silver triangle and a clear stone at the apex.
- ❑ Earrings: gold and silver plate, pierced or clip-on (also in 14K gold by Lincoln Enterprises) $15-17
- ❑ Necklaces: 1/2" to 2" in size (also in 14K gold) $7-15
- ❑ Pin: gold and silver plate (also in 14K gold by Lincoln Enterprises) $8-10
- ❑ Ring: gold and silver plate, men & women's styles, adjustable $20-22

Keychains

AVIVA — 1979 $5-7 each
- ❑ Square 1 1/2" lucite with two-sided translucent pictures
- ❑ Enterprise: oval blue background
- ❑ Kirk & Spock with Enterprise
- ❑ Spock: "Live Long and Prosper" printed semicircle
- ❑ Spock Bust: with uniform insignia, white & gray
- ❑ Spock Salutes

BUTTON UP
- ❑ Beam Me Up, Scotty: yellow background, 1980 $3-5

CALIFORNIA DREAMERS — 1987
Original series color photos, 1 1/2" x 2" plastic holders $5-8 each
- ❑ Chekov: "I Hate Mondays"
- ❑ Kirk: "Beam Me Up, Scotty"
- ❑ Kirk: "The Captain"
- ❑ Kirk, Spock & McCoy: "Fire All Phaser Weapons"
- ❑ Kirk, Spock, & Uhura: "Keep Your Shields Up"
- ❑ Kirk, Spock, & Uhura: "Seek Out Strange New Worlds"
- ❑ Spock: "Hang In There"
  - ❑ "I Need Space"
  - ❑ "Spock for President"
  - ❑ "Live Long and Prosper"
  - ❑ "Superior Being"

INTERSTELLAR PRODUCTIONS, INC. — 1994
Six keychains with sound effects, three in each of the original Star Trek & Next Generation series.
- ❑ Original Star Trek: 8 sound effects keyed by buttons $12-14
- ❑ Classic Communicator $12-14
- ❑ Classic Tricorder $12-14

PINNACLE DESIGNS
Rectangular metal keychain, gold plated designs with engraved & enameled designs.
- ❑ U.S.S. Enterprise NCC-1701: ship designation with red border $5-6
- ❑ "Star Trek": movie Enterprise in white above the name $5-6

RAWCLIFFE
Pewter keychains $7-8
- ❑ Live Long & Prosper Vulcan Salute
- ❑ Tricorder: original design
- ❑ U.S.S. Enterprise NCC-1701

Key Rings: Left: U.S.S. Enterprise NCC-1701 (1988); Right: Star Trek with movie Enterprise (1989) by Pinnacle Designs. *Courtesy of the Collection of Jeff Maynard — New Eye Studio*

Miscellaneous Keychains
- ❑ Delta Shield: cloisonne key ring, gold with black $5-6
- ❑ Enterprise: brass, metal cast, oval $5-6
- ❑ Enterprise: cloisonne original ship cutout $5-6
- ❑ Enterprise: original design in round hologram keychain $3-4
- ❑ Enterprise: "Star Trek & "Starship Enterprise," navy background $10-15
- ❑ Klingon Battlecruiser: original series design in round hologram keychain $3-4
- ❑ Romulan Bird of Prey: original series design in round hologram keychain $3-4
- ❑ "Star Trek": cloisonne key ring $5-6
- ❑ Spock: with original series Enterprise on back, gold-plated silver by Rarities Mint $30-50
- ❑ Star Fleet Headquarters insignia: movies design, gold-plated metal, 1 1/4" $5-10
- ❑ "Star Trek Adventure" with insignia: brass oval $5-10
- ❑ UFP: cloisonne key ring $5-6

Necklaces
- ❑ Khan's Pendant: bronze dipped in acid by Don Post Studio, 1982 $20-30
- ❑ Mount Seleya Symbol Necklace: by Lincoln Enterprises $8-9
- ❑ Enterprise Orbiting: Pewter medallion by Goodtime Jewelry $4-6
- ❑ Enterprise Orbiting Ringed Planet: by American Miss $10-15
- ❑ Phaser Pendant: gold or silver by Star Trek Galore $3-5
- ❑ Spock or Kirk & Spock: on original series insignia in pewter by Goodtime Jewelry $4-6
- ❑ Spock on a Chain: lightweight gold-plated by American Miss $3-5
- ❑ Star Trek Logo: by American Miss $3-5
- ❑ Vulcan Salute: stamped metal, flat gold $3-5

Pendants
- ❑ Filigree: U.S.S. Enterprise, original series design, firing phasers, orbiting planet $8-9
- ❑ Filigree: "Where No Man Has Gone Before": around edges with castle on Rigel in center $8-9
- ❑ Sparkle Necklace: circular pendant, black background, silver movie command insignia with gold or silver beveled frame $3-4
- ❑ Sparkle Necklace: circular pendant, black background, silver outline of Enterprise on gold or silver beveled frame $3-4
- ❑ Sparkle Necklace: circular pendant, black background, silver outline of UFP emblem on silver beveled frame $3-4
- ❑ Try Trekking: quartz crystal, changes color with mood, by Lincoln Enterprises $4-5
- ❑ UFP Security Badge: Star Trek IV, hinged, two-piece by Lincoln Enterprises $12-18

Uniform Insignia

- Star Trek: The Motion Picture: star insignia in circle, bronze, by Don Post, 1982 — $10-15
- Star Trek: The Motion Picture: by Lincoln Enterprises — $20-30
- Star Trek II-VI Movie Insignia: circle design superimposed on bar, bronze, by Don Post — $20-30
- Star Trek II-VI Movie Insignia: lightweight plated & painted metal in 2 sizes by Lincoln Enterprises — $6-9
- Uniform Belt Buckles: Star Trek II-VI in brushed bronze or gold-plated metal, 2 1/2" in diameter by several manufacturers — $18-20

Uniform Rank Insignia

Early designs were painted cast fiberglass and very fragile. More recent examples are plated and painted metal insignias produced by a number of manufacturers. Examples were produced reflecting Star Trek II through VI designs and for Star Trek: The Next Generation series (see also Next Generation Uniform Insignia section).

- Admiral — $6-7
- Captain — $12-14
- Commander — $9-10
- Commodore — $15-17
- Fleet Admiral — $8-9
- Lieutenant — $9-10
- Lieutenant Commander — $9-10
- Lieutenant J.G. — $6-7
- Uniform Shoulder Strap Back Pin: eight-sided ridged metal pin, unpainted or gold plated — $3-5
- Uniform Sleeve Pips: round or oblong, ridged metal, unpainted or gold plated. — $2-4
- Uniform Twist Tab: for shoulder strap as seen in films II-VI — $15-17

Watches

BRADLEY TIME COMPANY
- Enterprise from Star Trek: The Motion Picture: starburst behind ship — $55-70
- Enterprise with Kirk & Spock from original series: faces below on rectangular face of an LCD display watch — $75-100
- Spock from Star Trek: The Motion Picture: appears on face — $55-70

COLLINS INDUSTRIAL — 1982
- Star Trek II: The Wrath of Khan art on the box of an LED game watch — $25-30

LEWCO — 1986
- Spock & Enterprise: relief on band of digital watch, 20th Anniversary packaging — $45-50

LINCOLN ENTERPRISES
- Enterprise & "Star Trek" on face: men's or ladies watches — $30-35

RARITIES MINT — 1989
- Enterprise, original series design: men's & women's limited edition gold-plated silver — $150-250

SERVICE TIME — 1989
All have painted faces — $50-70 each
- Enterprise, original design: with "Star Trek" below in gold, black plastic band
- Enterprise, original design, three-quarters view: same as above
- Enterprise, original design: orbiting planet
- Enterprise & Klingon Bird of Prey: movie designs

TIMEX
Star Trek Command Watch
- NCC 1701" & "Star Trek" in relief on wrist bands: digital watch & stop watch with delta shield on face — $30-33

UNIDENTIFIED MANUFACTURERS
- Kirk, Spock, & McCoy: original series pictures on men's & women's watches — $25-30
- Kirk, Spock, & McCoy: original series pictures on a pocket watch — $30-40

Enterprise. The Magazine for Star Trek Fans. 1985. *Courtesy of the Collection of Jeff Maynard — New Eye Studio*

MAGAZINES

As with the books before, no attempt will be made here to separate the magazines listed here between the various series. Great care must be taken when collecting paper products. The magazines in which Star Trek articles include:

- Accent West — $3-5
- Aerospace Education — $3-5
- All About Star Trek Fan Club: Ego Enterprises, NY, 1976, No. 1-6 — $10-15
- American Cinematographer — $5-25
- Bananas — $4-6
- Best of Starlog: No. 1-3 — $25-30
- Byte, The Small System Journal Computer Magazine — $3-5
- Castle of Frankenstein — $10-20
- Cinefantastique — $6-20
- Cinefex — $5-55
- Cue — $5-8
- Cinemagic — $5-10
- The Communicator — $3-10
- Cracked — $15-25
- Crawdaddy — $5-10
- Dynamite — $3-5
- The Electric Company — $3-6
- Enterprise: HJS Publications, No. 1-13 — $3-5
- Enterprise Spotlight 2: New Media Publishing memory book — $4-5
- Enterprise Incident: Star Trek Federation of Fans: No. 1-36, name changed to SF Movieland on issue No. 28. Six Collectors Editions & four Spotlight issues on Leonard Nimoy, Star Trek personalities, technical details, & William Shatner. — $5-10

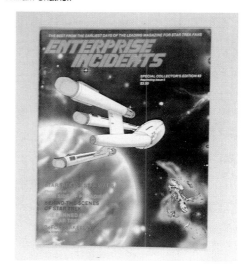

Enterprise Incidents, Reprint Issue #5, 1984. *Courtesy of the Collection of Jeff Maynard — New Eye Studio*

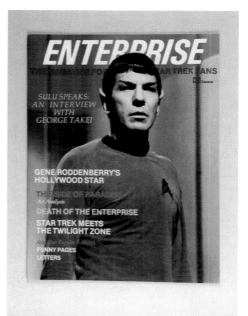

Star Trek: The Next Generation. The Official Magazine Series #2, 1987. *Courtesy of the Collection of Jeff Maynard — New Eye Studio*

Star Trek V: The Final Frontier. The Official Movie Magazine, 1989. *Courtesy of the Collection of Jeff Maynard — New Eye Studio*

Star Trek Town Mook Japanese Super Visual Magazine 7, 1981. *Courtesy of the Collection of Jeff Maynard — New Eye Studio*

❑ Entertainment	$4-8
❑ Famous Films	$4-10
❑ Famous Monsters	$4-8
❑ Fantasy Enterprises: New Media Publishing, 1985	$4-5
❑ Fantasy Image No. 2: Spock & Enterprise on cover, March 1985	$5-10
❑ Future	$3-5
❑ Games	$3-5
❑ Globe	$3-4
❑ Hollywood Studio Magazine	$5-7
❑ Journal of Popular Film & Television	$5-10
❑ Mad Magazine	$5-10
❑ Mediascene Preview	$4-10
❑ Media Spotlight: Issues 1-5, J. Schuster Publishers, 1975-1977	$8-10
❑ Megastars Poster Magazine	$3-5
❑ Monster Magazine	$3-8
❑ Monsterland No. 16	$4-8
❑ Monsters of the Movie	$5-7
❑ Monster Times: newspaper format	$50-55
❑ Muppet Magazine	$3-7
❑ National Enquirer	$3-10
❑ Newsweek	$5-10
❑ Officers of the Bridge	$10-15
❑ Parade Magazine	$5-8
❑ People	$5-10
❑ Preview	$3-5
❑ Questar	$5-7
❑ Science and Fantasy Film Classics	$4-8
❑ Science Fiction Horror and Fantasy	$5-8
❑ Science Fiction Blockbusters	$3-5
❑ Science Fiction Now	$3-5
❑ Sci-Fi Monthly	$4-6
❑ Sesame Street	$3-5
❑ Sick	$4-8
❑ Space Odyssey	$4-8
❑ Space Trek	$3-5
❑ Space Wars	$5-10
❑ Spectrum 30	$4-8
❑ Star Battles	$3-5
❑ Starblaster Special	$3-5
❑ Starblazer Special	$3-5
❑ Starburst	$4-15
❑ Stardate	$3-6
❑ Star Force	$3-5
❑ Starlog: features regular Star Trek columns	$5-6
❑ Star Trek Files Magazine	$6-15
❑ Starlog Poster Magazine	$10-15
❑ Star Trek II: The Wrath of Khan Official Movie Magazine: Starlog, 1982	$5-10
❑ Star Trek III: The Search for Spock Official Movie Magazine: Starlog, 1984	$5-10
❑ Star Trek IV: The Voyage Home Official Movie Magazine: Starlog, 1986	$5-10
❑ Star Trek V: The Final Frontier Official Movie Magazine: Starlog, 1989	$4-6
❑ Star Trek: The Next Generation Official Magazine Series: Starlog, No. 1-16, 1987-1991	$5-8
❑ Star Trek Voyager Magazine: No. 1, 1995	$7-8
❑ Super Visual: Japanese publication, complete visual guide of Star Trek, Vol. 1-3	$25-50
❑ Time	$3-6
❑ Trek: fanzine gone pro by G.B. Love & W. Irwing, Houston, Texas, published 1974-1981. No. 1-19	$50-110
with Special Issues No. 1, Feb. 1977& No. 2, Nov. 1978	$15-20
❑ TV Gold	$4-7
❑ TV Guide	$2-50
❑ TV Showpeople	$3-5
❑ Twilight Zone	$4-7
❑ US Magazine	$3-8
❑ Videogaming	$5-7
❑ Video Viewing	$3-5
❑ World of Horror	$3-5

Trek Special #2, 1978. *Courtesy of the Collection of Jeff Maynard — New Eye Studio*

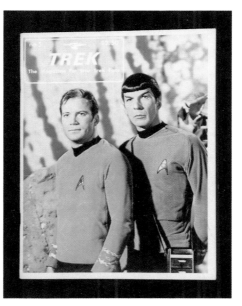

Trek. The Magazine for Star Trek Fans #5, 1976. *Courtesy of the Collection of Jeff Maynard — New Eye Studio*

The Monster Times Special Star Trek Issue. *Courtesy of the Collection of Jeff Maynard — New Eye Studio*

Star Trek Communicator. The Magazine of Star Trek: The Official Fan Club. *Courtesy of the author's collection*

Trek. The Magazine For Star Trek Fans. Number 2. *Courtesy of the Collection of Jeff Maynard — New Eye Studio*

Starlog Number 1. *Courtesy of the Collection of Jeff Maynard — New Eye Studio*

Magazines featuring Star Trek stories (Entertainment & TV Guide). *Courtesy of the Collection of John E. Balbach*

MODELS & MODEL ROCKET KITS

AMT (Aluminum Model Toy Corporation) produced the first licensed Star Trek model kits in America. Their first was the Enterprise and measured 18" long. AMT's first models were packaged in boxes with painted artwork in a vertical format, measuring 14 1/2" x 10". Early ships were lighted. Later runs were packaged in horizontally formatted boxes with photographs of completed models without lighting. A third change placed the models in boxes only half the size of the horizontally formatted box measuring 8 1/2" x 10", also without lighting. Ertl purchased AMT and with their original molds has reissued a number of original Star Trek models and has also added new models to the line.

Estes produced Enterprise and Klingon Battle Cruiser model rocketry starter kits in 1975 and 1976.

Model kits are considered to be most valuable in their original condition, packed and unassembled. Assembled models are only worth a fraction of those left unassembled. Note here as well that a model kit can be shrink wrapped by machine easily and quickly today. Shrink wrapped boxes are not necessarily indicative of models in original condition.

AMT/ERTL — The Original Series
- ☐ Enterprise: large box with lights by AMT, 1966, vertical
  box art $200-300

Star Trek U.S.S. Enterprise Space Ship Model Kit by AMT, 1968. *Courtesy of the Collection of Jeff Maynard — New Eye Studio*

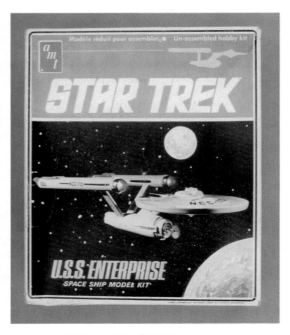

Star Trek U.S.S. Enterprise Space Ship Model Kit, by AMT Corporation. *Courtesy of the Collection of John E. Balbach*

- ❑ Enterprise: large box without lights by AMT, photo of the model against planet & stars background in a horizontal format $150-200
- ❑ Enterprise: small box without lights by AMT, 1968, same box art as horizontal format second issue $145-160
- ❑ Enterprise: small box with the same box art as AMT's 1968 release but by ERTL with printed "ERTL" beneath AMT logo, 1983 $100-150
- ❑ Enterprise: by ERTL, 1989 $9-11
- ❑ Exploration Set: large boxed set featured child-sized communicator, tricorder, & phaser with hand grip by AMT, 1974 $150-300
- ❑ Exploration Set: small boxed set by AMT with the same box art, not reissued by ERTL $100-200
- ❑ Galileo 7: large box with artwork of shuttlecraft by AMT, 1974 $200-220
- ❑ Galileo 7: small box version $100-200
- ❑ Galileo 7 Shuttlecraft, Special Edition: 25th anniversary release by ERTL, 1991 $10-11
- ❑ K-7 Space Station: produced in the small box only by AMT in 1976 without an ERTL reissue $65-75
- ❑ Klingon Battle Cruiser: with lights, large box packaging, horizontal format, Klingon engaging Enterprise in phaser fight, by AMT, 1966 $400-500
- ❑ Klingon Battle Cruiser: large box version without lights by AMT in 1968 $95-105

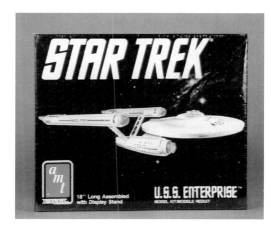

Star Trek U.S.S. Enterprise model kit by AMT/ERTL*, 1989. *ERTL bought out AMT, added their own name to the AMT logo, used the AMT molds, & reissued some of the AMT models. *Courtesy of the Collection of Jeff Maynard — New Eye Studio*

Star Trek Galileo 7 Shuttlecraft model kit by AMT, 1974. *Courtesy of the Collection of Jeff Maynard — New Eye Studio*

Star Trek K-7 Space Station model kit by AMT, 1976. *Courtesy of the Collection of Jeff Maynard — New Eye Studio*

Star Trek Special Edition Galileo II Shuttlecraft 25th anniversary reissue model kit by AMT/ERTL, 1991. *Courtesy of the Collection of Jeff Maynard — New Eye Studio*

Star Trek Klingon Battle Cruiser model kit in the large horizontal format box by AMT, 1968. *Courtesy of the Collection of Jeff Maynard — New Eye Studio*

Star Trek Klingon Battle Cruiser model kit by AMT, boxed in the smallest and last packaging of the model by AMT, 1968. *Courtesy of the Collection of Jeff Maynard — New Eye Studio*

Star Trek Original Klingon Cruiser 25th anniversary reissue model kit by AMT/ERTL, 1991. *Courtesy of the Collection of Jeff Maynard — New Eye Studio*

Star Trek U.S.S. Enterprise Command Bridge model kit by AMT, 1975. *Courtesy of the Collection of Jeff Maynard — New Eye Studio*

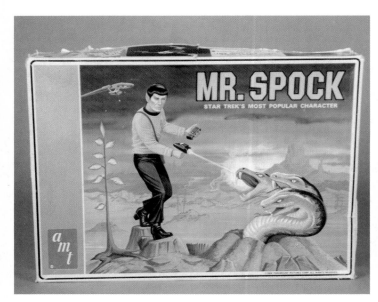

Mr. Spock (original series Spock) model kit by AMT, 1968. *Courtesy of the Collection of Jeff Maynard — New Eye Studio*

Star Trek U.S.S. Enterprise Command Bridge 25th anniversary reissue model kit by AMT/ERTL, 1991. *Courtesy of the Collection of Jeff Maynard — New Eye Studio*

ERTL 12" vinyl model kits — 1994:
- ❑ Captain James T. Kirk: holding phaser, vertical box showing
  model $19-22
- ❑ Dr. Leonard McCoy: with medical tricorder, vertical packaging $19-22
- ❑ Chief Engineer Montgomery Scott: vertical packaging $19-22
- ❑ Mr. Spock: newly added in 1995 $19-22

AURORA
- ❑ Enterprise: identical model and box art as the AMT
  product, made for British market in 1966 $100-200
- ❑ Mr. Spock: identical model and box art as the AMT
  product, made for the British market, 1972 $75-150

ESTES
- ❑ Enterprise: model rocket fired with tail motor from stands
  and landed by parachute, packaged in a plastic bag
  with a cardboard header, 1975 $55-60
- ❑ Enterprise: special 25th anniversary edition, boxed, 1991 $25-30
- ❑ Klingon Battle Cruiser: model rocket fired from a stand &
  landing via parachute, packaged in a plastic bag
  with a cardboard header, 1975 $55-60
- ❑ Klingon Battle Cruiser: special 25th anniversary edition,
  boxed, 1991 $25-30

MEDORI
- ❑ Enterprise: Japanese model with a propeller added to
  the ship. Kirk & Spock on the box. 1969 $150-300

Star Trek Movie Models

AMT/ERTL
AMT produced its last models prior to the ERTL purchase for Star Trek: The Motion Picture.
- ❑ Enterprise: Star Trek: The Motion Picture ship with lighted
  saucer section by AMT, 1979 $100-125
- ❑ Enterprise: Star Trek II model with the same box art as
  AMT's last design, even showing the saucer lights
  although the lights were no longer part of the set,
  by ERTL, 1983 $55-80
- ❑ Enterprise: Star Trek III, the box no longer indicates saucer
  lights available, by ERTL, 1984 $50-60
- ❑ Enterprise: Star Trek IV with new box art depicting the
  NCC-1701-A designation on the identical model by
  ERTL, 1986 $45-50
- ❑ Enterprise: Star Trek V with new box art and the
  inclusion of a small shuttlecraft model by ERTL, 1989 $20-25
- ❑ Enterprise: Star Trek VI model of the NCC-1701-A, 22"
  long, with small shuttlecraft model, by ERTL, 1991 $10-11

Star Trek Space Ship Set model kit (original Enterprise, Klingon Battle Cruiser, & Romulan Bird of Prey) by AMT/ ERTL, 1989. *Courtesy of the Collection of Jeff Maynard — New Eye Studio*

Captain James T. Kirk 12" tall vinyl model kit by AMT/ ERTL, 1994. *Courtesy of the Collection of Jeff Maynard — New Eye Studio*

Star Trek Flying Model Rocket Starship Enterprise by Estes, 1975. *Courtesy of the Collection of Jeff Maynard — New Eye Studio*

Star Trek VI: The Undiscovered Country U.S.S. Enterprise model kit by AMT/ERTL, 1991. *Courtesy of the Collection of Jeff Maynard — New Eye Studio*

Star Trek: The Motion Picture Klingon Cruiser model kit by AMT, 1979. *Courtesy of the Collection of Jeff Maynard — New Eye Studio*

❏ Enterprise: Special edition with lights & sound by ERTL, 1991 $30-35
❏ Klingon Cruiser: from Star Trek: The Motion Picture by AMT, 1979 $20-50
❏ Klingon Cruiser: slightly different box art released by ERTL in 1984 $10-15
❏ Mr. Spock: remodeled version of the original series model mold with a different base without serpents by AMT, 1979 $80-100
❏ U.S.S. Excelsior: model depicted on cover against dark background of planet & moon, 18" long, by ERTL, 1994 $19-21
❏ U.S.S. Reliant: snap together model, 1995 $18-20
❏ Vulcan Shuttle: AMT & ERTL model with detachable warp drive sled, 1979. Box art revised from Star Trek: The Motion Picture to Star Trek III in 1984. Production run finished in 1989 $30-60

Die cast ships from Star Trek V by Ertl
❏ U.S.S. Enterprise NCC-1701-A: fully painted & decaled, packaged in shrink wrap against color card stock $20-11
❏ Klingon Bird of Prey: fully painted & decaled, packaged in shrink wrap against color card stock $20-22

Star Trek Special Edition U.S.S. Enterprise (movie version NCC-1701-A) with lights & sound effects model kit released as a 25th anniversary kit by AMT/ERTL, 1991. *Courtesy of the Collection of Jeff Maynard — New Eye Studio*

Star Trek: The Motion Picture Vulcan Shuttle by AMT/ ERTL, 1979. *Courtesy of the Collection of Jeff Maynard — New Eye Studio*

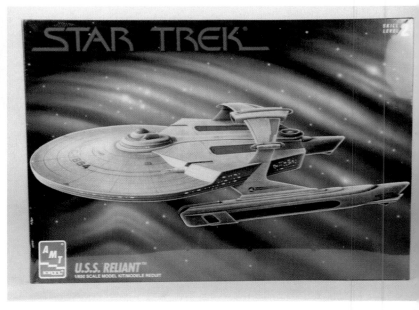

Star Trek U.S.S. Reliant model kit by AMT/ERTL, 1995. *Courtesy of the Collection of Jeff Maynard — New Eye Studio*

MATCHBOX

Lesney was the parent company for both Matchbox and AMT when Star Trek: The Motion Picture was produced. Matchbox created models for the European market, featuring box art appealing to the European, rather than the American, market.

- ❑ Klingon Battle Cruiser: packaged in a 10" x 12 1/2" box with
   instructions in multiple languages, 1980 $55-75
- ❑ Vulcan Shuttle: packaged in a 10" x 12 1/2" box $55-75

PATCHES

Embroidered patches, largely, still in production. Patches are easily copied and will not appreciate in value much over time.

- ❑ Alpha Centauri Symbol: gold & purple from Tech Manual $3-5
- ❑ Commendation Ribbons: set of nineteen small triangular
   patches from the original series $3-5
- ❑ Dreadnought: NCC-1707 blue & yellow $3-5
- Enterprise:
   - ❑ Black background by Lincoln Enterprises $2-4
   - ❑ Black background with white silhouette & "Star Trek" $3-5
   - ❑ Dark blue background, cutout $3-5
   - ❑ Orbiting planet in a six color, fan-shaped patch
      from Star Trek Welcommittee, 4 1/2" $2-5
   - ❑ White or black background, ship's name & number,
      from Star Trek Welcommittee, 4" $2-5
- ❑ Enterprise Cutout: movie design by Lincoln Enterprises $9-12
- ❑ Federation: name with Enterprise from Star Trek
   Welcommittee, 3" $2-5
- ❑ Figure Patch Cutouts: original series characters: $2-5 each
   - ❑ Kirk
   - ❑ Spock
   - ❑ McCoy
   - ❑ Uhura
- ❑ Galileo: name, number & picture from Star Trek
   Welcommittee, 2" $2-5
- ❑ IDIC Symbol: "Peace In Our Galaxy" by Lincoln Enterprises $2-4
- ❑ Insignia Patches: original series, center delta shield, black
   star over circular background: $2-4
   - ❑ White background $2-4
   - ❑ Red background $2-4
   - ❑ Orange background $2-4
   - ❑ Green background $2-4
   - ❑ Yellow background $2-4
   - ❑ Blue background $2-4
- ❑ Insignia Patches: original series: $2-4 each
   - ❑ Command
   - ❑ Engineering
   - ❑ Nursing
   - ❑ Science
- ❑ Insignia patches: Star Trek: The Motion Picture, 1979 $2-4 each
   - ❑ Command
   - ❑ Engineering
   - ❑ Medical
   - ❑ Operations
   - ❑ Science
   - ❑ Security
- ❑ Keep on Trekkin': rectangle, red background, from Star Trek
   Welcommittee, 3 1/2" $2-5
- ❑ Klingon Battle Cruiser: with Klingon text from Star Trek
   Welcommittee, 3" $2-5
- ❑ Live Long and Prosper: phrase & Vulcan salute by Thinking
   Cap Company, 3" diameter circle $4-5
- ❑ Live Long and Prosper: phrase & Vulcan salute from Star Trek
   Welcommittee, 4" $3-6
- ❑ Mascot Patch: showing tribbles $2-5
- ❑ Medical Caduceus: in green by Lincoln Enterprises $3-4
- ❑ Phaser Cutout $2-4
- ❑ Photo Patches from Star Trek: The Motion Picture by
   Aviva, 1979: $3-5 each
   - ❑ Admiral Kirk
   - ❑ Kirk in dress uniform
   - ❑ Spock, Kirk, & McCoy
   - ❑ Spock & Kirk
   - ❑ Spock in white
- ❑ Romulan Bird of Prey: with phrase from Star Trek
   Welcommittee, 3" $2-5
- ❑ Space Station K-7 image & name: from Star Trek
   Welcommittee, 3" $2-5
- ❑ Spock with "Live Long and Prosper": square $2-4

- ❑ Spock Lives: by Thinking Cap Company, 3" diameter $3-6
- ❑ 61 Cygni Symbol: planetary system, copper bird from
   Tech Manual $4-5
- ❑ Star Trek III Commemorative Patch: by Lincoln Enterprises $6-8
- ❑ Star Trek IV: Enterprise & whales, by Lincoln Enterprises $9-12
- ❑ Star Trek IV: Bird of Prey & whale, by Lincoln Enterprises $9-10
- ❑ Star Trek IV: whales & insignia by Lincoln Enterprises $8-10
- ❑ Star Trek 20th Anniversary Patch: by Lincoln Enterprises $6-8
- ❑ UFP Headquarters Patch: name with blue background &
   central symbol $4-5
- ❑ United Federation of Planets:
   - ❑ Silver & red banner from original series $4-5
   - ❑ Silver & black banner $2-4
   - ❑ Silver & blue circle from Tech Manual, 4" $6-7
   - ❑ Silver & blue circle from the movies by Thinking
      Cap Co., 3" diameter $2-5
- ❑ U.S.S. Enterprise:
   - ❑ Light blue background, dark blue border, orange
      lettering, silver ship $3-5
   - ❑ Yellow background, light blue border, orange lettering,
      silver & gray ship $3-5
   - ❑ Black background & border, silver & red ship, red &
      white stars $3-4
   - ❑ Name & insignia in red by Thinking Cap Co., 3" circle $2-5
   - ❑ Name on yellow rectangular felt background $3-5
   - ❑ "Zap": with Enterprise firing phasers from the
      Star Trek Welcommittee, four-color, rectangular, 3 1/2" $3-5

PEWTER FIGURINES

FRANKLIN MINT

Star Trek ship pewter replicas are mounted on hardwood bases, accented with inset crystals and gold-plated trim. Periodically, the firm also has offered chess sets in one form or another.

- ❑ Enterprise: original series design, measuring 10" in length $125-200
- ❑ Klingon Cruiser: original series design, measuring 9" in
   length $125-200
- ❑ Romulan Ship: original television design, measuring 9"
   in length $195-210
- ❑ Three Ship Set: miniature versions of the original design.
   Enterprise, Klingon Cruiser, and Romulan Ship, all
   mounted on a single base. $190-210

RAWCLIFFE

Under FASA's license, Rawcliffe produced their first series of pewter figurines in 1988. These were basically the same ships FASA had produced in base metals manufactured in pewter. Paramount took issue with this licensing arrangement and production of this first series ceased. More recently, Rawcliffe has reached a licensing agreement with Paramount and produces several pewter Star Trek lines based on the various television series and films.

1988 — Ships licensing through FASA $25-75 each
- ❑ Chandley: 3" in length (the ships of this series were packed in clear plastic
   boxes with blue velveteen inserts with silver embossed labels)
- ❑ Enterprise: original series design, measuring 3" in length
- ❑ Enterprise: movie design, 3" in length
- ❑ Excelsior: movie ship, 4 3/4" in length
- ❑ Grissom: movie ship, 2" in length
- ❑ Klingon Bird of Prey (L-42): movie ship, 1 3/4" in length
- ❑ Klingon Cruiser: original series design, 2 1/2"in length
- ❑ Regula 1: movie space laboratory, 2" in height
- ❑ Reliant: movie ship, 2 1/2" in length

1991-onward—Ships & figures licensed through Paramount

Rawcliffe issued a new line of ships (including those previously produced) under new licensing beginning in 1991.
- ❑ U.S.S. Enterprise NCC-1701: original series design $16-17
- ❑ U.S.S. Enterprise NCC-1701-A: movie ship $16-17
- ❑ U.S.S. Excelsior: movie ship $20-22
- ❑ U.S.S. Grissom: movie ship $16-17
- ❑ U.S.S. Reliant: movie ship $16-17
- ❑ Regula 1 Space Laboratory: movie station $20-22
- ❑ Klingon Battle Cruiser: original series design $16-17
- ❑ Klingon Bird of Prey: as seen in films & on The Next
   Generation $16-17

Larger ship figurines with greater detail, approximately 4 1/2" long or wide
- ❑ U.S.S. Enterprise NCC-1701: original series design with
   red jeweled nacelle forward ends, gold plated sensor
   array, custom delta shield stand $45-50

U.S.S. Enterprise NCC-1701, 2 3/4" x 1 1/2" high (left); Klingon Battle Cruiser, 2" x 1 1/8" high, by Rawcliffe, 1991. *Courtesy of the Collection of John E. Balbach*

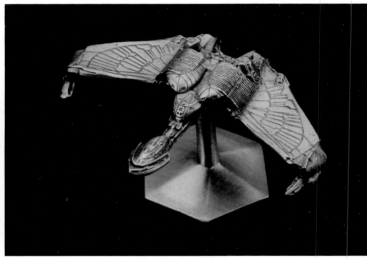

Various incarnations of the Enterprise in pewter by Rawcliffe: the original series Enterprise (left & center) and the Enterprise-A from the movies (right). *Courtesy of the Collection of Jeff Maynard — New Eye Studio*

Klingon Bird of Prey in pewter by Rawcliffe, 1991, measuring 2 1/4" x 1 5/8", x 1 1/4" high. *Courtesy of the Collection of John E. Balbach*

Star Trek ships of the line in pewter by Rawcliffe: top: Klingon Battle Cruiser, U.S.S. Grissom, U.S.S. Enterprise, U.S.S. Enterprise-A, U.S.S. Reliant, Klingon Bird of Prey; bottom: U.S.S. Enterprise-D, U.S.S. Enterprise, U.S.S. Excelsior, & Deep Space Nine Runabout. *Courtesy of the Collection of Jeff Maynard — New Eye Studio*

Pewter 4 1/2" original series Enterprise with jeweled engine nacelles and gold plated main sensor array by Rawcliffe. *Courtesy of the Collection of Jeff Maynard — New Eye Studio*

Star Trek crew (original series) by Rawcliffe, in pewter, 2 1/2" high: left to right: Kirk, Spock, McCoy, Scotty, Uhura, Sulu, & Chekov. *Courtesy of the Collection of Jeff Maynard — New Eye Studio*

❑ U.S.S. Enterprise NCC-1701-A: movie design with blue
   enameled sensor array & bridge, with custom delta
   shield stand, detachable saucer $55-60
❑ Klingon Bird of Prey: movable wings, 4 1/2" wide, gold
   plated disrupters, custom Klingon Empire symbol stand. $65-75

Original Enterprise Crew — 2 1/2" high
The classic crew, a set of seven:
   ❑ Kirk $17-19
   ❑ Spock $17-19
   ❑ McCoy $17-19
   ❑ Scotty $17-19
   ❑ Uhura $17-19
   ❑ Sulu $17-19
   ❑ Chekov $17-19

Larger, More Detailed 3 1/2" High Original Crew Members
See The Next Generation and Deep Space Nine for additional large figurines
❑ Kirk $35-40
❑ Spock $35-40

POSTCARDS

ANABAS
British firm, produced two different color photo postcards in 1987 $3-5 each
   ❑ Enterprise & Kirk
   ❑ McCoy & Uhura

CALIFORNIA DREAMERS — 1985 $2-4 each
   ❑ Enterprise: (all are color photos with captions) "To seek
      strange new worlds - like you!"
   ❑ Kirk: "Screens up full, magnification 10"
   ❑ Kirk at party with aliens: "...Call me. We'll have lunch."
   ❑ Kirk holding communicator: "Lock me in and beam me up,
      baby, I'm yours."
   ❑ Spock: "Bizarre...but I like it."
   ❑ Spock: touching wall
   ❑ Spock with earphone: "Batteries may fail, but rock & roll will
      never die!"
   ❑ Sulu: "Control systems out, navigation out. Directional
      systems out...I'm so confused."

CLASSICO SAN FRANCISCO, INC.
   ❑ Star Trek Classic Postcard Set 1: set of 15 cards,
      numbered 000-000 $10-11
   ❑ Star Trek Classic Postcard Set 2: set of 15 cards, 000-004 $10-11
   ❑ Star Trek 8" x 10" Postcards from the original series in
      color & numbered:
         ❑ Crew: 220-111, 1991 $3-4
         ❑ Kirk: 220-110, 1991 $3-4
         ❑ Spock: 220-109, 1991 $3-4
         ❑ Spock: 220-112, 1991 $3-4
         ❑ Spock: 220-113, 1991 $3-4
         ❑ U.S.S. Enterprise: 220-143 $3-4

ENGALE — 1989
   ❑ Original series full color photographs along with the first
      two seasons of The Next Generation series. On the
      backs, they are identified as sets of 16. At least 30
      different Star Trek cards among these. $3-5

FOTO PARJETAS
   ❑ Spanish brown & white picture postcard of the original crew
      on the bridge $3-5

Captain James T. Kirk pewter figure measuring 3 1/2" high by Rawcliffe. *Courtesy of the Collection of Jeff Maynard — New Eye Studio*

Star Trek crew members Uhura, McCoy, Spock, & Kirk, 8" x 10" postcard, 220-111, by Classico San Francisco, Inc., 1991. *Courtesy of the Collection of John E. Balbach*

LINCOLN ENTERPRISES
Sold in three different color sets which remain on the market. $3-5 each
- ❑ Original series cast: Kirk, Spock, McCoy, Scott, Sulu, Uhura, Chekov
- ❑ Star Trek: The Motion Picture cast: Kirk, Spock, McCoy, Scott, Sulu, Uhura, Chekov, Chapel, Rand, Decker, Ilia, & Enterprise
- ❑ Star Trek III: The Search for Spock: Kirk, Spock, McCoy, Scott, Sulu, Uhura, Chekov, Saavik, Sarek, & Tilar

IMPACT
- ❑ Movieland Wax Museum Star Trek exhibit, 1979 $3-5

NATIONAL AIR AND SPACE MUSEUM
- ❑ color photo, original Enterprise model hanging in the museum $3-5

PRIME PRESS
- ❑ Star Trek Postcard book with 48 color photo postcards of original series, cards in book format, 1977 $45-50

SIMON AND SCHUSTER
- ❑ Star Trek III: The Search for Spock Postcard Book: 22 color cards in book format, 1984 $10-12

STAR TREK LASERGRAM POSTCARDS
- ❑ Kirk, Spock, McCoy, & Uhura $4-5
- ❑ Spock $4-5
- ❑ U.S.S. Enterprise NCC-1701 $4-5

TK GRAPHICS
Sets of eight postcards, silkscreened in assorted colors $3-6
- ❑ UFP banner: "Star Fleet Headquarters Tactical Center"
- ❑ UFP emblem: "Star Fleet Headquarters Official Mail"

POSTERS
Original Series Posters

Captain Kirk poster, artwork signed by the artist, Drew, 1991 *Courtesy of the Collection of Jeff Maynard — New Eye Studio*

Mr. Spock by Drew, 1991. *Courtesy of the Collection of Jeff Maynard — New Eye Studio*

DARGIS ASSOCIATES
- ❑ Kirk: all posters in this series are 17" x 30", black & white, 1976 $8-12
- ❑ Spock $8-12
- ❑ McCoy $8-12
- ❑ Sulu $8-12
- ❑ Kirk, Spock, Enterprise & Klingon: 6' door poster $8-12

DREW
- ❑ Kirk: color art by Drew, signed, 39" x 28", 1991 $10-11
- ❑ Spock: color art by Drew, signed, 39" x 28", 1991 $10-11
- ❑ McCoy: color art by Drew, signed, 39" x 28", 1991 $10-11
- ❑ Bridge Crew of the Enterprise: color art, 39" x 28", 1991 $10-11

DYNAMIC PUBLISHING
- ❑ Kirk: all in this series are black light-flocked posters, 1976 $10-12
- ❑ Spock $10-12
- ❑ Enterprise $10-12

HEINEKEN
- ❑ Three Spock Faces, with Ears Drooping to Pointed as Sips Beer: thought balloon over Spock after sip states, "Illogical", below "Heineken. Refreshes the parts other beers cannot reach.", color promotional in Europe, 10" x 18", 1975 $15-17

HUCKLEBERRY DESIGNS
- ❑ Spock in Pain: artwork by M. Beard, 29" x 23" poster, 1972 $10-12

JERI OF HOLLYWOOD
- ❑ Kirk: all in this series are 22" x 33", black & white posters from early promotional pictures, 1967 $5-7 each
- ❑ Spock
- ❑ McCoy

LANGLEY ASSOCIATES
- ❑ Castle on Rigel: most are color posters 20" x 24", 1976 $5-8 each
- ❑ Crew on bridge
- ❑ Crew on transporter pads

- ❑ Enterprise & crew
- ❑ Enterprise & Klingon: two-sided 11" x 15", black & white poster
- ❑ Enterprise fires on enemy ships
- ❑ Enterprise fires phasers
- ❑ Enterprise with enemy ships
- ❑ Spock & Kirk
- ❑ Spock & Kirk (art)
- ❑ Kirk: door poster, 6' $10-11
- ❑ Spock: door poster, 6' $10-11

LINCOLN ENTERPRISES
- ❑ Kirk masquerades as Romulan: artwork by Little, 17" x 22" $4-7 each
- ❑ Spock: two faces artwork
- ❑ Kirk collage: 2' x 3' color poster
- ❑ Spock collage: 2' x 3' color poster
- ❑ Character collage: 16" x 20" color art

PORTAL PUBLICATIONS LTD.
- ❑ "All I need to know about life I learned from Star Trek": original Enterprise in center, phrase above & lists below, 1992 $6-7

STAR TREK: THE OFFICIAL FAN CLUB
- ❑ UFP Symbol in a fold out poster, 1994   market value

STAR TREK GALORE
- ❑ Kirk with Lirpa: unlicensed color posters, 19" x 23", 1976 $4-10 each
- ❑ Kirk
- ❑ Spock with Vulcan harp
- ❑ Bridge crew
- ❑ Enterprise firing phasers
- ❑ "Journey to Babel" party scene
- ❑ "A Taste of Armageddon" city scene
- ❑ Landing party meets Klingons
- ❑ Federation recruiting poster
- ❑ Klingon recruiting poster
- ❑ Character collage: black & white art
- ❑ Character collage with ship: black & white art

- ❑ **STERANKO, JIM**: crew members & ships color art collage, 23" x 32", 1974 $8-12

- ❑ **U.S.S. ENTERPRISE NCC-1701**: unsigned original art of Enterprise viewed from a forward angle below the saucer, traveling at warp speed, 27" x 40", 1991 $10-11

- ❑ **VIDEO POSTERS**: American color posters from television episodes $15-20

Dr. McCoy by Drew, 1991. *Courtesy of the Collection of Jeff Maynard — New Eye Studio*

Kirk with Lirpa. Star Trek Galore, 1976. *Courtesy of the Collection of Jeff Maynard — New Eye Studio*

Star Trek Fan Club Poster. *Courtesy of the author's collection.*

Sat Nam Kaur created this fan art poster using Star Trek II movie characters. 1982. *Courtesy of the Collection of Jeff Maynard — New Eye Studio*

Star Trek Movie Posters

- **SAT NAM KAUR**: fanzine cover original color art based on movie characters, 22" x 30", 1982 — $8-12

- **SEGA**: movie Enterprise & Klingon cruiser engaged, "Star Trek" above, Sega logo below, promotional — $5-10
- Enterprise & Klingon cruisers (2) engaged, "Star Trek Strategic Operations Simulation" above, & "Sega The Arcade Experts" below, with Regula 1 science station from Star Trek II in background 1983 — $5-10

Star Trek: The Motion Picture

COCA-COLA
- Enterprise overhead, insets of crew below it, 18" x 24" color promotional poster — $5-10

Star Trek: The Motion Picture promotional poster by Coca-Cola. *Courtesy of the Collection of Jeff Maynard — New Eye Studio*

LINCOLN ENTERPRISES
- Spock weeps: 2' x 3' — $5-6
- Enterprise: 2' x 3' — $5-6
- Bridge Crew: 17" x 22" — $2-3
- Crew & Ship: "Human Adventure is Just Beginning," 17" x 22" — $2-3
- Kirk: 17" x 22" — $2-3
- Kirk, Spock, & Enterprise: 17" x 22" — $2-3
- McCoy: 17" x 22" — $2-3
- Kirk: art by Little, 17" x 22" — $3-4
- Spock: two faces, art by Little, 17" x 22" — $3-4
- Kirk & Spock: art by Little, 17" x 22" — $3-4
- Character Portfolio: twelve color art posters, 11" x 14", sold in sets only — $9-10

PROCTOR AND GAMBLE
- No. 1 Enterprise: all of these are 17" x 22" color promotional posters — $5-7
- No. 2 Spock & Kirk — $5-7
- No. 3 Enterprise & Crew — $5-7
- Complete Set — $15-30

SALES CORPORATION OF AMERICA
Character collage: alien landscape & ships in background:
- Regular view — $4-6
- Reversible 3-D, with glasses — $5-10

Sega Star Trek Strategic Operations Simulator. 1983. *Courtesy of the Collection of Jeff Maynard — New Eye Studio*

Captain James T. Kirk. Lincoln Enterprises. 1982. *Courtesy of the Collection of Jeff Maynard — New Eye Studio*

Star Trek II. 1982. *Courtesy of the Collection of Jeff Maynard — New Eye Studio*

Star Trek II: The Wrath of Khan. 1982. *Courtesy of the Collection of Jeff Maynard — New Eye Studio*

Star Trek III: The Search For Spock. 1984. *Courtesy of the Collection of Jeff Maynard — New Eye Studio*

❑ Cutaway poster: color cross-section of Enterprise in
    22" x 48" regular or mylar and 11" x 23" Coca-Cola
    promotional poster $15-25
❑ Enterprise: Mylar, 22" x 29" $20-35

Star Trek II: The Wrath of Khan
LINCOLN ENTERPRISES
❑ Kirk: 2' x 3' $5-6
❑ Crew: with color movie insets, 2' x 3' $5-6
❑ Khan: with muppet, 17" x 22" color art by Doug Little $3-4
❑ Spock: 17" x 22" color art by Doug Little $3-4
❑ Spock & Enterprise: 17" x 22" color art by Doug Little $3-4

SALES CORPORATION OF AMERICA
❑ Enterprise: with character insets, 22" x 30" color, 1982 $6-7
❑ Logo: 22" x 30" color, 1982 $5-6

Star Trek III: The Search for Spock
❑ **BENNETT**: color art, montage similar to overseas one-sheet,
    22" x 28", 1982 $5-10

Star Trek III: The Search For Spock. 1984. *Courtesy of the Collection of Jeff Maynard — New Eye Studio*

Star Trek IV: The Voyage Home. Art signed "Freundt." *Courtesy of the Collection of Jeff Maynard — New Eye Studio*

LEVER BROTHERS: color promotionals, 16" x 22", 1984 $6-10 each
- ❑ Bird of Prey with logo
- ❑ Crew
- ❑ Enterprise with logo
- ❑ Kirk & Kruge

Star Trek IV: The Voyage Home
LINCOLN ENTERPRISES
- ❑ Crew, ship, & whales montage: 18" x 28" color art $6-8
- ❑ One-sheet art: 24" x 36" $12-13

❑ **MIND'S EYE PRESS:** Enterprise cutaway poster reprint, updated with Star Trek IV logo, 24" x 36" $10-20

❑ **ONE STOP PUBLISHING:** Enterprise, angled, inset photo, 23" x 35" color poster $5-6

Star Trek IV: The Voyage Home movie poster, 1986. *Courtesy of the Collection of Jeff Maynard — New Eye Studio*

Twentieth Anniversary Posters
❑ **ANABAS:** Kirk, Spock, & McCoy from original series, 24" x 35" color British poster, 1987 $5-8

❑ **PERSONALITIES:** Enterprise over planet with crew & logo, color art by Gibson, heavy paper stock, 22" x 28", 1986 $10-20

❑ **VERKERKEY PUBLISHING:** Kirk, Spock, McCoy, & Uhura from original series, color, 36" x 24", 1986 $6-12

❑ **VIDEO POSTER:** original Enterprise & characters with 20-years logo, promotional color art, 26" x 39", 1987 $10-15

Star Trek IV: The Voyage Home teaser movie poster, 1986. Smallest of the posters at 20" x 13 1/2". *Courtesy of the Collection of Jeff Maynard — New Eye Studio*

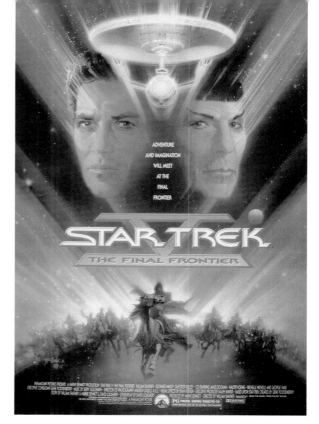

Star Trek V: The Final Frontier movie poster, 1989. *Courtesy of the Collection of Jeff Maynard — New Eye Studio*

Star Trek, Twenty Years, 1966-1986 poster featuring Uhura, McCoy, Spock, & Kirk by Verkerke Publications, Inc. 1986. 36" x 24". *Courtesy of the Collection of Jeff Maynard — New Eye Studio*

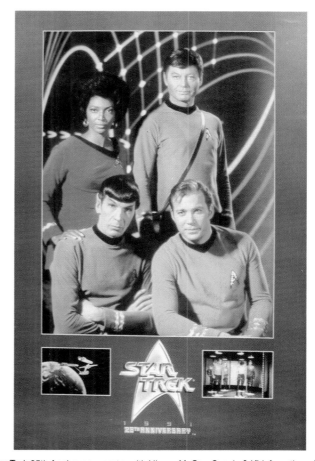

Star Trek 25th Anniversary poster with Uhura, McCoy, Spock, & Kirk from the original series by Portal Publications Ltd., 1991. *Courtesy of the Collection of Jeff Maynard — New Eye Studio*

Star Trek V: The Final Frontier

❑ **LINCOLN ENTERPRISES:** one-sheet art, 27" x 40", 1989 $10-11

Twenty-fifth Anniversary Posters

❑ **PORTAL PUBLICATIONS LTD.:** Kirk, Spock, McCoy, & Uhura above 25th anniversary logo & two color original series insets, 24" x 36", 1991 $6-7

    ❑ 25th anniversary logo in large size with four small insets of Kirk, Spock, McCoy, & Scott from the original series, 24" x 36", 1991 $6-7

Star Trek Giant Poster Book #1 (1976), #3 (1976), & #17 (1978). *Courtesy of the Collection of Jeff Maynard — New Eye Studio*

Movie Poster Books

- ❑ Star Trek: The Motion Picture: identical format to the original series poster books, cover and poster of Enterprise & crew, by Paradise Press, 1979 $10-20
- ❑ Star Trek II: The Wrath of Khan: identical format to the poster books, produced by Walkerprint Publications in England, 1982, with cover showing Enterprise & Kirk, poster showing collage, 23" x 32" fold out. $8-12

PROPS & PROP REPRODUCTIONS

While obtaining original props from any of the television series or feature films is next to impossible (Paramount does not give their property away), there are any number of anonymous artists out there producing quality prop reproductions. Paramount frowns but these people continue to produce. Some can be better in quality and appearance than the actual props as these pretenders will stand up to close examination. Original props were never designed for close scrutiny. Some reproductions come with electronics for sound and light effects. Reproduction props have been created for both the original television series, the first six films, and for Star Trek: The Next Generation. Happy Hunting!
The reproductions listed here are of high quality.

Star Trek: The Motion Picture Exclusive Collectors Issue magazine, 1979. *Courtesy of the Collection of Jeff Maynard — New Eye Studio*

Artist produced reproduction communicators, Type 1 phaser, and Type 2 phaser. *Courtesy of the Collection of Jeff Maynard — New Eye Studio*

Star Trek VI: The Undiscovered Country

- ❑ **Star Trek VI:** one-sheet with title & Enterprise (aft-view) above, Klingon face below, 27" x 40", 1991 $12-14
- ❑ **Star Trek VI:** one-sheet with moving Enterprise, rainbow with crew faces, explosion with title, & Klingon Bird of Prey, 27" x 41" $12-14

Star Trek Poster Books

Original Series Poster Books, Paradise Press — 1976-1978

Publications series printed in color on both sides of a 22" x 33" sheet. A poster covers one side, pictures and articles are printed on the other. Sold folded into an 8 1/2" x 11" format for seventeen issues.

❑	Voyage 1, 1976	$35-40
❑	Voyage 2-4, 1976	$6-35
❑	Voyage 5-14, 1977	$6-35
❑	Voyage 15-17, 1978	$35-40

Captain's Command Chair
- ❑ Original series: lights & special effects. While this would be a very difficult item to find or purchase, one such fan reproduction was borrowed by Paramount to recreate the original bridge on the holodeck during a Star Trek: The Next Generation episode. Mr. Scott arrived in the 24th century via a transporter trick of his own design.   market value

Chess Set, 3-D
- ❑ Original series 3-D chess set: handmade painted wooden armature, silkscreened lucite playing fields, pieces, instructions. $100-120

Communicators
- ❑ Original series: flip up grid, non-functioning (no electronics) $75-150
- ❑ Original series: flip up grid, flashing lights, & sound effect "chirp" $125-200
- ❑ Original series: flip up grid, flashing lights, sound effect, & one voice $225-250
- ❑ Original series: flip up grid, flashing lights, sound effect, & two voices $250-275

Dr. McCoy's Medical Equipment
- ❑ Original series hypo spray: machined metal, working plunger, hissing sound, two vials of "medicine" — $110-120
- ❑ Original series medical scanner: battery powered hand unit with holographic spinning sensor within lucite dome — $60-70

Phasers
- ❑ Original series Type 1 hand phaser: non-functioning, solid cast unit, painted & finished — $50-75
- ❑ Original series Type 1 hand phaser: working unit with stun & disrupt settings, beam emitter changes color — $125-200
- ❑ Original series Type 1 phaser kits: solid cast resin kit with instructions — $15-17
- ❑ Original series Type 2 phaser: power pack hand grip attachment for the Type 1 (adding power & range), detachable Type 1 phaser, non-functioning — $200-275
- ❑ Original series Type 2 phaser: light & sound effects — $225-250
- ❑ Movie ("movie" here spans from The Motion Picture to Star Trek VI) Type 3 phaser: solid cast, streamlined with hand grip, non-functioning, fully painted — $175-300
- ❑ Movie Type 3 phaser kit: solid cast resin kit with instructions — $90-100
- ❑ Movie Type 4 phaser: two piece solid cast, non-functioning, with removable Type 1-4 unit, painted & detailed — $200-250
- ❑ Movie Type VI heavy duty assault weapon: exact replica, one piece solid cast non-functioning unit, detailed, painted, machined metal beam emitter — $200-250
- ❑ Movie Type VI weapon kit: ready to assemble & paint with instructions — $150-175

Tricorders
- ❑ Original series tricorder: non-functioning, compartment opens, storage compartments — $150-200
- ❑ Original series tricorder: rotating viewer head, scanner sound, flashing lights, compartment opens, storage compartments, metal & plastic — $250-350

Vulcan Harps
- ❑ Movie Vulcan harp: Paramount approved working model, produced by the artist who created them for the movies, rosewood, mahogany, & ash, numbered & signed — $350-400

PROMOTIONAL ITEMS

Artifacts (press kits, lobby cards, restaurant displays...) produced for the promotion of current and upcoming releases which were not intended for public release. They find there way into the market as distributors (movie theaters, etc.) have very little use for them.

Star Trek: The Original Series
- ❑ Advance Brochure: booklet, twelve-page, introducing the series to NBC affiliates, 1966 — $350-400
- ❑ Promotional Flyer: nervous NBC network early promotional art, Spock's pointed ears airbrushed into human form (fear of scaring off advertisers) — $200-300
- ❑ Second Season Publicity Folder: promotional for NBC affiliates, 1967 — $300-350
- ❑ Star Trek Mail Call: NBC booklet for affiliates, twenty-page, containing viewers' letters, 1967 — $300-350
- ❑ Star Trek Syndication Package: artwork of cast & demographics, folder designed to sell stations on syndication — $75-100

Star Trek: The Movies
Lobby Cards (11" x 14") & Stills (8" x 10") for Theaters
- ❑ Star Trek: The Motion Picture:
  - ❑ Cards (foreign counterparts of each are also produced) — $60-80
  - ❑ Stills — $50-70
- ❑ Star Trek II: The Wrath of Khan:
  - ❑ Cards — $60-80
  - ❑ Stills — $50-70
- ❑ Star Trek III: The Search for Spock:
  - ❑ Cards — $50-70
  - ❑ Stills — $45-60
- ❑ Star Trek IV: The Voyage Home:
  - ❑ Cards — $50-60
  - ❑ Stills — $50-60
- ❑ Star Trek V: The Final Frontier:
  - ❑ Cards — $45-55
  - ❑ Stills — $25-35
- ❑ Star Trek VI: The Undiscovered Country:
  - ❑ Cards — $35-45
  - ❑ Stills — $15-25

Press Books & Kits
- ❑ Star Trek: The Motion Picture:
  - ❑ Book — $35-40
  - ❑ Giant Kit Including Novel — $150-175
  - ❑ Kit — $80-100

Star Trek: The Motion Picture Press Information Pack, 1979. *Courtesy of the Collection of Jeff Maynard — New Eye Studio*

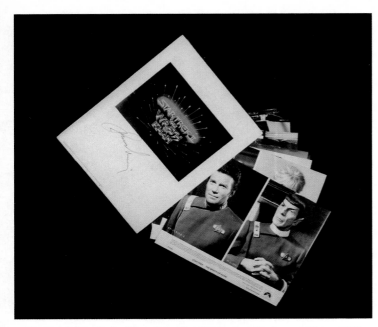

Star Trek II: The Wrath of Khan Promotional folder signed by Leonard Nimoy, 1982. *Courtesy of the Collection of Jeff Maynard — New Eye Studio*

- ❏ Star Trek II: The Wrath of Khan:
    - ❏ Book ... $35-45
    - ❏ Kit ... $100-150
    - ❏ (signed by Nimoy) ... $200-220
- ❏ Star Trek III: The Search for Spock:
    - ❏ Book ... $15-20
    - ❏ Kit ... $50-75
- ❏ Star Trek IV: The Voyage Home:
    - ❏ Book ... $10-15
    - ❏ Kit ... $40-60
- ❏ Star Trek V: The Final Frontier:
    - ❏ Book ... $8-12
    - ❏ Kit ... $25-40
- ❏ Star Trek VI: The Undiscovered Country:
    - ❏ Book ... $7-10
    - ❏ Kit ... $25-35

Standees
Die-cut color cardboard figures or scenes for theater displays.
- ❏ Star Trek: The Motion Picture ... $200-300
- ❏ Star Trek II: The Wrath of Khan ... $200-300
- ❏ Star Trek III: The Search for Spock ... $150-250
- ❏ Star Trek IV: The Voyage Home ... $100-200
- ❏ Star Trek V: The Final Frontier ... $75-125
- ❏ Star Trek VI: The Undiscovered Country ... $50-100

Program Books
Promotional 8" x 11" books with poster art & pictures sold directly to the public at the theaters. Popularity for these items is increasing in markets outside of the United States while slipping in the U.S.
- ❏ Star Trek: The Motion Picture ... $25-30
- ❏ Star Trek II: The Wrath of Khan ... $25-30
- ❏ Star Trek III: The Search for Spock ... $25-30
- ❏ Star Trek IV: The Voyage Home ... $15-25
- ❏ Star Trek V: The Final Frontier ... $15-20
- ❏ Star Trek VI: The Undiscovered Country ... $10-15

Star Trek: The Motion Picture Magazine, 1979. *Courtesy of the Collection of Jeff Maynard — New Eye Studio*

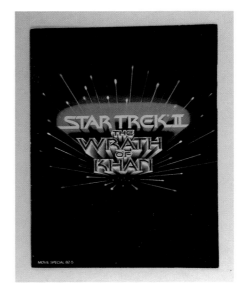

Star Trek II: The Wrath of Khan magazine, movie special, 1982. *Courtesy of the Collection of Jeff Maynard — New Eye Studio*

PUZZLES

Puzzles must have undamaged boxes and all of their pieces to be collectibles with more than sentimental value.
AVIVA — 1979
- ❏ Star Trek: The Motion Picture: color jigsaw puzzles of various crew members, 551 pieces, 18" x 24" ... $30-35
    - ❏ Spock ... $30-35
    - ❏ U.S.S. Enterprise NCC-1701 ... $30-35

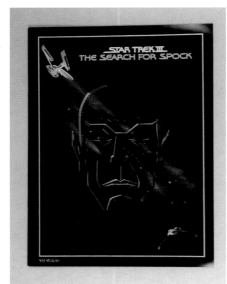

Star Trek III: The Search for Spock magazine, movie special, 1984. *Courtesy of the Collection of Jeff Maynard — New Eye Studio*

GOLDEN — 1993
- ❑ Kirk, Spock, & Enterprise: color art of the original series,
  300 pieces, 36" x 24" $10-30

H.G. TOYS
First Series: cartoon art, in color, two sizes — 1974
- ❑ Battle on the Planet Klingon: 150 pieces, 10" x 14" $20-30
- ❑ Battle on the Planet Romulan: 150 pieces, 10" x 14" $20-30
- ❑ Captain Kirk & Officers Beam Down: 150 pieces, 10" x 14" $20-30
- ❑ Attempted Hijacking of the U.S.S. Enterprise & Its Officers:
  300 pieces, 14" x 18" $25-35
- ❑ Starship U.S.S. Enterprise & Its Officers: 300 pieces,
  14" x 18" $25-35

Second Series: more realistic color art, boxes marked Series II,
150 pieces, 14" x 10" size.
- ❑ The Alien $25-27
- ❑ Captain Kirk, Mr. Spock, & Dr. McCoy $25-27
- ❑ Force Field Capture $25-27

LARAMI — 1979
- ❑ Star Trek: The Motion Picture: 15 piece sliding puzzles $20-30 each
  - ❑ Kirk
  - ❑ Spock
  - ❑ Enterprise

MILTON BRADLEY — 1979
- ❑ Star Trek: The Motion Picture: 250 piece color photo
  designs, 19 7/8" x 13 7/8" $20-25 each
  - ❑ Faces of the Future
  - ❑ Sickbay & Ilia
  - ❑ U.S.S. Enterprise

MIND'S EYE PRESS — 1986
- ❑ U.S.S. Enterprise NCC 1701-A: 551 pieces of color cutaway art from Star Trek IV, 18" x 24" $30-35

SPRINGBOK — 1993
- ❑ Star Trek. Journey to the Undiscovered Country: crew
  portrait art with Enterprise & planet, puzzle $10-30

WHITMAN JIGSAW PUZZLES — 1978
Cartoon art in color featuring collages of crew members,
vessels, & alien planetscapes, 200 pieces, 14" x 18" $20-22 each
- ❑ Yellow Boxed Puzzle
- ❑ Red Boxed Puzzle
- ❑ Green Boxed Puzzle
- ❑ Purple Boxed Puzzle

WHITMAN FRAME TRAY PUZZLES
Cartoon art in color within a 8 1/2" x 11" tray. $20-22
- ❑ Bridge
- ❑ Kirk in Space Suit
- ❑ Kirk, Spock & Enterprise
- ❑ Transporter Room

Star Trek puzzle by Golden, 1993. *Courtesy of the Collection of Jeff Maynard —
New Eye Studio*

Star Trek puzzle by Whitman, 1978. *Courtesy of the Collection of Jeff Maynard —
New Eye Studio*

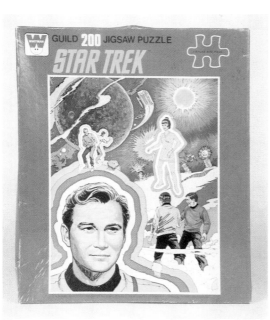

Star Trek puzzle by Whitman, 1978. *Courtesy of the Collection of Jeff Maynard —
New Eye Studio*

Inside Star Trek record, Columbia Records. *Courtesy of the Collection of Jeff Maynard — New Eye Studio*

Trek Bloopers by Blue Pear Records. *Courtesy of the Collection of Jeff Maynard — New Eye Studio*

RECORDS, TAPES, & COMPACT DISCS

With the advent of the CD, records and record players themselves have now fallen by the wayside. Albums will be harder to find as the years go by and ever more collectible.

SIMON & SCHUSTER Audio Novels
Based on Star Trek novels by Pocket Books and narrated by cast members. Recorded on tape only.

❑	Enterprise: The First Adventure: Nimoy & Takei, 1988	$10-12
❑	Entropy Effect: Nimoy & Takei, 1988	$10-12
❑	Final Frontier: Nimoy & Doohan, 1989	$10-12
❑	Kobayashi Maru: Doohan, 1990	$11-13
❑	Lost Years: Nimoy & Doohan, 1989	$16-18
❑	Prime Directive: Doohan	$15-17
❑	Spock's World: Nimoy & Takei, 1995	$15-17
❑	Strangers from the Sky: Nimoy & Takei, 1987	$9-11
❑	Time for Yesterday: Nimoy & Doohan, 1989	$11-13
❑	Web of the Romulans: Nimoy & Takei, 1988	$10-12
❑	Yesterday's Son: Nimoy & Doohan, 1988	$10-12
❑	Star Trek IV: The Voyage Home: Nimoy & Takei, 1986	$9-11
❑	Star Trek V: The Final Frontier: Nimoy & Takei, 1989	$10-12
❑	Ashes of Eden: Shatner, 1995 (based on his own book)	$18-20

Audio Grab Bag

	Captain of the Starship: two 12" LP albums, Canadian pressing of William Shatner-"Live" Two pressings were made:	
❑	Imperial Music	$30-35
❑	K-TEL Record	$30-35
❑	The Green Hills of Earth & Gentlemen, Be Seated: by Robert A. Heinlein & read by Nimoy, 12" LP album or cassette by Caedmon Records	$20-25
❑	Halley's Comet: Once in a Lifetime: Nimoy narrated with space music & sound effects by Geodesium, audio cassette by Caedmon Cassettes, 1986	$20-25
❑	The Illustrated Man: by Ray Bradbury, read by Nimoy, 12" LP album by Caedmon Records	$20-25
❑	Inside Star Trek: recorded by Gene Roddenberry, featuring Shatner, Isaac Asimov, Lenard, & Kelley. Discuss series origins, personalities, & additional insider information. Columbia Records	$50-55
❑	The Martian Chronicles: by Ray Bradbury: read by Nimoy, 12" LP album, by Caedmon Records	$25-35
❑	Mimsy Were the Borogoves: by Henry Kuttner: read by Shatner, 12" LP album, by Caedmon Records	$25-35
❑	The Mysterious Golem: Jewish folklore narrated by Nimoy, 12" LP album, by JRT Records	$25-35
❑	The Psychohistorians: by Isaac Asimov, read by Shatner, 12" LP album or cassette, by Caedmon Records	$25-35
❑	Star Fleet Beat, Phasers on Stun: special 20th anniversary 12" LP album by Penguin Records	$25-35
❑	Star Trek Comedy: The Unofficial Album: comedy songs & skits about Star Trek, 12" album or cassette by Vince Emery Productions	$15-25
❑	Star Trekkin' by "The Firm": Star Trekkin' & Dub Trek on 12" 45 rpm & 7" 45 rpm records by Precision Records & Tapes	$15-25
❑	The Star Trek Philosophy & Star Trek Theme: performed by Gene Roddenberry & Inside Star Trek Orchestra from the Inside Star Trek album, 7" 45 rpm record by Columbia Records	$20-40
❑	Star Trek Tapes: compiled official press recordings with the cast of the original series, produced by Jack M. Sell Tape Cassettes, Inter Audio Associates: Star Trek parody, four tapes begun in 1973 for college radio, Vols. I-IV.	$45-50
❑	The Transformed Man: performed by William Shatner, Captain Kirk reads 6 selections with chorus & instrumental background, 12" LP album by Decca Records	$40-70
❑	The Transformed Man & How Insensitive: from Transformed Man album, 7" 45 rpm by Decca Records	$20-30

William Shatner "Live" dramatic narratives with musical accompaniment by Lemli Records. *Courtesy of the Collection of Jeff Maynard — New Eye Studio*

- ❏ Trek Bloopers: unedited tapes of six third season episodes of the original Star Trek. 12" LP album & cassette by Blue Pear Records $20-30
- ❏ Voice Tracks, U.S. Marine Corps Toys for Tots: readings by Nimoy, and other notables, music by U.S. Marine Band, 7" 33 1/3 rpm album, by Warner Bros.-Seven Arts Records. $20-30
- ❏ The Voyage of Star Trek: 60 minute radio special from The Source, NBC Radio's Young Adult Network, promotional copy, discusses Star Trek original series & Star Trek II. 12" LP album, 1982 $30-40
- ❏ The War of the Worlds: by H.G. Wells, read by Nimoy, 12" LP album by Caedmon Records $30-40
- ❏ William Shatner-"Live": 2 record LP, dramatic narratives recited with musical accompaniment from Shatner's college tour by Lemli Records $50-70
- ❏ Whales Alive: by Paul Winter & Paul Halley, narrations by Nimoy accompanied by humpback whales, 12" album by Living Music $30-40

"Captain, I have an incoming transmission...badly garbled!" Star Trek Personalities Sing

A number of these original "gems" have been reissued by Rhino Records on several "Golden Throats" tapes and CDs.

- ❏ Beyond Antares & Uhura's Theme: by Nichols, 7" 45 rpm by R-Way Records $10-20
- ❏ Consilium & Here We Go 'Round Again: by Nimoy from album The Way I Feel, 7" 45 rpm by Dot Records $30-40
- ❏ Dark Side of the Moon: by Nichols, two 7" 45 rpm, 4 songs with album jacket unfolding to reveal inside poster, by Americana Records $20-30

Leonard Nimoy sings and waxes poetic! Several of Nimoy's albums. *Courtesy of the Collection of Jeff Maynard — New Eye Studio*

Star Trek record singles, from vocal to comic. *Courtesy of the Collection of Jeff Maynard — New Eye Studio*

Star Trek Original Television Soundtrack by GNP Crescendo Records *Courtesy of the Collection of Jeff Maynard — New Eye Studio*

❏ Disco Trekkin' & Star Child: by Grace Lee Whitney, 7" 45 rpm
 by GLW Star Enterprises $20-30
❏ Down to Earth: 8 popular songs by Nichols, 12" LP album by
 Epic Records $30-40
❏ Leonard Nimoy: 12" Sears album, reissues Dot records $25-30
❏ Leonard Nimoy Presents Mr. Spock's Music From Outer
 Space: Nimoy sings & recites 11 songs, 12" LP album
 by Dot Records $35-40
  ❏ British version released in 1973 $35-40
❏ Leonard Nimoy, You Are Not Alone: Nimoy's previously
 recorded material, cassette by MCA $12-14
❏ The New World of Leonard Nimoy: Nimoy sings 8 popular
 songs, 12" LP album by Dot Records $50-55
❏ Outer Space/Inner Mind: 2 record album with all of Leonard
 Nimoy Presents Mr. Spock's Music From Outer Space &
 cuts from The Two Sides of Leonard Nimoy, The Touch
 of Leonard Nimoy, The Way I Feel, & The New World of
 Leonard Nimoy, 12" LP albums by Paramount Records
 Famous Twinsets $30-40
❏ Please Don't Try to Change My Mind, & I'd Love Making
 Love to You: Nimoy songs from The Way I Feel, 7"
 45 rpm by Dot Records $10-15
❏ Space Odyssey: 9 pieces from Nimoy's 5 albums by Dot
 Records. Pickwick/33 Records produced $25-30
❏ The Sun Will Rise, & Time to Get It Together: Nimoy sings
 from album The New World of Leonard Nimoy, 7" 45 rpm
 by Dot Records $10-15
❏ Take a Star Trip: by Grace Lee Whitney, 45 rpm $10-15
❏ The Touch of Leonard Nimoy: 11 songs by Nimoy on Dot
 Records $30-35
❏ Two Sides of Leonard Nimoy: 13 songs sung or recited by
 Nimoy, 12" LP album by Dot Records $25-30
❏ Uhura Sings: 9 songs by Nichols on cassette by AR-WAY
 Productions $25-30
❏ Visit to a Sad Planet, & Star Trek Theme: by Nimoy from
 Leonard Nimoy Presents Mr. Spock's Music from
 Outer Space, 7" 45 rpm by Dot Records $10-15
❏ The Way I Feel: 12 songs narrated or sung by Nimoy on a
 12" LP album or reel-to-reel tape by Dot Records $40-45

Soundtracks & Themes
❏ The Cage & Where No Man Has Gone Before: original series
 soundtrack, Alexander Courage composed & conducted
 music, 12" LP album, CD, & cassette by GNP Crescendo
 Records $10-25
❏ The Cage & Where No Man Has Gone Before: 33 1/3 rpm
 album with the cover art printed directly on the record,
 by Precision Records & Tapes Ltd., 1986 $35-40
❏ Charlie X, The Corbomite Maneuver, The Doomsday
 Machine, & Mudd's Women: recorded by the Royal
 Philharmonic Orchestra, Fred Steiner conductor, 12"
 LP album, CD, cassette by Varese Sarabande Records $10-25
❏ The Colors of Love, & Only Star Can Last: original words &
 music on a fan-produced 12" LP album by Omicron
 Ceti Three   market value
❏ Dementia Royale: Dr. Demento compilation with Star
 Trek parody, 12" LP album by Rhino Records $20-25

Star Trek The Original Television Soundtrack photo record by Precision Records & Tapes Ltd. *Courtesy of the Collection of Jeff Maynard — New Eye Studio*

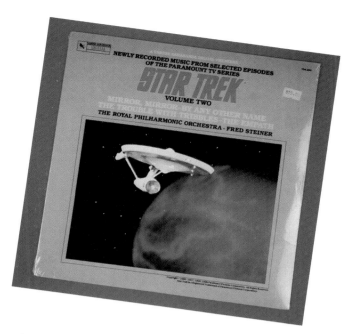

Star Trek Volume Two scores from series episodes by Varese Sarabande. *Courtesy of the Collection of Jeff Maynard — New Eye Studio*

Star Trek record singles. *Courtesy of the Collection of Jeff Maynard — New Eye Studio*

Star Trek: The Motion Picture Original Movie Soundtrack by Columbia Records. *Courtesy of the Collection of Jeff Maynard — New Eye Studio*

Star Trek IV: The Voyage Home Original Motion Picture Soundtrack by MCA. *Courtesy of the Collection of Jeff Maynard — New Eye Studio*

Star Trek II Original Motion Picture Soundtrack by Atlantic Records. *Courtesy of the Collection of Jeff Maynard — New Eye Studio*

- ❏ 50 Popular TV Themes: The Bruce Baxter Orchestra performs the original series theme, among others, on two 12" LP albums by Pickwick Records $12-22
- ❏ Genesis Project: expanded soundtracks never heard in Star Trek II & III, two 12" LP albums or cassette by Sonic Atmo Spheres $15-30
- ❏ I, Mudd, The Enemy Within, Spectre of the Gun, & Conscience of the King: Vol. II., symphonic suites from original series by the Royal Philharmonic Orchestra, Tony Bremner conductor, 12" LP album, CD or cassette by Label X Record $10-25
- ❏ Is There in Truth No Beauty?, & Paradise Syndrome: Vol I., symphonic suites from original series by the Royal Philharmonic Orchestra, Tony Bremner conductor, 12" LP album, CD or cassette by Label X Record $22-24
- ❏ Love Theme From Star Trek: The Motion Picture (A Star Beyond Time): Shuan Cassidy sings, 7" 45 rpm by Warner Brothers Records $10-20
- ❏ Main Theme from Star Trek: The Motion Picture: Bob James arranged & conducted, 7" 45 rpm by Tappan Zee Records $10-15
- ❏ Main Theme from Star Trek: The Motion Picture: from Music From the Original Soundtrack, composed & conducted by Jerry Goldsmith, 7" 45 rpm by Columbia Records $10-15
- ❏ Masterpiece: contains theme from Star Trek original series, 12" LP album by Ranwood Records $20-25
- ❏ Mirror, Mirror, By Any Other Name, The Trouble With Tribbles, & The Empath-Vol. II: symphonic suites from the original series, 12" LP album, CD or cassette by Varise Sarabande, 1986 $22-24
- ❏ Music From Return of the Jedi & Other Space Hits: by Odyssey Orchestra, including the original series theme, 12" LP album by Sine Qua Non Records $20-25
- ❏ Music From Star Trek & the Black Hole: Meco Monardo disco music by Casablanca Records $20-25
- ❏ Music From the Original Soundtrack-Star Trek: The Motion Picture: Jerry Goldsmith music, 12" LP album by CBS/SONY Record $30-35
- ❏ 1984-A Space Odyssey: John Williams & The Boston Pops Orchestra perform the main themes from the original series & The Motion Picture, 12" LP album by J & B Records $20-25
- ❏ Out of This World: John Williams & The Boston Pops Orchestra again performed the main themes from the original series & The Motion Picture, by Phillips Digital Recording $20-25
- ❏ Starship: fan-produced Frank Argus 45 rpm, 1984 $10-15
- ❏ Star Tracks: The Cincinnati Pops Orchestra, Erich Kunzel conductor, with main theme from original series by Telarc Digital Records $30-35
- ❏ Star Trek: The Motion Picture: 7" 45 rpm by Capital Exposition Record, 1981 $10-15
- ❏ Star Trek: The Motion Picture: original soundtrack music, Jerry Goldsmith composed & conductor, 12" LP album, CD or cassette by Columbia Records $12-22
- ❏ Star Trek-Main Theme From The Motion Picture: The Now Sound Orchestra performs A Star Beyond Time-The Motion Picture love theme-and original series theme, 12" LP album by Synthetic Plastics Record $20-25
- ❏ Star Trek-21 Space Hits: theme from the original series, 12" LP album by Music World $30-35
- ❏ Star Trek II: original motion picture soundtrack, James Horner composed & conducted, 12" LP album by Atlantic Records $25-30
- ❏ Star Trek III: The Search for Spock, The Audio Movie Kit: transcripts of "The Movie for Radio" & "Behind the Scenes", 2 audio tapes with same material, script folder, by Riches/Rubinstein & Radio, Inc. $70-80
- ❏ Star Trek III: original motion picture soundtrack, two 12" LP albums, CD or cassette, by Capital-EMI Record $12-22
- ❏ Star Trek IV: original motion picture soundtrack, 12" LP album, CD or cassette by MCA $12-22
- ❏ Star Trek V: movie soundtrack in CD or cassette by Epic $12-22
- ❏ Star Trek VI: movie soundtrack in CD or cassette $12-22
- ❏ Star Trek Sound Effects: original series soundtrack, 12" LP album, CD or cassette by GNP Crescendo $12-22
- ❏ Theme From Star Trek TV: from album Masterpiece, 7" 45 rpm by Ranwood Records $10-15
- ❏ Theme From Star Trek, Greatest Science Fiction Hits: Neil Norman & His Cosmic Orchestra, 12" LP album or cassette $20-25

- ❏ Theme From Star Trek: Tristar Orchestra & Chorus, John Townsley producer, 7" 45 rpm by Tristar Records $10-15
- ❏ Theme From Star Trek: The Jeff Wayne Space Shuttle by Wonderland Records $20-25
- ❏ Theme From Star Trek: Warp Nine fan-produced, synthesizer space music, sold to get the series back on TV, 7" 45 rpm by Privilege Records $10-15
- ❏ Theme From Star Trek: Ferrante & Teicher, 7" 45 rpm by United Artists Records $10-15
- ❏ Theme From Star Trek: Meco Monardo, 7" 45 rpm by Casablanca Records $10-15
- ❏ Theme From Star Trek: Gene Page & His Orchestra, 7" 45 rpm by Arista Records $10-15
- ❏ Theme from Star Trek: Billy Strange, 7" 45 rpm by GNP Crescendo Records $10-15
- ❏ Theme From Star Trek: The Motion Picture: Neil Norman & His Cosmic Orchestra, 12" LP album by GNP Crescendo Records $20-25
- ❏ Theme From Star Trek II: James Horner & Orchestra, 7" 45 rpm by Atlantic Records $20-25
- ❏ Theme From Star Trek III: James Horner, 7" 45 rpm by Capital Records $15-20
- ❏ TV Themes: the Ventures, contains original series theme, 12" LP album by United Artists Records $20-25

Two Star Trek story records with 16 page color comics by Power Records. *Courtesy of the Collection of Jeff Maynard — New Eye Studio*

Stories From Star Trek

- ❑ Star Trek: The Motion Picture: read-along adventure record, 24 page book, color illustrations, 7" 33 1/3 rpm or cassette by Buena Vista Records $20-25
- ❑ Star Trek II: read-along adventure record 24 page book, color illustrations, 7" 33 1/3 rpm by Buena Vista Records $20-25
- ❑ Star Trek III: read-along adventure record 24 page book, color illustrations, 7" 33 1/3 rpm by Buena Vista Records $20-25
- ❑ Star Trek IV: read-along adventure record 24 page book, color illustrations, 7" 33 1/3 rpm by Buena Vista Records $20-25
- ❑ Star Trek: book & record set with Passage to Moauv adventure, 7" 45 rpm & 20 page illustrated book:
  - ❑ Kirk, Spock, & alien beast art by Power Records, 1975 $10-15
  - ❑ Spock, Kirk & Enterprise color cover by Peter Pan, 1979 $10-15
- ❑ Star Trek: Dinosaur Planet adventure, book & record set, 7" 45 rpm record, 20 page color illustrated book by Peter Pan Records $10-15
- ❑ Star Trek: The Robot Masters adventure, book & record set, 7" 45 rpm record & 20 page color illustrated book by Peter Pan Records $10-15
- ❑ Star Trek: A Mirror for Futility & The Time Stealer adventures, book & record set, 12" LP album & 16 page color comic by Power Records $15-18
- ❑ Star Trek: The Crier in Emptiness & Passage to Moauv adventures, book & record set, 12" LP album & 16 page color comic by Peter Pan Records $15-18
- ❑ Star Trek: The Time Stealer, In Vino Veritas, To Starve a Fleaver, Dinosaur Planet, & Passage to Moauv adventures, 12" LP album by Peter Pan Records $15-18
- ❑ Star Trek: original stories for children inspired by In Vino Veritas, 7" 45 rpm by Power Records $5-10
- ❑ Star Trek: original stories for children inspired by The Human Factor, 7" 45 rpm by Power Records $5-10
- ❑ Star Trek: original stories for children inspired by The Time Stealer, 7" 45 rpm by Power Records $5-10
- ❑ Star Trek: original stories for children inspired by To Starve a Fleaver, 7" 45 rpm by Power Records $5-10
- ❑ Star Trek: The Time Stealer, To Starve a Fleaver, The Logistics of Stampede, & A Mirror of Futility adventures, 12" LP album by Power Records $15-18
- ❑ Star Trek: The Man Who Trained Meteors, The Robot Masters, Dinosaur Planet, & The Human Factor adventures, 12" LP album by Peter Pan Records $25-30
- ❑ Star Trek & Other Movie Songs: original series theme along with other television themes by Kid Stuff Records, 1978 $20-25

SCRIPTS

It is virtually impossible to authenticate a script from the various Star Trek series or films as the genuine articles. Scripts are merely photocopies and photocopies do tend to look alike. Copies of scripts do crop up, although Paramount is trying hard to prevent this. One week prior to the release of Star Trek: Generations, a copy of the script was found at a convention while another was making its way through the internet.

However, now there are now Paramount approved *Premier Collector's Scripts* available each Star Trek film from The Motion Picture to The Undiscovered Country, complete with background information, photos, and film credits.

STILLS (printed lithographs), SLIDES, & PHOTOGRAPHS

- ❑ **Disney/MGM Studios:** black & white cards with cast pictures, made for autographing by cast members at events $3-5
- ❑ **Fantasy House:** mini-poster set with six 4" x 6" posters with Kirk, Spock, Spock up close & personal, McCoy, Kirk & Chekov, & Sulu $5-8
- ❑ **Kelly Freas Portfolio:** seven color art stills of cast, 1976, 8 1/2" x 11" $25-28

Langley & Associates $4-6 each
- ❑ Kirk: head only
  - ❑ head cocked
  - ❑ smiling
  - ❑ Tribble bound
  - ❑ dress uniform
  - ❑ with communicator
- ❑ Spock: color portrait
  - ❑ smiling
  - ❑ bearded from Mirror, Mirror
  - ❑ Vulcan salute
- ❑ Kirk & Spock
- ❑ Kirk, Spock, McCoy, & Scott at conference table
- ❑ McCoy: close up
- ❑ Chekov: portrait
- ❑ Uhura: color portrait
- ❑ Scott: in dress uniform
- ❑ Sulu: on the bridge
- ❑ Crew on alien planet
- ❑ Crew on bridge
- ❑ Crew on transporter pads
- ❑ Enterprise: alien vessels surround
- ❑ Enterprise: firing phasers
- ❑ Enterprise: follows another Federation vessel
- ❑ Enterprise: in starburst
- ❑ Enterprise: with "Star Trek"

Lincoln Enterprises Art Prints
- ❑ Probert color original series cast including Chapel, Chekov, Enterprise, Kirk, McCoy, Scott, Spock, Sulu, & Uhura, 8 1/2" x 11" $3-5
- ❑ Doug Little color art of cast from Star Trek: The Motion Picture, including Chapel, Chekov, Decker, Ilia, Klingon, McCoy, Saavik, Scott, Spock, Sulu, & Uhura, 11" x 14" $3-5
- ❑ **Lincoln Enterprises, Evolution of the Enterprise:** starship takes place through twelve phases to final series form $4-6
- ❑ **Lincoln Enterprises, Wallet Pictures,** sets of 15 color 2" x 3" photos: $2-4 each
  - ❑ Costumes No. 1
  - ❑ Costumes No. 2
  - ❑ Kirk
  - ❑ Spock
  - ❑ Makeup & aliens
  - ❑ Action scenes from Star Trek: The Motion Picture
  - ❑ Scenes from Star Trek: The Motion Picture
  - ❑ Stars & groups
  - ❑ Star Trek: The Wrath of Khan, sets No. 1-4
  - ❑ Star Trek original series No. 1-3
  - ❑ Star Trek III: The Search for Spock, No. 1-4
- ❑ **Lincoln Enterprises, Weapons & Field Equipment:** 12 color pictures per set $3-5
- ❑ **Star Trek Episode Cards:** large, color, fan-produced pictures with 3 small insets on each card, 1978 $4-6 each
  - ❑ All Our Yesterdays
  - ❑ Amok Time
  - ❑ Bloopers
  - ❑ The Cage
  - ❑ City on the Edge of Forever
  - ❑ Doomsday Machine
  - ❑ Journey to Babel
  - ❑ Mirror, Mirror
  - ❑ Paradise Syndrome
  - ❑ Patterns of Force
  - ❑ Star Trek
  - ❑ Tholian Web
  - ❑ Trouble With Tribbles
  - ❑ What Are Little Girls Made Of?
  - ❑ Where No Man Has Gone Before

Star Trek Galore: unlicensed color photos, 8" x 10" or 8 1/2" x 11", 1976 $2-4 each
- ❑ Alien ship fires weapons
- ❑ Captain Pike (Jeffrey Hunter)
- ❑ Captain Kirk: Tribble buried
- ❑ Captain Kirk
- ❑ Captain Kirk & Federation flag
- ❑ Captain Kirk & Spock: fire on Horta
- ❑ Chekov portrait
- ❑ Chekov & Sulu on the bridge
- ❑ Kirk, Spock, Uhura & Chekov on the bridge
- ❑ Crew: without Kirk
- ❑ Crew: on bridge
- ❑ Crew: portrait on bridge
- ❑ Crew: tension on the bridge
- ❑ Enterprise: firing phasers
- ❑ Enterprise: viewed from below
- ❑ Enterprise: alien vessels surround

- ❑ Galileo: in space
- ❑ McCoy, Kirk, & Spock
- ❑ Scott: concerned
- ❑ Scott: on the bridge
- ❑ Spock: bearded
- ❑ Spock: takes aim with phaser
- ❑ Spock: Vulcan greeting
- ❑ Spock: drives home his point
- ❑ Spock: emotionally charged
- ❑ Spock: with Vulcan child
- ❑ Spock: plays 3-D chess
- ❑ Spock: plays Vulcan harp
- ❑ Sulu: portrait
- ❑ Transporter room: Kirk, McCoy, Uhura, & Scott beam away
- ❑ Tribbles: Kirk regards his furry nemeses
- ❑ Uhura & Chekov: good humor on the bridge

TOYS and CRAFTS

Toys fire the collector's passion more than any other collectibles category. The toy lines in Star Trek are growing continually now, offering many opportunities for collecting. Star Trek toys also interest general toy collectors, making them a fine investment. Adding to the interest is the fact that toy lines seldom stay on the market long. Competition keeps manufacturers on their toes, constantly changing their offerings.

When collecting toys, keep them in their boxes for added value. Complete and packaged toys garner the highest interest and value in the collecting world.

Star Trek Communicators working communicators packed first in a box and later in a blister pack by Mego, 1976. *Courtesy of the Collection of Jeff Maynard — New Eye Studio*

From the Quartermaster: Communicators, Phasers, and Tricorders

Star Trek V: The Final Frontier promotional communicator walkie-talkies with retractable antennae for Proctor & Gamble. Produced by P.J. McNerney & Associates, 1989. *Courtesy of the Collection of Jeff Maynard — New Eye Studio*

Communicators

- ❑ "Star Trek Astro-Walkie Talkies": blue plastic cups with hand grips connected by string. Cardboard header with Kirk, Spock & Enterprise line art, blister packed, by Remco, 1967. $75-85
- ❑ "Star Trek Inter-Space Communicator": black & yellow plastic cups, hand grips, connecting strings, packaged in a 6" x 9 1/2" box with Kirk, Spock & Enterprise line art, by the British firm Lone Star, 1974. $50-55
- ❑ "Star Trek Communicators": working toy walkie-talkies (no cups & string here) sold in pairs, blue plastic with flip-up grid & retractable antennae. Early models packaged in boxes, later packed on a 9" x 14" header. Both packages had Kirk & Spock color art. By Mego, 1976. $250-275
- ❑ "Command Communications Console": blue plastic, light-up screen toy, working toy base station for use with walkie-talkies, by Mego, 1976 $175-200
- ❑ "Star Trek: The Motion Picture Wrist Communicators": plastic wrist band walkie-talkies sold in pairs, attached with a wire to a battery belt pack, by Mego, 1980 $65-75
- ❑ Communicators, Star Trek V Promotional for Proctor & Gamble: black plastic with flip-up grid, working walkie-talkies with retractable antennae, sold in pairs packed in plain white boxes, by P.J. McNerney & Associates, 1989 $85-95
- ❑ "Classic Star Trek Communicator, Starfleet Standard Communication Device: flip-up metallic grid, signal lights, & three sound effects by Playmates, 1995 $50-55

Phasers

- ❑ "Star Trek Astro Buzz-Ray Gun": three color flash beams in an ray-gun design, boxed with color original series art, by Remco, 1967 $200-250
- ❑ Phaser: flashlight with the Star Trek logo, white plastic casing, by Larami, 1968 $50-70
- ❑ "Star Trek Phaser Gun": flashlight in black plastic, phaser pistol shaped, outfitted with "electronic sound," projects targets, by Remco, 1975 $150-200
- ❑ Phaser: Star Trek logo on the side of this plastic toy, blister packed, Enterprise header art, by Azrak-Hamway, 1976 $50-60
- ❑ "Star Trek Super Phaser II Target Game": reflector target game with black plastic pistol phaser style flashlight, when light hits reflector worn by another, reflector buzzes, Klingon cruiser on the reflector, by Mego, 1976 $60-70
- ❑ Phaser, electronic dueling game: Star Trek: The Motion Picture set included two gray plastic phasers by South Bend, 1979 $195-215

Official Star Trek Electronic Phaser Gun by Remco, 1975. *Courtesy of the Collection of Jeff Maynard — New Eye Studio*

- Phaser, Star Trek III: blue & white plastic phasers with lights & sound effects, Star Trek logo adorns hand grip, packed in 6 1/2" x 10 1/2" window box with color art of movie Kirk, Spock, & Klingon, by Daisy, 1984 $80-90
- Phaser Battle Game: electronic target game (batteries not included), black plastic, LED scoring lights, sound effects, speed controls, aiming at a screen in the 13" high box, packaged in a large red box with color art of child, Spock, & toy, by Mego, 1976 $595-650
- Classic Star Trek Phaser, Starfleet Standard Issue Side-arm: Type 2 pistol grip phaser with sound effects & adjustable beam emitter, packed in box with toy's picture on front with the Enterprise, by Playmates, 1995 $30-40

Guns, Saucers & Tracers
- Saucer Gun: plastic phaser-shaped gun, shot plastic 2" spinner discs (3 discs per set), color header of Kirk & Spock on blister pack, by Azrak-Hamway, 1976 $50-60
- Tracer Gun: plastic pistol firing colored plastic discs (included), blister packed with Kirk, Spock & Enterprise on the color header, by Rayline, 1966 $35-50
- Tracer Gun Discs: one hundred replacement discs for the "Tracer Gun", packaged in blister pack with color header of the gun, Rayline, 1966 $5-15
- Tracer Scope: "Tracer Gun" rifle, fires colored plastic discs (included). Blister packed with Kirk, Spock, & Enterprise on header, by Rayline, 1968 $35-40

Tricorders
- "Star Trek Tricorder": battery powered blue plastic tape recorder with black plastic shoulder strap & flip-up top. Included taped portions of the original series episode, "The Menagerie." By Mego, 1976 $150-165
- "Classic Star Trek Science Tricorder": black plastic design with flip-up display, opening cabinet, light-up viewscreen, flashing tricorder lights, & three sound effects, black shoulder strap, by Playmates, 1995 $20-22

Star Trek Super Phaser II Target Game by Mego, 1976. *Courtesy of the Collection of Jeff Maynard — New Eye Studio*

Star Trek Tricorder with unboxed tape player toy with tape by Mego, 1976. *Courtesy of the Collection of Jeff Maynard — New Eye Studio*

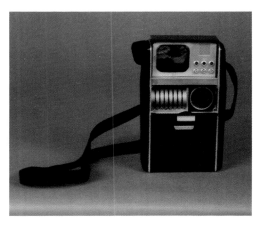

Classic Star Trek Classic Science Tricorder toy by Playmates, 1995. *Courtesy of the Collection of Jeff Maynard — New Eye Studio*

Utility Belt
- ❑ Black plastic miniature communicator, phaser, & tricorder on a belt with a "Star Trek" buckle, window box packaging with Kirk, Spock, & Enterprise on box, by Remco, 1975 $200-220

Water Pistols
- ❑ Water Pistol, phaser design: plastic packed in blister pack with color header with original series characters, by Azrak-Hamway, 1975 $70-75
- ❑ "U.S.S. Enterprise Water Gun": Enterprise-shaped white plastic pistol, blister packing with Enterprise & photos of Kirk & Spock on the color header, by Azrak-Hamway, 1976 $70-75
- ❑ Water Pistol, Star Trek: The Motion Picture gray plastic phaser design: header with art of Enterprise & Kirk on blister pack, by Aviva, 1979 $40-45

From the Space Dock: Starships and Their Interiors

On The Bridge
- ❑ "U.S.S. Enterprise Action Playset": blue plastic fold-out with carrying handle, designed for use with 8" action figures. Accessories included transporter, plastic stools, captain's chair, helm console, & three screen scenes, by Mego, 1975 $200-220
- ❑ "U.S.S. Enterprise Bridge" from Star Trek: The Motion Picture: white, molded plastic set for use with 3 3/4" action figures by Mego, 1980 $150-200

Star Trek U.S.S. Enterprise Action Playset of the bridge with a "spin action" transporter by Mego, 1974. *Courtesy of the Collection of Jeff Maynard — New Eye Studio*

Star Trek U.S.S. Enterprise Controlled Space Flight toy by Remco, 1976. *Courtesy of the Collection of Jeff Maynard — New Eye Studio*

Flying Ships
- ❑ "Controlled Space Flight": counterbalanced white plastic Enterprise with a fan in the saucer section, a wire from the saucer to a hub, a controller wired from the hub. Picks up three objects off a color printed space background board. By Remco (Burbank in England), 1976 $185-205

In the Transporter Room

❑ Transporter: figures "beam out" in a spinning cylinder. This toy is the transporter from Mego's 1976 bridge set, packaged in a box with color art, by Palitoy (Britain), 1976 $95-105

Starships Of The Line & Of Alien Races

1970s

❑ Enterprise, disc firing: original series die-cast metal ship, 9" in length, firing plastic colored discs from the saucer, includes discs & a plastic shuttlecraft. First packed in a solid box with toy art, followed by a window box package with color photo of Kirk & Spock, by Dinky (Meccano, British manufacturer), 1975 $75-100

❑ Klingon Cruiser, disc firing: blue original series die-cast metal ship, 9" long, fires discs from the bow, sold with discs in a window box with a color photo of Kirk & Spock, by Dinky, 1977 $75-100

❑ Enterprise & Klingon Gift Set: both disc firing die-cast vessels packed together in the familiar window box, adding the ships to the color photo, by Dinky, 1978 $300-350

❑ Klingon Cruiser: from Star Trek: The Motion Picture, blue die-cast metal, 4" long vessel, blister packed with Kirk, Spock, & Enterprise on color header, by Dinky, 1979 $20-25

❑ Star Trek Electronic U.S.S. Enterprise: from Star Trek: The Motion Picture, white plastic, battery powered lights & sound effects. Modular design allowing for conversion to many ship configurations, 20" in length, by South Bend, 1979 $200-220

Star Trek Klingon die-cast disc shooting toy ship by Dinky Toys, 1977. *Courtesy of the Collection of Jeff Maynard — New Eye Studio*

Star Trek Electronic U.S.S. Enterprise (movie version) modular toy ship by South Bend, 1979. *Courtesy of the Collection of Jeff Maynard — New Eye Studio*

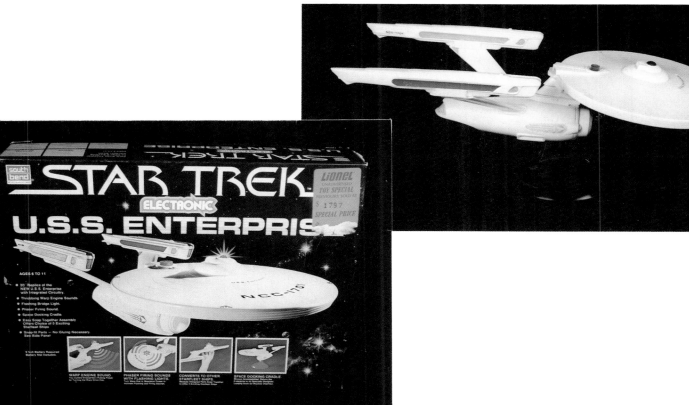

Classic Star Trek U.S.S. Enterprise NCC-1701 toy with working lights & sound effects by Playmates, 1995. *Courtesy of the Collection of Jeff Maynard — New Eye Studio*

Four MicroMachine Star Trek ships: left: Klingon Bird of Prey; center bottom: U.S.S. Reliant; center top: Enterprise-D; right: Enterprise-B. *Courtesy of the Collection of Michael W. Snyder*

1980s

❑ Enterprise: Star Trek: The Motion Picture design in white plastic, saucer section detaches, 12" long, marketed to Pacific coast, by Mego, 1980 — $200-225

❑ Klingon Cruiser: The Motion Picture design in green plastic, 8" long, marketed to the Pacific coast, by Mego, 1980 — $200-225

❑ Vulcan Shuttle: The Motion Picture design in yellow plastic, 8" long, detachable warp sled, marketed to the Pacific coast, by Mego, 1980 — $200-225

❑ Enterprise: Star Trek II design, die-cast metal, 3" long, blister packed ship with Kirk & Spock on the header, by Corgi (Mettoy, Britain), 1981 — $30-40

❑ Klingon Cruiser: Star Trek II design, die-cast metal, black & yellow decals, 3" long, blister packed with Kirk & Spock on header, by Corgi, 1981 — $30-40

❑ Enterprise & Klingon Cruiser Double Pack: Both Corgi Star Trek II designed die-cast vessels packed together in blister packing, by Corgi, 1981 — $60-70

❑ Enterprise: Star Trek III Enterprise, die-cast metal, 4" long, blister packed with black plastic stand, by ERTL, 1984 — $20-30

❑ Excelsior: Star Trek III design, die-cast metal, 4" long, blister packed with black plastic stand, by ERTL, 1984 — $20-30

❑ Klingon Bird of Prey: Star Trek III design, blue die-cast metal, 3 1/2" wide, "Star Trek" logo across wings, blister packed with black plastic stand, by ERTL, 1984 — $20-30

❑ Enterprise, Inflatable, Sterling: silver plastic Star Trek IV promotional with movie & Paramount 75th Anniversary logos on top & bottom of saucer section, 1986 — $40-44

❑ Enterprise, Inflatable, Sun: blue plastic promoting Star Trek IV & Paramount's 75th Anniversary with logos on saucer, 1986 — $39-42

❑ Enterprise, Paramount Promotional: die-cut cardboard color movie Enterprise in five pieces for assembly, 4 1/2" long with "The Star Trek Video Collection" printed on the sides, 1988 — $75-100

❑ Enterprise NCC-1701-A: from Star Trek V, reissue of Star Trek III 4" die-cast ship, blister packed with black plastic base, by ERTL, 1989 — $10-15

❑ Klingon Bird of Prey: reissue of Star Trek III 4" die-cast ship for Star Trek V, blister packed with black plastic stand, by ERTL, 1989 — $10-15

1990s

❑ Classic Star Trek U.S.S. Enterprise NCC-1701: white plastic, battery-powered, with lights & sound effects on a gold delta shield stand, by Playmates, 1995 — $30-40

❑ U.S.S. Excelsior NCC-2000: movie vessel, limited collector's edition of 10,000, sound effects & lights, by Playmates, 1995 — $30-40

❑ MicroMachines Star Trek Space Series by Galoob
  ❑ Original Star Trek Series #1: includes Botany Bay, Klingon Battlecruiser, & Romulan Bird of Prey — $8-9
  ❑ Original Star Trek Series #2: includes Galileo II, Space Station K-7, U.S.S. Enterprise NCC-1701 — $8-9
  ❑ Star Trek The Movies #1: includes movie ships, Reliant, Space Dock, Klingon Bird of Prey — $8-9
  ❑ Star Trek The Movies #2: Excelsior, Grissom, Vulcan Shuttle — $8-9

Toys, Crafts and The Twenty-Third Century: Miscellany

❑ Action Fleet: color cardboard mobile of ships from Star Trek: The Motion Picture, candy promotion, 1979 — $25-28

❑ Astrotank: original series toy including three figures & four shells for the gun, boxed with color photos from series, very rare, by Remco, 1967 — $1000-1500

❑ Belt, Buckle, & Insignia: thermal strip & storage compartment in buckle, for Star Trek: The Motion Picture, boxed with color photos, by South Bend, 1979 — $25-40

❑ Binoculars: white & orange with "Star Trek" logo, blister packed with header showing Spock, by Larami, 1968 — $60-70

❑ Bop Bag: inflatable plastic Spock by Azrak-Hamway, 1975 — $100-150

❑ Cartoon Capers: battery-powered light box overlays & colored pins, made in France for British consumption by Wiggins Teape, 1978 — $75-125

- Colorforms Star Trek Adventure Set: plastic stick-ons & color cardboard bridge scene, by Colorforms, 1975 — $30-40
- Color N' Recolor Game Cloth, Star Trek: plastic reusable game cloth with 8 crayons & sponge, by Avalon, 1979 — $30-40
- Figurine Painting: from Star Trek: The Motion Picture, plastic figurines, brush, & five paints, by Whiting (Milton Bradley division), 1979 — $30-40
- Frisbee, U.S.S. Enterprise: with "Star Trek" & Spock decal, by Remco, 1967 — $40-50
- Happy Meals: Star Trek: The Motion Picture McDonald's premium, highly colored cardboard meal boxes with games, included small prizes, five in all with a mobile display showing each below a cardboard movie Enterprise, by McDonald's, 1979 — $10-15
- Helmet: a flashing red light tops this plastic helmet, included character decals, & electronic sound, by Enco (Remco), 1976 — $100-110
- I.D. Set: red plastic folder for Star Trek: The Motion Picture, by Larami, 1979 — $10-15
- Kite: original series Enterprise or Spock pictured, by Hi-Flyer, 1979 — $20-25
- Kite: Star Trek III promotional picturing Spock, assorted colors, by Lever Brothers, 1984 — $20-25
- Magic Putty: putty packed in blue plastic egg, released for Star Trek: The Motion Picture, blister packed with a tube of transfer solution, by Larami, 1979 — $10-15
- Magic Slates: 4 designs, classic Enterprise, Kirk, Spock, or Kirk & Spock, by Whitman, 1979 — $10-15
- Metal Detector: working toy, white with "Property of U.S.S. Enterprise" decal, by Jetco, 1976 — $300-350
- Mission to Gamma VI: plastic "Cave Creature" playset for Mego action figures, creature with movable jaws, trap door, manipulator glove, four small "Gamma people," & cardboard base, by Mego, 1976 — $1000-1200
- Mix 'n Mold: plaster casting set with character mold, molding compound, paint, & brush. 3 kits: Kirk, Spock, & McCoy, by Catalog Shoppe, 1975 — $50-60
- Movie Viewer: red & black plastic viewer toy (3") with toy film strips, by Chemtoy, 1967 — $35-40
- Paint by Numbers: canvas paint & instructions in two sizes: large 12" x 19" box with Kirk, Spock, & Enterprise on the box; small 11" x 11" box with Kirk, Spock, & Enterprise on the box, by Hasbro, 1972 — $40-50/$70-75
- Pen & Poster Kit: four posters: Enemies of the Federation, Journeys of the Enterprise, Star Trek Lives, & Tour of the Enterprise. Line posters, 14" x 22", felt-tip pens, by Open Door, 1976 — $35-40
- Pen & Poster Kit: "How Do You Doodle" 2 original series posters & pens, Open Door — $20-25
- Pen & Poster Kit: Star Trek: The Motion Picture, one 14" x 20" poster & 5 pens, by Aviva, 1979 — $20-25
- Pen & Poster Kit: Star Trek III: 3-D poster set, with poster, 3-D plastic overlay, 3-D glasses, 4 felt-tip pens, by Placo, 1984 — $20-25
- "Star Trek Intergalactic Planetarium": large plastic toy planetarium, very rare & maybe only prototypes produced, by Mego, 1976 — $1500-1800
- Pocket Flix: hand-held movie viewer with film cartridge & scenes from original series episode "By Any Other Name", battery powered, by Ideal, 1978 — $40-50
- Space Design Center: craft kit based on Star Trek: The Motion Picture contains blue plastic tray, crew member cutouts, pens, crayons, paints, & a project book, by Avalon, 1979 — $185-215
- Space Viewer: from Star Trek: The Motion Picture, domed viewer with 2 film strips, by Larami, 1979 — $25-30
- Sky Diving Parachutist: painted & weighted 4 1/2" figure of Kirk or Spock attached to a plastic parachute with "Star Trek", by Azrak-Hamway, 1974 — $35-40
- Star Trekulator: blue plastic, battery-operated desktop calculator with LED & sound effects. Console with bridge scene from original series, by Mego, 1976 — $150-180
- String Art Kit: create Star Trek pictures with pins & colored strings, by Open Door, 1976 — $60-75
- Telescreen: 14" x 10" plastic, battery-powered console target game with lights & sound effects, by Mego, 1976 — $200-220
- Trek Menagerie: plush toys, baby Targ, Capellian Power Cat, baby Mugato, or Selat kitten, handmade, fan produced — $55-60

Star Trek: The Motion Picture Space Design Center by Avalon, 1979. *Courtesy of the Collection of Jeff Maynard — New Eye Studio*

- Tribbles: the favorite fur-balls from the original series, in several sizes & colors, fan produced — $8-10
- View-Master: three reels with scenes from original episode "Omega Glory", 16 page story booklet, by GAF, 1968 — $20-25
- View-Master: "Mr. Spock's Time Trek," 3 viewer reels with scenes from "Yesteryear" animated episode, with 16 page story booklet, by GAF, 1974 — $15-20
- View-Master, Talking: "Mr. Spock's Time Trek," 3 viewer reels for talking viewer with scenes from "Yesteryear" animated episode, with 16 page story booklet, by GAF, 1974 — $20-25
- View-Master: Star Trek: The Motion Picture 3 reels with scenes from movie, & story booklet, by GAF, 1979 — $15-17
- View-Master Double-Vue: Star Trek: The Motion Picture double plastic cassette with 2 film strips, by GAF, 1981 — $20-25

Star Trek Telescreen Console by Mego, 1976. *Courtesy of the Collection of Jeff Maynard — New Eye Studio*

❑	View-Master Gift Pak: Star Trek: The Motion Picture, viewer, 3 reels, 3-D poster, & glasses, by GAF, 1979	$60-80
❑	View-Master: Star Trek II, 3 viewer reels by View-Master International, 1982	$10-15
❑	Yo-Yo: Star Trek: The Motion Picture blue sparkle plastic with Enterprise & logo on side, by Aviva, 1979	$25-30

TRADING CARDS and STICKERS
American Gum Cards

Star Trek: The Original Series
- ❑ **LEAF** Photo Cards: Star Trek original series 72 card set, black & white photos, 2 3/8" x 3 7/16", 1967:
  - ❑ Single Card — $25-30
  - ❑ Set — $1200-1500
  - ❑ Wrapper — $125-150
  - ❑ Display Box — $100-110
- ❑ **TOPPS** Photo Cards: 88-card set, color photos from original series, 2 1/2" x 3 1/2", "captain's log" narratives & character profiles on back, 1976:
  - ❑ Single Card — $6-10
  - ❑ Set — $275-300
  - ❑ Wrapper — $15-20
  - ❑ Display Box — $30-33
  - ❑ Unopened Pack — $30-33
  - ❑ Unopened Box — $900-1200
- ❑ **TOPPS** Stickers: Compliments card set, original series stickers, 1976:
  - ❑ Single Card — $6-8
  - ❑ Set — $75-100

Star Trek: The Motion Picture
- ❑ **TOPPS** Photo Cards: 88-card set with color photos & white borders, captioned, 1979:
  - ❑ Single Card — $3-5
  - ❑ Set — $50-75
  - ❑ Wrapper — $3-5
  - ❑ Display Box — $9-12
  - ❑ Unopened Pack — $20-25
  - ❑ Unopened Box — $300-350
- ❑ **TOPPS** Stickers: Compliments card set, The Motion Picture stickers, 1979:
  - ❑ Single Card — $3-5
  - ❑ Set — $40-60

Promotional & Foreign Cards
Star Trek: The Original Series
- ❑ **MORRIS:** Canadian brown backed sticker, 4 1/2" x 3 1/4", puzzle card, series scenes or new art, no gum, 1975:

❑	Set	$75-120
❑	Album for 35 stickers	$40-60
❑	**PANINI:** Italian 400 stickers & album, for European market	$150-200
❑	**PHOENIX** Candy Company: boxes from the U.S., front color photo 3" x 2 1/4" approximately, numbered photos, labeled Enterprise photo on back, released as individual candy boxes with two plastic prizes, eight boxes per set, 1976	$10-15
❑	**PRIMROSE** Confectionery: candy cigarette boxes of thin white stock with color art on front, a number & story printed on box back, mint remainder cards are on the market from this British firm, 12 cards per set, 1970	$30-40
❑	**TOPPS A & BC:** hard to find color photos cards measuring 3 1/4" x 2 1/4" with blue borders & captions in white, rockets at the bottoms, stories & numbers on pale aqua backs, issued in bubble gum packs, 55 card sets, English cards, 1969:	
❑	Single Card	$15-18
❑	Wrapper	$150-200

Star Trek: The Motion Picture — International
- ❑ **GENERAL MILLS** Collectors' Series: U.S. & English sales, plain-backed heavy stock cards, color photos, silver & white borders, numbered, issued on backs of General Mills cereal boxes, 1979 — $18-20
- ❑ **GENERAL MILLS** Starship Door Signs: U.S. & England, plain-backed heavy cards, angled corners, orange & silver borders, art & photos, no numbers, issued on backs of Cheerios boxes, 1979 — $12-15
- ❑ **LYONS MAID:** English, color photos, numbers & story backs, issued on back of Lyons Maid Ice Lollies, 1979 — $50-60
- ❑ **RAINBOW BREAD:** 33 card series, white borders, red or yellow trim, movie photographs, one card per loaf of bread, 1979:
  - ❑ Single Card — $2-3
  - ❑ Set — $15-17
- ❑ The same applies to **KILPATRICK'S, COLONIAL, & MONITOR** Bread, both U.S. — $15-17
- ❑ **SWIZZELS** Refresher Sticks: English stickers, 88-card set, rounded corners, color pictures with captions below, numbers on side, issued in Swizzels Star Trek Refreshers packs, 1979 — $12-14
- ❑ **TOPPS** United Kingdom T.M.P.: English, same format as U.S. cards, bright red & blue backs, no stickers, 1979 — $60-90
- ❑ **VENDING STICKERS:** U.S., color photos with gold borders, no numbers, made to stick to windows or outside glass, 1979:
  - ❑ Set — $40-50

Topps Star Trek Picture Cards bubble gum cards display box. *Courtesy of the Collection of Jeff Maynard — New Eye Studio*

- **WEETABIX:** U.K., color art & captions on front, color photo in oval on purple back, cards scored at base to stand up, issued in Weetabix cereal, strips of 3 perforated cards, 18 card sets:
  - Single card $3-5
  - Set $60-70

Star Trek II: The Wrath of Khan
- **MONTY GUM:** English, 100 card set:
  - Set $25-28

Collectors' Cards and Stickers (no gum, sold to collectors)

Star Trek II: The Wrath of Khan
- **FANTASY TRADING CARD CO.:** 30 card set, color photos, 5" x 7", no stickers or captions, limited 7500 set possible print run, 1982:
  - Single Card $3-5
  - Set $60-70
  - Wrapper $3-5
  - Display Box $12-18

Star Trek III: The Search for Spock
- **FANTASY TRADING CARD CORP.:** 60 scene cards & 20 spaceship cards with glossy finish, 2 1/2" x 3 1/2", subject titles on card backs, 1984:
  - Single Card $4-6
  - Set $75-85
  - Wrapper $6-10
  - Display Box $12-20
  - Unopened Pack $30-50
  - Unopened Box $300-350

Star Trek IV: The Voyage Home: 60 card set, 1986:
  - Single Card $3-5
  - Set $35-40
  - Wrapper $5-8
  - Display Box $10-15
  - Unopened Pack $30-33
  - Unopened Box $90-100

25th Anniversary Star Trek Trading Cards
Cards had been lacking for Star Trek V & VI. The younger viewers most likely to buy cards were impressed with The Next Generation series effects and pleased with the fact that this was not their parents' Star Trek. While these young buyers were not particularly keen on cards from the movies, cards combining the two series in celebration of Star Trek's 25th anniversary were quite welcome.
- **IMPEL** (now Skybox) distributed card sets incorporating both the original and the then fairly new Next Generation series. A 310 card, two series set wrapped in silver (Series I) & black (Series II) plastic packs, introducing hologram cards (Classic Enterprise, Enterprise-D, Kirk, Picard, Bird of Prey, Klingon Cruiser, Romulan Ship, Ferengi Ship) to collectors, was released in 1991.
  - Single Card $15-35
  - Hologram Card $35-40
  - Wrapper
  - Display Box
  - Unopened Pack
  - Unopened Box Series I $18-20; Series II $18-20

Star Trek: The Next Generation and Star Trek: Generations

ACTION & COLLECTORS' FIGURES
First Next Generation Action Figures

GALOOB — 1988, 3 3/4" Next Generation Action Figures
Of these, Picard, Riker, LaForge and Worf are the most commonly found figures. Data and Lt. Yar are rare and the aliens are the most difficult to find. Serious collectors of action figures also consider the packages more valuable if the punch-out tab at the top of the package is in place.
The Next Generation Crew
- Captain Jean Luc Picard $60-65
- Commander William Riker $60-45
- Lt. Commander Data: this android's face has color variations-speckled, blue, & white $35-40
- brown-faced Data $45-50
- Lt. Tasha Yar $30-33
- Lt. Worf $60-65
- Lt. Geordi La Forge $60-65

Star Trek: The Next Generation 3 3/4" high action figures by Galoob, 1988. The crew: top: Picard, Riker, & Data; bottom: Yar, Worf, & La Forge. *Courtesy of the Collection of Jeff Maynard — New Eye Studio*

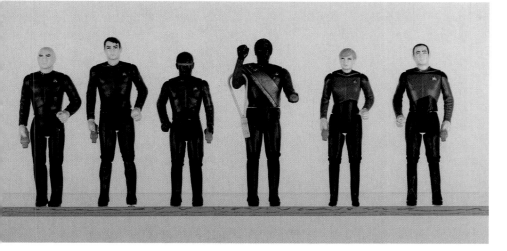

The first plastic Next Generation action figures (Picard, Riker, LaForge, Worf, Yar, & Data - not ordered by rank in this photo) with phasers molded to hands and extra molded plastic opened tricorder with shoulder strap. Manufactured by Galoob, 1988 license. These vary in height from 3 7/8" to 3 1/2" high. A die-cast metal Enterprise-D was also part of this series. *Courtesy of the Collection of Bob Hoag*

Star Trek: The Next Generation 3 3/4" high action figures by Galoob, 1988. The alien figures shown here are (left to right): Antican, Selay, & "Q." *Courtesy of the Collection of Jeff Maynard — New Eye Studio*

Playmates first series 4 1/2" tall action figures included: top: Gowron the Klingon, Borg; bottom: Ferengi, & Data. 1992. *Courtesy of the Collection of Jeff Maynard — New Eye Studio*

The Next Generation Aliens
Of the aliens, Q and the Ferengi are the most valued.

❑ Antican	$50-55
❑ Ferengi: large lobes, striped vest, olive pants	$75-80
❑ Q: judge's outfit with hat from the series opener, the two part "Encounter at Farpoint"	$75-80
❑ Selay	$50-55

PLAYMATES Next Generation Action Figures
Playmates entered the action figures line in 1992, beginning with Next Generation figures. Their line of small action figures measure approximately 4 1/2" tall.

First Series — 1992

❑ Picard: uniform jacket	$25-28
❑ Riker: torn uniform	$15-17
❑ Data: gold uniform	$15-17
❑ La Forge: gold uniform, T2 phaser	$25-28
❑ Troi: gray jump suit	$50-55
❑ Worf: gold uniform	$25-27
❑ Borg	$25
❑ Ferengi: energy whip & blaster	$25-27
❑ Gowron: Klingon uniform	$40-44
❑ Romulan: phaser rifle	$50-55

Star Trek: The Next Generation action figures by Playmate, 1992. Top: Romulan; Ferengi; Bottom: Gowron The Klingon; Borg. (10 figures in the complete set) *Courtesy of the Collection of Bob Hoag*

Star Trek: The Next Generation action figures by Playmate, 1992. (with accessories). Top: Captain Jean-Luc Picard with Captain's Log Adventure Book; Commander William Riker; Lieutenant Commander Data; Bottom: Lieutenant Commander Geordi La Forge; Lieutenant Worf. *Courtesy of the Collection of Bob Hoag*

Second Series — 1993

- Aged McCoy: 137 years old from cameo appearance in "Encounter at Farpoint", this series came with trading cards ... $8-9
- Ambassador Spock ... $15-17
- Benzite ... $15-17
- Borg ... $8-9
- Data ... $15-17
- Dathon ... $8-9
- Dr. Crusher ... $8-9
- Guinan ... $15-17
- K'Ehleyr ... $15-17
- La Forge: dress uniform ... $8-9
- La Forge ... $15-17
- Lore ... $15-17
- Picard: holster ... $8-9
- Picard as Locutus ... $25-28
- Q ... $15-17
- Riker ... $8-9
- Scotty ... $8-9
- Sela ... $15-17
- Troi: maroon uniform ... $15-17
- Vorgon ... $15-17
- Wesley Crusher: academy uniform ... $15-17
- Worf: red uniform ... $8-9
- Worf: ceremonial robe ... $25-28

Third Series — 1994

Most of this series came with photo cards with center punch-out "space caps" (pogs).

- Barclay ... $8-9
- Data: gold Generations movie uniform, late 1994-early 1995 release, trading card, no pog ... $12-13
- Data: red uniform, rare ... $35-40
- Data as Romulan ... $15-17
- Data: dress uniform, no pog ... $15-17
- Dr. Crusher ... $8-9
- Dr. Noonian Soong ... $15-17
- Ensign Ro: this character introduced the Bajorans to the series $25-28
- Esoqq ... $25-28
- Gowron: in robes, no pog ... $25-28
- Guinan ... $8-9
- Hugh Borg ... $10-11
- K'Ehleyr ... $15-17
- La Forge: as alien ... $15-17
- La Forge: gold dress uniform ... $15-17
- La Forge: movie uniform, trading card, no pog ... $15-17
- Lore ... $8-9
- Lwaxana Troi ... $12-13
- Nausicaan ... $15-17
- Picard: as Dixon Hill ... $15-17

Playmates Star Trek: The Next Generation Second Series 1993 action figures include: top: K'ehleyr, Ambassador Spock, Dathon; bottom: Counselor Deanna Troi, Captain Scott, & Dr. Beverly Crusher. Trading cards were included. *Courtesy of the Collection of Jeff Maynard — New Eye Studio*

Star Trek: The Next Generation third series action figures by Playmates, 1994. Most of these came with pogs: Picard (no pog), Ensign Ro Laren; bottom: Guinan & Lt. Barclay. *Courtesy of the Collection of Jeff Maynard — New Eye Studio*

Star Trek: The Next Generation action figure, Captain Jean-Luc Picard as Dixon Hill with pog, by Playmates, 1994. *Courtesy of the Collection of Jeff Maynard — New Eye Studio*

Star Trek: The Next Generation fourth series action figures by Playmates, 1995: top: Lt. Worf (holodeck series), Nausicaan; bottom: Lwaxana Troi & Data (holodeck series). These figs came with a trading card, the backs of which are much revised from the earlier cards. *Courtesy of the Collection of Jeff Maynard — New Eye Studio*

☐	Picard: as Romulan	$10-11
☐	Picard: red uniform, T2 phaser, holster on left, no pog	$8-9
☐	Q: Star Fleet uniform	$15-17
☐	Q: judges robes	$15-17
☐	Riker: as Malcorian	$8-9
☐	Riker: red uniform (rare)	$45-50
☐	Sarek	$12-14
☐	Spock	$15-17
☐	Sela	$8-9
☐	Tasha Yar	$12-13
☐	Troi: blue uniform	$25-28
☐	Wesley Crusher	$15-17
☐	Wesley Crusher: Star Fleet uniform, no pog	$25-28
☐	Worf: black combat uniform	$15-17

Fourth Series — 1995

☐	Admiral Riker: from final episode "All Good Things"	$10-11
☐	Borg	$10-11
☐	Data	$10-11
☐	Data: gangster garb	$10-11
☐	Dr. Crusher: duty uniform	$10-11
☐	Dr. Crusher: gangster moll	$10-11
☐	Dr. Katherine Pulaski	$10-11
☐	Dr. Noonien Soong	$10-11
☐	Ensign Ro	$10-11
☐	La Forge: Generations movie uniform	$10-11
☐	La Forge: "All Good Things" episode	$10-11
☐	Picard: "All Good Things" episode	$10-11
☐	Picard: as Galen	$10-11
☐	Picard: metallized Borg	$10-11
☐	Worf: western sheriff	$10-11
☐	The Traveler	$10-11
☐	Troi: western garb	$10-11
☐	Vash	$10-11
☐	Worf	$10-11
☐	Worf: governor from "All Good Things"	$10-11
☐	Worf: metallized Klingon garb	$10-11

Star Trek: Generations Movie Figures — 1994

☐	BeTor: Klingon sister: all of these Generations figures are rare	$15-17
☐	Chekov: red Star Fleet uniform	$30-33
☐	Data: gold Star Fleet uniform	$10-11
☐	Dr. Crusher	$15-17
☐	Dr. Soran	$15-17
☐	Guinan	$15-17
☐	Kirk: red Star Fleet uniform	$15-17
☐	Kirk: silver space suit, never seen in the movie	
☐	La Forge	$12-14

Star Trek: Generations action figures by Playmates, 1994 (all rare): top: Kirk in a silver space suit (never in movie), Pavel A. Chekov; bottom: Guinan & Lursa. *Courtesy of the Collection of Jeff Maynard — New Eye Studio*

Star Trek: The Next Generation Playmates variations of their popular Deanna Troi figure: 1992 purple uniform; 1993 red uniform; 1994 green Starfleet uniform with pog; & 1994 Generations movie uniform. *Courtesy of the Collection of Jeff Maynard — New Eye Studio*

❑	Lursa: Klingon sister	$15-17
❑	Picard: red Star Fleet uniform	$10-11
❑	Riker: bearded, red Star Fleet uniform	$12-14
❑	Scotty: silver haired	$30-33
❑	Troi: green uniform	$15-17
❑	Worf: gold Star Fleet uniform	$12-14
❑	Worf: gold vest	$8-9

PLAYMATES Space Talk Series — 1995

Each 7" tall figure features the cast members' voices, three phrases, accessories, & action adventure booklet. The ship itself has many more voices & sounds available.

❑	Borg	$20-40
❑	Picard	$20-40
❑	Q	$20-40
❑	Riker	$20-40
❑	Enterprise-D: 100 voices & sound effects	$40-45

Star Trek Collector's Series — Playmates

Playmates extended its line of small Next Generation action figures with 9 1/2" high Alien, Command, Starfleet, & Movie Edition Collectors Series (Deep Space Nine figures were also produced)

Alien Edition

❑	Borg: 1995	$23-25

Star Trek: The Next Generation Space Talk Series (included the actual voices of the actors), 7" action figures, top: Picard with jacket 6081; Riker, 6082; bottom: Borg, 6085; "Q," 6086. *Courtesy of the Collection of Jeff Maynard — New Eye Studio*

Star Trek Space Talk Series, action figures by Playmates with the voices of the cast members, 1995. *Courtesy of the Collection of Jeff Maynard — New Eye Studio*

Star Trek Collector Series, Alien Edition Borg by Playmates, 1995. *Courtesy of the Collection of Jeff Maynard — New Eye Studio*

Star Trek Collector Series, Command Edition Captain Jean-Luc Picard by Playmates, 1994. *Courtesy of the Collection of Jeff Maynard — New Eye Studio*

Star Trek Collector Series, Starfleet Edition Commander William Riker by Playmates, 1995. *Courtesy of the Collection of Jeff Maynard — New Eye Studio*

Command Edition
- ❏ Captain Jean-Luc Picard: 1994, Kirk & Sisko make up the rest of this edition $23-25/each

Starfleet Edition
- ❏ Commander William Riker: 1995 $23-25
- ❏ Dr. Beverly Crusher: 1995 $23-25

Movie Edition
- ❏ Captain James T. Kirk: 1994 $23-25
- ❏ Captain Jean-Luc Picard: 1994 $23-25
- ❏ Lieutenant Commander Geordi LaForge: 1994 $23-25
- ❏ Lieutenant Commander Data: 1994 $23-25

Star Trek: Generations Collector Series, Movie Edition Captain Jean-Luc Picard by Playmates, 1994. *Courtesy of the Collection of Jeff Maynard — New Eye Studio*

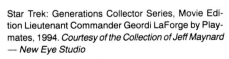

Star Trek Collector Series, Starfleet Edition Dr. Beverly Crusher by Playmates, 1995. *Courtesy of the Collection of Jeff Maynard — New Eye Studio*

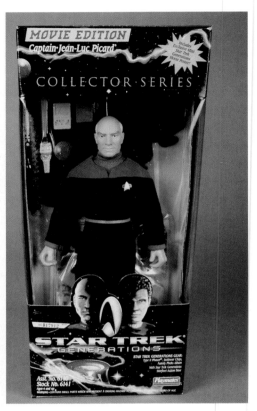

Star Trek: Generations Collector Series, Movie Edition Lieutenant Commander Geordi LaForge by Playmates, 1994. *Courtesy of the Collection of Jeff Maynard — New Eye Studio*

Star Trek: Generations Collector Series, Movie Edition Lieutenant Commander Data by Playmates, 1994. *Courtesy of the Collection of Jeff Maynard — New Eye Studio*

HAMILTON GIFTS PVC Figurines
Hamilton Gifts produced series of 3 1/2" tall PVC figurines for the crews of the original series, The Next Generation, Generations, and Deep Space Nine. These are simple, molded, unarticulated figures in full color.

The Next Generation Crew & Aliens

❑ Data		$4-5
❑ LaForge		$4-5
❑ Picard		$4-5
❑ Riker		$4-5
❑ Troi		$4-5
❑ Worf		$4-5
❑ Borg		$4-5
❑ Ferengi		$4-5
❑ Klingon		$4-5
❑ Q		$4-5

Star Trek: Generations Crew & Aliens

❑ Data		$4-5
❑ Guinan		$4-5
❑ Kirk		$4-5
❑ LaForge		$4-5
❑ Picard		$4-5
❑ Riker		$4-5
❑ Worf		$4-5
❑ B'Etor		$4-5
❑ Dr. Soran		$4-5
❑ Lursa		$4-5
❑ Also available in a six figure boxed set containing Data, Kirk, LaForge, Lursa, Picard, and Worf		$18-20

Dolls

HAMILTON GIFTS
By 1994, Hamilton Gifts was manufacturing a line of 9" - 12" vinyl dolls of characters from Star Trek, The Next Generations, Star Trek: Generations, and Deep Space Nine.

The Next Generation

❑ Data		$10-11
❑ Ferengi		$10-11
❑ LaForge		$10-11
❑ Picard		$10-11
❑ Riker		$10-11
❑ Troi		$10-11
❑ Worf		$10-11

Star Trek: Generations

❑ Data		$10-11
❑ LaForge		$10-11
❑ Picard		$10-11
❑ Riker		$10-11
❑ Worf		$10-11

BLUEPRINTS

Blueprints specifically related to Star Trek: The Next Generation

❑ Enterprise 1701-D: 14" x 18" three full color posters		$25-27
❑ Olympus Class Battle Dreadnought: 20" x 26" one-sheet poster similar in design to future Enterprise in final TV episode "All Good Things ..."		$14-16
❑ Romulan L-85 Battleship: 20" x 26" one sheet poster		$14-16
❑ Star Fleet Tactical Database: five poster of the U.S.S. Stargazer, Klingon Bird of Prey, Klingon Empire Class Heavy Cruiser, Ferengi Cruiser, Class 1 Shuttlecraft by Larry Miller		$13-15

BOOKS

Childrens' Books
Game Books

❑ Star Trek: The Next Generation Starship Enterprise Make A Model, Chatham River Press, 1990		$10-11

Star Trek: The Next Generation Starfleet Academy Paperbacks

❑ #1 Worf's First Adventure		$4-5
❑ #2 Line of Fire		$4-5
❑ #3 Survival		$4-5
❑ #4 Capture The Flag		$4-5
❑ #5 Atlantis Station		$4-5

Star Trek: Generations

❑ Novelization of the seventh feature film for young readers, complete with eight pages of color movie stills.		$4-5

Novels

Pocket Books Star Trek: The Next Generation Paperback Novels
Each of these books are organized by number from the first to the most recent release rather than by alphabetical title listing. Issue #1 was released in 1988.

❑ #0 Encounter at Farpoint: Novelization of the series pilot episode produced separtely from the numbered novels which follow		$6-7
❑ #1 Ghostship		$6-7
❑ #2 The Peacekeepers		$6-7
❑ #3 Children of Hamlin		$6-7
❑ #4 Survivors		$6-7
❑ #5 Strike Zone		$6-7
❑ #6 Power Hungry		$6-7
❑ #7 Masks		$6-7
❑ #8 Captains Honor		$6-7
❑ #9 A Call to Darkness		$6-7
❑ #10 Between a Rock and a Hard Place		$6-7
❑ #11 Gulliver's Fugitives		$6-7
❑ #12 Doomsday World		$6-7
❑ #13 The Eyes of the Beholders		$6-7
❑ #14 Exiles		$6-7
❑ #15 Fortune's Light		$6-7
❑ #16 Spartacus		$6-7
❑ #17 Contamination		$6-7
❑ #18 Boogeyman		$6-7
❑ #19 Q-in-Law		$6-7
❑ #20 Perchance to Dream		$6-7
❑ #21 Chains of Command		$6-7
❑ #22 Imbalance		$6-7
❑ #23 War Drums		$6-7
❑ #24 Nightshade		$6-7
❑ #25 Grounded		$6-7
❑ #26 Romulan Prize		$6-7

Jackill's Star Fleet Reference Manual, Volume 1(1992), Volume 2 (1993), & Volume 3 (1995). *Courtesy of the Collection of Jeff Maynard — New Eye Studio*

❑	#27 *Guises of the Mind*	$6-7
❑	#28 *Here There Be Dragons*	$6-7
❑	#29 *Sins of Commission*	$6-7
❑	#30 *Debtor's Planet*	$6-7
❑	#31 *Foreign Foes*	$6-7
❑	#32 *Requiem*	$6-7
❑	#33 *Balance of Power*	$6-7
❑	#34 *Blaze of Glory*	$6-7
❑	#35 *The Romulan Strategem*	$6-7
❑	#36 *Into the Nebula* $6-7	

References, Manuals, & Memoirs

❑ *Jackill's Star Fleet Reference Manual.* Volumes 1-3 by Eric Kristiansen, 1992-1995 $15-17

❑ *The Next Generation Companion* by Larry Nemecek, Pocket Books, 1995 $13-15

❑ *The Next Generation Tribute Book 1* by Larry Nemecek, self-published, 1989   market value

❑ *The Next Generation Tribute Book 2* $15-17

❑ *The Nitpickers Guide for Next Generation Trekkers* by Phil Farrand $13-15

❑ *Star Trek: The Next Generation. Technical Manual* by Rick Sternback & Michael Okuda, Pocket Books, 1991 $13-15

❑ *Star Trek: The Next Generation. The voyage continues ...* by James Van Hise $15-17

CALENDARS

❑ 1989 Pocket Books: Star Trek: The Next Generation Calendar. Group shot on cover with first season TV stills within $20-22

❑ 1990 Pocket Books: Star Trek: The Next Generation Calendar. Enterprise-D on cover. TV stills within. $15-17

❑ 1991 Pocket Books: ST:TNG Calendar, color stills from third season. $15-17

❑ 1992 Pocket Books: ST:TNG Calendar, orbiting Enterprise-D on cover, stills from the series within. $15-17

❑ 1993 Pocket Books: ST:TNG Calendar, stills from the series within $15-17

❑ 1994 Pocket Books: ST:TNG Calendar, stills from the series within $11-12

❑ 1995 Pocket Books: ST:TNG Calendar, Enterprise-D & shuttle on cover, stills from the series within $11-12

❑ 1996 Pocket Books: Star Trek: Generations Calendar with movie poster art on cover, movie stills within. $12-14

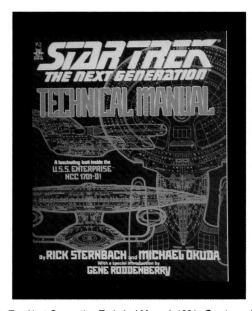

Star Trek: The Next Generation Technical Manual, 1991. *Courtesy of the Collection of Jeff Maynard — New Eye Studio*

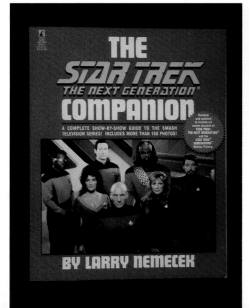

The Star Trek: The Next Generation Companion, 1995. *Courtesy of the Collection of Jeff Maynard — New Eye Studio*

Star Trek: The Next Generation 1989 calendar. *Courtesy of the Collection of Jeff Maynard — New Eye Studio*

Star Trek: The Next Generation 1992 Calendar. *Courtesy of the Collection of Jeff Maynard — New Eye Studio*

Star Trek: The Next Generation Platinum rimmed Picard plate by Ernst, 1989. *Courtesy of the Collection of Jeff Maynard — New Eye Studio*

CERAMICS

Collector's Plates, Dining & Serving Wares

HAMILTON/ERNST
Hamilton/Ernst Commemorative Plates
This partnership began to produce plates for Star Trek: The Next Generation in 1989. These were numbered and never finished. The edges were decorated in platinum and carried the title, "Star Trek: The Next Generation." This was Hamilton and Ernst's third series together, but their first The Next Generation series.

- ❏ Picard $35-40
- ❏ Data $35-40
- ❏ Riker $35-40

HAMILTON
Hamilton Commemorative Plates
Fifth Anniversary Commemorative Series
Hamilton's fifth anniversary plates featuring the crew of The Next Generation as depicted by artist Thomas Blackshear. Gilt-edged and individually numbered.

- ❏ Captain Picard (second series with nebula background rather than 1989 Ernst Picard with Enterprise bridge background) $35-40
- ❏ Commander Riker $35-40
- ❏ Lt. Commander Data $35-40
- ❏ Lt. Worf $35-40
- ❏ Counselor Troi $35-40

Star Trek Voyages Commemorative Series
Hamilton's 1994 plates largely dealing with Star Trek: The Next Generation, but beginning with the starship that started it all. Gold gilt edged plates numbered on the backs.

- ❏ #1 U.S.S. Enterprise NCC-1701 $35-40

Star Trek: The Next Generation Riker plate by Hamilton, 1993. *Courtesy of the Collection of Jeff Maynard — New Eye Studio*

Star Trek: The Next Generation Data plate by Hamilton, 1993. *Courtesy of the Collection of Jeff Maynard — New Eye Studio*

The Hamilton Collection Plate, Star Trek Voyagers Commemorative Series, U.S.S. Enterprise NCC-1701-D, 8 1/2" in diameter, 1994. *Courtesy of the Collection of John E. Balbach*

Star Trek mugs, left: by Pfaltzgraff, USS Enterprise NCC-1701-A as seen in the movies, 1993; right: by Centric, 1993 Star Trek: The Next Generation mug with Riker & Troi. Left: 4 1/4" high; right: 3 3/4" high. Both measure 3 1/8" in diameter.
Courtesy of the Collection of Bob Hoag

	#2 U.S.S. Enterprise NCC-1701-D	$35-40
	#3 Klingon Battle Cruiser	$35-40
	#4 Romulan Warbird	$35-40

Star Trek:The Next Generation, The Episodes

Hamilton Commemorative Plate Collection with art produced by Keith Birdsong. Gilt edged, numbered on back.

	Best of Both Worlds	$35-40
	Encounter at Far Point	$35-40
	Unification	$35-40

Miniature Commemorative Plates

❑ Hamilton also produced a series of 4 1/4" diameter miniature plates of The Next Generation crew. These were sold boxed with small plastic display stands. $8-10/each

Mugs

CENTRIC — 1993

Centric produced a set of mugs with two images printed on opposite sides for both Star Trek and The Next Generation.

Two-sided Mugs

	Enterprise-D & Romulan Warbird	$10-11
	Picard & LaForge	$10-11
	Riker & Troi	$10-11
	Data & Worf	$10-11

IMAGE DESIGN CONCEPTS, INC.

Image Design produced a series of Star Trek "Magic Mugs" with designs produced from heat sensitive materials which disappeared or appear when hot beverages were added to the mugs. The mugs measure roughly 3 1/4" in diameter and 3 5/8" high. They produced mugs for both the original series and The Next Generation.

Magic Mugs: Transporter room

Crew members beam off of the transporter pad when the mugs are heated.

	Captain Picard	$12-14
	Commander Riker	$12-14
	Lt. Commander Data	$12-14
	Geordi LaForge	$12-14
	Dr. Crusher	$12-14
	Counselor Troi	$12-14

Magic Mugs: Holodeck Mugs

ST:TNG characters appear in garb from various holodeck adventures when hot liquids applied. Holodeck grid, shown in background, provides square outline of the printed pattern on the mugs. When cold, the closed doors to the holodeck are visible.

	Picard as Dixon Hill	$12-14
	Picard & Data as Musketeers	$12-14
	Troi as the Goddess of Empathy	$13-15
	Worf as a Merry Man	$13-15
	Data as Sherlock Holmes	$13-15

Star Trek pyramid of Magic Mugs: bottom left: Troi on transporter pad; bottom right Riker on transporter pad; top: Enterprise Evolution by Image Design Concepts, 1992. *Courtesy of the Collection of Jeff Maynard — New Eye Studio*

Applause, Inc. — 1994
Star Trek Figural Mugs: Sculpted three dimensional busts of characters from Star Trek, ST:TNG, & DS9. The entire bust is hollow and open at the top of the head, forming the mug.

- ❏ Data — $15-17
- ❏ LaForge — $15-17
- ❏ Borg — $15-17
- ❏ Troi — $15-17
- ❏ Worf — $15-17

CHRISTMAS ORNAMENTS

HALLMARK
Hallmark first produced Christmas tree ornaments in 1991 for Star Trek's 25th anniversary. The first two of this Keepsake Ornament - Magic line are from the original series. In 1995, Hallmark produced two different ornament types, all continuing under the "Keepsake Magic Ornament" line. One was the next in this series, a Romulan Warbird and the other was a small set of three ornaments "The Ships of Star Trek" (see Crossover products).

- ❏ U.S.S. Enterprise NCC-1701-D: 1993 — $85-95
- ❏ Klingon Bird of Prey: 1994 — $30-40
- ❏ Romulan Warbird: 1995 — $30-40

CLOTHING & ACCESSORIES

Caps
- ❏ Star Trek: The Next Generation: embroidered logo on a baseball cap. — $12-14

Jackets
The Next Generation Logo
- ❏ TNG Logo: embroidered across the back of a wool jacket with black leather sleeves. — $225-250
- ❏ TNG Logo: embroidered in red on back of black denim jackets. — $90-100
- ❏ TNG Logo: embroidered red logo on back of black satin jackets. — $90-110

Tee Shirts
Tee shirts are produced quickly, cheaply, and in large quantities. Licensed and unlicensed Star Trek tee shirts abound. Silkscreening allows small runs of many different designs. With this situation there has been an eye-popping proliferation of tee shirts over the past thirty years of Star Trek. By in large, tee shirts will never become great collectibles and, as such, they will not be covered here.

Silk Ties
Colorful silk ties have been recently offered for both Star Trek and The Next Generation.
- ❏ The Next Generation Crew — $14-26
- ❏ Picard — $14-26
- ❏ Borg — $14-16
- ❏ Combination Ships: outlines of the original, movie, and Next Generation Enterprise overlaid over each other. — $20-22

COINS & MEDALLIONS

The Next Generation Limited Silver Coin Set: One ounce silver coins, limited to 10,000 total pieces minted. Numbered and sold in sets of three. The fronts feature Captain Picard, Troi & Riker, or Worf, Data, and LaForge. The backs are all the same, displaying the Enterprise-D.
- ❏ Picard
- ❏ Troi & Riker
- ❏ Worf, Data, & LaForge
- ❏ Set of three — $120 per set

COMICS
DC Comics introduce Star Trek: The Next Generation to the comic universe in February of 1986.

DC COMICS
Star Trek: The Next Generation — 1986-1988
- ❏ A six issue limited series based on the characters and concepts

Star Trek: The Next Generation tee shirt. *Courtesy of the Collection of Jeff Maynard — New Eye Studio*

of the television series. Issues were written by Mike Carlin and drawn by Pablo Marcos. — $10-30

Star Trek: The Next Generation — 1989-present
- ❏ Begun in October 1989, this continuing comic series supplies original stories based on the characters and concepts of the television show. — $3-6

Star Trek: Generations — 1994
- ❏ Comic rendition of the Generations film. — $3-5

COSTUMES, PATTERNS, & MAKEUP KITS

Ben Cooper
Halloween costumes packaged on hangers, 1988 — $20-25 each
- ❏ Ferengi
- ❏ Klingon

Lincoln Enterprises
Patterns in several sizes released in 1988 of the first season design including:
- ❏ Men's jump suit — $13-15
- ❏ Women's jump suit — $13-15
- ❏ Men's skant — $9-10
- ❏ Women's skant — $9-10

Patterns by Lincoln from 1990 in several sizes reflecting the third season costume redesign:
- ❏ Men's third season top — $8-10
- ❏ Women's third season top — $8-10
- ❏ Pants — $6-8
- ❏ Visor: released by Lincoln in 1989 in plastic in the design worn by the character Geordi LaForge. — $4-5

Simplicity
Patterns produced in 1989 with first season low collar design jump suit. Packaged in pattern envelope with color cover photo. Several sizes in each package.

Star Trek: The Next Generation Klingon Complete Character Headpiece & Make-Up Kits, both large & small by Rubies, Small #18250, Large #2581, 1994. *Courtesy of the Collection of Jeff Maynard — New Eye Studio*

Star Trek: The Next Generation costume, men's uniform shirt, third season onward design. *Courtesy of the Collection of Jeff Maynard — New Eye Studio*

❑ Men's jump suit: costumed man & woman on cover	$6-7
❑ Women's jump suit: costumed man & woman on cover	$6-7
❑ Children's jump suit: two costumed children on cover	$6-7

Rubies
Star Trek: The Next Generation Complete Character Headpiece and Make-Up Kit.

❑ Klingon	$55-60
❑ Ferengi	$40-44

Star Trek PVC Masks
Colorful masks with elastic cords to hold them in place, designed for children. Masks made for characters from both The Next Generation and Deep Space Nine.

❑ Picard	$4-5
❑ Data	$4-5
❑ Worf	$4-5
❑ Borg	$4-5

Star Trek: The Next Generation Deluxe Uniform Shirts & Jump Suit
Third through seventh season designed costumes in red, gold, and blue.

❑ Men's shirt	$48-53
❑ Women's jump suit	$60-70

DECALS & STICKERS

Lincoln Enterprises

❑ United Federation of Planets sticker in The Next Generation design.	$2-3

A.H. Prismatic

❑ Star Trek: The Next Generation Hologram Stickers: eight scenes in a cartoon format.	$6-7

FILM & VIDEO

PARAMOUNT HOME VIDEO

❑ Star Trek: The Next Generation TV episodes: the first 66 of the 177 episodes (from the "Encounter at Farpoint" two part opener to "Allegiance") are available on video tape as of this writing.	$12-15 each
❑ Star Trek: Generations: the movie that passed the torch from Captain Kirk and the original crew to Captain Picard and the Next Generation cast.	$15-20/each
❑ From Here to Infinity. The Ultimate Voyage: Patrick Stewart hosts.	$20-25

As of this writing, the first 66 episodes of The Next Generation are available on video. *Courtesy of the Collection of Jeff Maynard — New Eye Studio*

Two tumblers by Zak Design Inc., 1994. Glitter in liquid between the tumbler walls. 3 1/2" in dia. 4" high. *Courtesy of the author's collection*

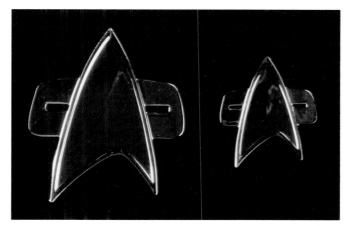

The Hollywood Commemorative Pins Company, enamel pins:
Communicators with delta shields as seen in the TV series Star Trek: Voyager (among others) (1994). *Courtesy of the Collection of Jeff Maynard — New Eye Studio*

JEWELRY
Cloisonne, Enamel, and Polychrome Pins
HOLLYWOOD COMMEMORATIVE PIN COMPANY

Star Trek: The Next Generation Pins:

❑ Generations Communicator Pin: full sized from the movie, 1994	$10-11
❑ Generations Communicator Pin: half size, 1994	$6-7
❑ Next Generation Communicator Pin: deluxe, 1989	$6-7
❑ Next Generation Communicator Pin: full sized deluxe, 1989	$10-11
❑ Next Generation Communicator Pin: small sized, 1988	$4-6
❑ Next Generation Communicator Pin: miniature	$5-6
❑ Next Generation Communicator Pin: The Future Imperfect Episode, 1990	$15-17
❑ Next Generation Communicator Pin: All Good Things Episode, 1994	$10-11
❑ U.S.S. Enterprise: NCC-1701-C: ship	$10-11
❑ U.S.S. Enterprise: NCC-1701-C: ship designator pins	$8-9
❑ U.S.S. Enterprise: NCC-1701-D: ship, 1988	$8-9
❑ U.S.S. Enterprise: NCC-1701-D: ship designator pins	$8-9
❑ Caution Force Field: 1989	$6-7
❑ Caution Antimatter: 1989	$6-7
❑ Borg Symbol: 1989	$6-7
❑ Borg Ship	$6-7
❑ "Engage!"	$8-9
❑ Ferengi Face	$6-7
❑ Ferengi Symbol: large, 1988	$6-7
❑ Ferengi Symbol: small, 1988	$4-5
❑ Fully Functional: 1989	$6-7
❑ Galaxy Class Starship Development Project: triangular pin	
❑ Horgon Idol	$6-7
❑ Klingon Face	$6-7
❑ Klingon Symbol	$8-9
❑ Locutus (Picard as)	$8-9
❑ Make It So: 1989	$6-7
❑ Next Generation Crew 1988-1989: 1990	$6-7
❑ Next Generation Cast & Crew 1989-1990: 1990	$6-7
❑ Next Generation Crew 1989-1990: 1989	$8-9
❑ Next Generation Cast & Crew Voyage Five 1991-1992: 1991	$6-7
❑ Next Generation Cast & Crew Voyage Six 1992-1993: 1992	$8-9

The Hollywood Commemorative Pins Company, enamel pins:
Left: Star Trek: The Next Generation, Voyage Five, Cast and Crew-1991-1992 (1991); Right: Star Trek: The Next Generation, The Final Season, Cast & Crew, 1993-1994 (1993). *Courtesy of the Collection of Jeff Maynard — New Eye Studio*

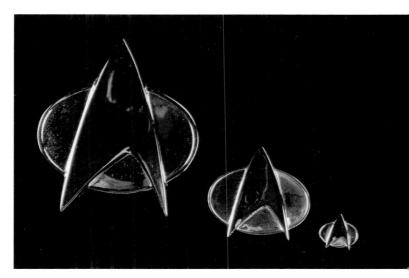

The Hollywood Commemorative Pins Company, enamel pins:
Communicators with delta shield from The Next Generation in full size, half size, & miniature (1988). *Courtesy of the Collection of Jeff Maynard — New Eye Studio*

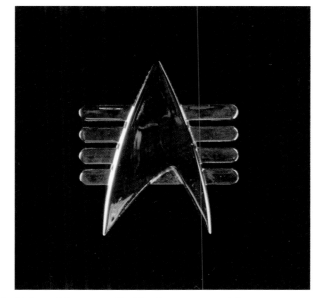

The Hollywood Commemorative Pins Company, enamel pins:
"Future Imperfect" Next Generation television episode insignia (1990). *Courtesy of the Collection of Jeff Maynard — New Eye Studio*

The Hollywood Pins Co., Key Rings:
Left: Borg symbol from Star Trek: The Next Generation, 1994. Right: Klingon Symbol & lettering, 1994. *Courtesy of the Collection of Jeff Maynard — New Eye Studio*

Star Trek: The Next Generation Key Chain with Sound FX. Push the buttons for different sound effects. 2 5/8" long. Interstellar Productions, Inc., 1994 *Courtesy of the Collection of Bob Hoag*

☐ Next Generation Cast & Crew The Final Season 1993-1994:	
1993	$6-7
☐ Next Generation Federation Symbol: 1988	$6-7
☐ Next Generation Logo: blue, 1988	$6-7
☐ Next Generation Logo: red, 1988	$6-7
☐ Next Generation Star Fleet Command: 1989	$6-7
☐ Next Generation 100 Episodes	$6-7
☐ Official Crew Member	$6-7
☐ Phasers: two different hand phaser cut outs	$6-8
☐ Romulan Bird of Prey Ship	$10-11
☐ Romulan Bird of Prey Symbol: 1989	$12-14
☐ Romulan Scout	$8-9
☐ Star Fleet Command Operations: green, 1989	$6-7
☐ Star Fleet Command Operations: red, 1989	$6-7

☐ Star Fleet Command Operations: yellow, 1989	$6-7
☐ Star Fleet Command Science: gold delta shields with cutout	
center symbols	$6-7
☐ Star Fleet Command Engineering: gold	$6-7
☐ Star Fleet Command Star Base: gold	$6-7
☐ Star Fleet Command Personnel: gold	$6-7
☐ Star Fleet Command Medical: gold	$6-7
☐ Starbase 74: 1989	$6-7
☐ Talarian Confederacy	$6-7

KOHN

☐ Next Generation Communicator Pin: with sound effects	$13-15
☐ Next Generation Communicator & Delta Shield: earrings	$18-20

LINCOLN ENTERPRISES — 1986-1990
These pins are valued at $8-10 each.

- ☐ Enterprise-D: blue
- ☐ Enterprise-D: white & black
- ☐ Enterprise-D: white, black, & orange
- ☐ Ferengi Ship
- ☐ Next Generation Communicator Pin: with logo
- ☐ Next Generation Logo: rainbow
- ☐ Next Generation Logo: blue, silver, & white
- ☐ "She Lives": Enterprise-D in orbit
- ☐ UFP Symbol: red & black

Enterprise Ship Jewelry

☐ Star Trek: The Next Generation Charm: 1" gold or silver	
plate, with or without chain	$10-12
☐ Star Trek: The Next Generation Earrings: 1" gold or silver	
plate, pierced or clip-ons	$17-22
☐ Enterprise-D: hologram earrings for pierced ears	$8-9
☐ Enterprise-D on delta shields: hologram earrings	$8-9

LINCOLN ENTERPRISES
Star Trek: The Next Generation 14K Gold:

☐ Charm	$150-175
☐ Charm with diamonds	$350-400
☐ Earrings	$300-325
☐ Earrings with diamonds	$650-700

Keychains

THE HOLLYWOOD PINS COMPANY
Rectangular gold-plated with enameled designs

☐ Borg Symbol: 1994	$5-6
☐ Klingon Symbol: with Klingon lettering, 1994	$5-6

INTERSTELLAR PRODUCTIONS, INC. — 1994
Six keychains with sound effects, three in each the original Star Trek & Next Generation series.

☐ Star Trek: The Next Generation Sound FX: 8 sounds	
triggered by buttons below delta shield	$12-14
☐ Star Trek: The Next Generation Phaser	$12-14
☐ Star Trek: The Next Generation Tricorder	$12-14

RAWCLIFFE
Pewter keychains, 1994-1995

☐ Klingon Bat'telh	$7-8
☐ Klingon Disrupter	$7-8
☐ Klingon Knife	$7-8
☐ Shuttlecraft 1701-D	$7-8
☐ Star Trek Generations Logo	$7-8
☐ Type 1 Phaser: palm-held	$7-8
☐ Type 2 Phaser: has a handle	$7-8
☐ U.S.S. Enterprise NCC 1701-D	$7-8

Miscellaneous Keychains

☐ Keychain Viewer: several Next Generation television stills	
seen within by Lincoln Enterprises	$4-8

Pendants

Next Generation Starcatchers: beveled crystal disks with central gold images, packed with "lanyard" & collectors' booklet:

☐ Delta Shield	$8-9
☐ Enterprise NCC-1701-D	$8-9
☐ UFP Symbol	$8-9

Uniform Insignia

- ❏ Star Trek: The Next Generation Communicator Insignia:
  metal, painted, & plated $15-17

Uniform Rank Insignia

- ❏ Next Generation Captain's collar pips: four on a base by
  Lincoln Enterprises $15-17
- Star Trek: The Next Generation pips: smaller pips were produced
  for the first two seasons, larger models were released
  for the third season onward. The pips are plain gold, silver,
  or "hollow" plated & painted:
  - ❏ Fleet Captain $14-17
  - ❏ Commodore $15-17
  - ❏ Captain $12-14
  - ❏ Commander $9-10
  - ❏ Lieutenant Commander $9-10
  - ❏ Lieutenant $9-10
  - ❏ Lieutenant JG $6-7
  - ❏ Ensign $3-4
  - ❏ Ensign JG $3-4
- ❏ Star Trek: The Next Generation Five Year Service Pips: set
  of four in gold $2-4
- ❏ Star Trek: The Next Generation Ten Year Service Pips, set
  of four with center delta shield, gold $2-4
- ❏ Star Trek: The Next Generation Commendation Bars: set
  of four, gold ridged $2-4

Watches

TIMEX

- ❏ Chronoscanner: "Star Trek: The Next Generation" written on
  band & face, multifunction digital watch $30-33
- ❏ "Command Watch": Delta Shield on sparkling face, white
  outer edge with "Star Trek," black wrist band $30-33
- ❏ Enterprise-D: forward view on the face of an Indiglo lighting
  for night reading watch $55-60
- ❏ Enterprise-D: rotating as seen from above on the second hand $40-45
- ❏ Enterprise-D: forward view on face above digital readout $30-33
- ❏ Klingon Chronometer: black with red circles on face,
  Klingon writing on wrist bands in red, black watch, digital
  readout $30-33
- ❏ Romulan Warbird: cloaking on watch face $40-45

Timex Indiglo U.S.S. Enterprise-D watch. *Courtesy of the Collection of Jeff Maynard — New Eye Studio*

MODELS and MODEL ROCKET KITS

AMT/ERTL — The Next Generation Television Series

- ❏ Adversaries Set: included three ships in scale, the Ferengi
  Marauder, Klingon Bird of Prey, & Romulan Warbird.
  Packaged in a 12" x 17 1/2" box in 1989 $15-17
- ❏ U.S.S. Enterprise Starship: an 18" model with a detachable
  saucer section, packaged in a 12" x 17 1/2" box, 1989 $15-17

Timex watches: Star Trek: The Next Generation sparkle face with delta shield; Star Trek: The Next Generation Cloaking Romulan Warbird; Star Trek: The Next Generation Rotating U.S.S. Enterprise-D; Star Trek: The Next Generation Chronoscanner; Star Trek: The Next Generation Klingon Chronometer; Star Trek: The Next Generation Indiglo U.S.S. Enterprise-D. *Courtesy of the Collection of Jeff Maynard — New Eye Studio*

Star Trek: The Next Generation 3 Piece Adversary Set model kit by AMT/ERTL, 1989. *Courtesy of the Collection of Jeff Maynard — New Eye Studio*

U.S.S. ENTERPRISE™ WITH FIBER OPTIC LIGHTS

❏ U.S.S. Enterprise with Fiber Optic Lights: includes lights & sound effects kit by ERTL, 1991 — $49-54

❏ U.S.S. Enterprise Three-Piece Set: includes in scale the original ship, the movie design, & the Enterprise-D. Packaged in a 12" x 17 1/2" box in 1989 — $15-17

❏ U.S.S. Enterprise Three-Piece Set: 25th anniversary special chrome edition — $25-28

❏ U.S.S. Enterprise Flight Display: features in scale the Enterprise-D, movie Enterprise NCC-1701, and the original series Enterprise, all held in flight by a clear plastic 13" disk, 1995 — $20-22

❏ Klingon Battle Cruiser: over 13" long with detachable weapons module, model shown on cover art, horizontal packaging, 1991 — $15-17

AMT/ERTL — Star Trek: Generations

❏ Klingon Bird of Prey: hinged, poseable wings, 10" long, 14 1/2" in width, cover art drawing of ship orbiting planet, horizontally packaged, 1994 — $18-20

❏ U.S.S. Enterprise NCC-1701-D: over 18" long, cover art drawing of the Enterprise-D in space, horizontal packaging, by ERTL, 1994 — $15-17

Star Trek: The Next Generation U.S.S. Enterprise with fiber optic lights model kit by AMT/ERTL, 1994. *Courtesy of the Collection of Jeff Maynard — New Eye Studio*

Star Trek: The Next Generation U.S.S. Enterprise Starship model kit by AMT/ERTL, 1988. *Courtesy of the Collection of Jeff Maynard — New Eye Studio*

Star Trek Special Edition 3-Piece U.S.S. Enterprise Chrome Set model kit (25th anniversary issue) by AMT/ERTL, 1991. *Courtesy of the Collection of Jeff Maynard — New Eye Studio*

Star Trek: The Next Generation Klingon Battle Cruiser model kit by AMT/ERTL, 1991. *Courtesy of the Collection of Jeff Maynard — New Eye Studio*

GEOMETRIC

1:6 scale vinyl model kits, cover art shows models of each figure, packaged in a vertical format.

❑ Captain Jean Luc Picard	$60-70
❑ Commander William Riker	$60-70
❑ Deanna Troi	$60-70
❑ Geordi LaForge	$60-70
❑ Lieutenant Commander Data	$60-70
❑ Lieutenant Worf	$60-70
❑ Locutus (Picard as a Borg)	$60-70
❑ Romulan	$60-70

PATCHES

Embroidered patches have been produced for both Star Trek and The Next Generation to date. Range from $3-12.

❑ Borg Ship: red symbol & gold background by Lincoln Enterprise
❑ Borg Symbol: symbol in front of their cube ship by Lincoln Enterprises
❑ Enterprise-D Cutout: by Lincoln Enterprises
❑ Enterprise-D Cutout: small sticky patches by Lincoln Enterprises

❑ Ferengi Ship Cutout: in orange by Lincoln Enterprises
❑ Next Generation Insignia Cutout: gold & silver by Lincoln Enterprises
❑ Next Generation Communicator Patch: white with gold background
❑ United Federation of Planets: Next Generation design of the UFP symbol in blue & red by Lincoln Enterprises

PEWTER FIGURINES

RAWCLIFFE

Under the new licensing agreement, Rawcliffe went on to produce detailed pewter figures and vessels for both The Next Generation and Deep Space Nine.

Ships — approximately 3 1/4" to 3 1/2" in length

❑ U.S.S. Enterprise NCC-1701-D: 1992	$25-28
❑ Ferengi Marauder: 1992	$25-28
❑ Romulan Warbird: 1992	$25-28

Larger Ships

❑ U.S.S. Enterprise NCC-1701-D: with detachable saucer section on custom delta shield stand	$55-60
❑ Borg Ship: on a square stand, 4 3/4" high	$70-80

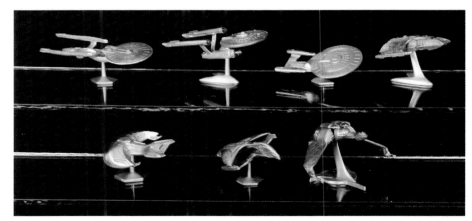

Star Trek ships of the line in pewter by Rawcliffe, 3" to 4 1/2" in length: top: U.S.S. Excelsior, U.S.S. Enterprise, U.S.S. Enterprise-D, Deep Space Nine Runabout; bottom: Ferengi Marauder, Romulan Warbird, & Klingon Bird of Prey. *Courtesy of the Collection of Jeff Maynard — New Eye Studio*

Next Generation ships in pewter by Rawcliffe: left: Romulan Warbird; right: U.S.S. Enterprise NCC-1701-D. Both were produced in 1992. *Courtesy of the Collection of John E. Balbach*

133

Limited Edition Ship

❑ U.S.S. Enterprise NCC-1701-D: 5" long, limited edition run
of 15,000 pieces, mounted on a black triangular stand
with a numbered plaque and delta shield.　　$100-110

The Next Generation Crew — a set of seven approximately

2 1/2" high, 1993　　$15-20 each

❑ Picard
❑ Riker
❑ Data
❑ Troi
❑ Worf
❑ LaForge
❑ Dr. Crusher

Additional Next Generation Figures — approximately 2 1/2" high

❑ Guinan: bartender in Ten Forward & Picard's confidant　　$18-20
❑ Klingon figure　　$18-20

Larger, More Detailed 3 1/2" High Next Generation Crew Members

❑ Picard　　$35-40
❑ Worf　　$35-40

Limited Edition Generations Pewter Sculpture

❑ Kirk & Picard Hanging From Broken Bridge: detailed pewter sculpture, Kirk
faces outward, hanging onto bridge railing & Picard (turned away), limited
run of 4500 pieces　　$100-110

Star Trek: The Next Generation crew by Rawcliffe, in pewter, 2 1/2" high: left to right: Picard, Riker, Data, Troi, Worf, La Forge, & Dr. Crusher. *Courtesy of the Collection of Jeff Maynard — New Eye Studio*

Large and small pewter figures of Captains Kirk and Picard by Rawcliffe. *Courtesy of the Collection of Jeff Maynard — New Eye Studio*

Rawcliffe Pewter, left: Captain Picard, 1993, 2 3/8" high; right: Dr. Crusher, 1993, 2 1/4" high. *Courtesy of the Collection of John E. Balbach*

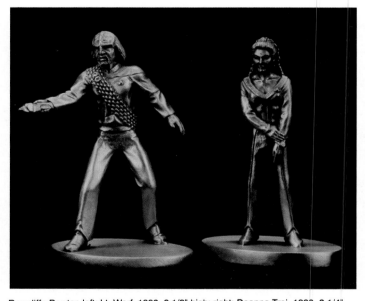

Rawcliffe Pewter, left: Lt. Worf, 1993, 2 1/2" high; right: Deanna Troi, 1993, 2 1/4" high. *Courtesy of the Collection of John E. Balbach*

POSTAGE STAMPS

From the Caribbean: St. Vincent & The Grenadines

Star Trek fans can now be found around the globe. St. Vincent & The Grenadines
have produced a set of commemorative stamps featuring scenes from the final
episode of Star Trek: The Next Generation, "All Good Things..."

❑ The Next Generation Limited Edition Gold Stamp Wallet: a 23K
gold stamp measuring 2 1/4" x 3 5/8", featuring a full color
inset of Captain Picard, a paper stamp on cache (envelope)
featuring the Enterprise-D crew, plus a cancelled first day
of issue. Limited edition set of 25,000, also includes a
numbered Certificate of Authenticity　　$60-70

❑ The Next Generation Gift Pack: nine stamp "sheetlet" showing
individual members of the crew & a souvenir crew sheet in
an album.　　$28-29

❑ The Next Generation First Day Covers: set of nine cache
envelopes with different stamps, all with first day of
issue cancellations.　　$50-55

❑ Souvenir Sheet: one large picture of the crew takes up the
entire sheet along with "Star Trek: The Next Generation,"
"1987-1994," "All Good Things...," "St. Vincent &
The Grenadines," & "$10."　　$10-11

The Next Generation Sheetlets: two sets of nine stamps each:

❑ Nine stamps, each featuring individual crew members　　$15-16
❑ Nine stamps, each featuring the entire crew (as on
souvenir sheet)　　$15-16

Republic of Guyana Official Postage Stamps — Star Trek: Generations

❑ Generations Limited Edition Gold Stamp Wallet: a 23K gold
stamp measuring 2 1/4" x 3 5/8" with a full color inset of
both Captains Picard & Kirk, a paper stamp on a cancelled
first day of issue cache showing the movie poster art. Limited

edition of 50,000, also includes numbered Certificate of
Authenticity $60-70
- ❏ Generations Tri-fold Gift Pack: two nine stamp sheetlets,
one featuring individual crew members in 19th century
sailing garb, the other with 23rd & 24th century individual
crew members, and a souvenir stamp sheet featuring the
movie poster art across the entire sheet, all held in a tri-
fold folder. $35-40
First Day Covers: two nine cache envelope sets with stamps from
both sheetlets, cancelled on the first day of issue:
- ❏ 19th century crew $50-55
- ❏ 23rd & 24th century crew $50-55
Nine Stamp Sheetlets:
- ❏ 19th century crew $15-16
- ❏ 23rd & 24th century crew $15-16
- ❏ Boldly Go poster art $15-16

POSTCARDS

CLASSICO SAN FRANCISCO, INC.
Color photo postcards from The Next Generation series, numbered cards
8" x 10" Postcards:
- ❏ The Next Generation Crew: color photo postcards,
numbered: 220-114, 1992 $3-4
- ❏ Data: 220-115, 1992 $3-4
- ❏ Picard: 220-116, 1992 $3-4
- ❏ Worf: 220-117, 1992 $3-4
- ❏ Troi: 220-118, 1992 $3-4
- ❏ The Next Generation Crew: 220-119, 1992 $3-4
- ❏ Beverly Crusher: 220-136, 1992 $3-4
- ❏ Wesley Crusher: 220-137, 1992 $3-4
- ❏ Riker: 220-138, 1992 $3-4
- ❏ Picard as Borg: 220-139, 1992 $3-4
- ❏ Romulan Warbird: 220-140, 1992 $3-4
- ❏ U.S.S. Enterprise NCC-1701-D: 220-141, 1992 $3-4
- ❏ The Next Generation Postcard Set: 14 card set $10-11
Star Trek: Generations 8" x 10" Postcards: color photo cards:
- ❏ Worf: 220-200, 1994 $3-4
- ❏ Data: 220-201, 1994 $3-4
- ❏ Kirk: 220-202, 1994 $3-4
- ❏ Kirk, Scotty, Chekov: 220-203, 1994 $3-4
- ❏ Picard: 220-204, 1994 $3-4
- ❏ Teaser: 220-205, 1994 $3-4

ENGALE — 1989
- ❏ Original series full color photographs along with the first
two seasons of The Next Generation series. On the
backs, they are identified as sets of 16. At least 30
different Star Trek cards among these. $3-5

Star Trek Lasergram Postcards
- ❏ The Next Generation Crew on the Bridge $3-5
- ❏ U.S.S. Enterprise NCC-1701-D $3-5
- ❏ Picard $3-5

POSTERS

The Next Generation Series

- ❏ **Enterprise-D:** ship above barely lit limb of a planet below,
unidentified manufacturer, 22" x 34", 1988 $6-7
- ❏ **Enterprise-D:** color ship cutaway technical poster, viewed
at an angle from above, 22" x 48" $20-22
- ❏ **Faces of the Next Generation:** characters from series with
brief biographies on one poster, 24" x 36" $6-7

- ❏ **GALOOB:** Enterprise-D & Galoob ad on opposite sides,
promotional poster, 1987 $10-12

- ❏ **HOLUSION ART:** Romulan Encounter poster with 3-D
computer image of an uncloaking Warbird in the center,
Enterprise-D in lower left $27-30

- ❏ **LIGHTRIX:** Three in one Red Beam® hologram poster, center
hologram shows either a Borg, Ferengi, or Klingon face,

Star Trek The Next Generation crew 8" x 10" postcard, 200-119, by Classico San
Francisco, Inc., 1992 (originally purchased for 2.99). *Courtesy of the Collection of
John E. Balbach*

Star Trek The Next Generation postcard (105-185) by Classico San Francisco,
Inc., 1992. *Courtesy of the Collection of Bob Hoag*

depending on which angle viewed from, with symbols from
each alien race down the right side $25-30

LINCOLN ENTERPRISES
- ❏ Enterprise-D: all posters in color, 23" x 34", 1987 $10-12
- ❏ Next Generation Crew on Transporter Pads $10-12

Next Generation Character Posters: each crew member, 36" x 11 3/4"
- ❏ Captain Picard $4-5
- ❏ Riker $4-5
- ❏ Data $4-5
- ❏ Troi $4-5
- ❏ Dr. Crusher $4-5

- ❏ **ONE STOP PUBLISHING:** collage art of crew, 22" x 35", 1988 $6-7

- ❏ **PORTAL PUBLICATIONS LTD.:** Enterprise-D cutaway
schematic of deck plans with inset photos from series,
22" x 48", 1993 $6-7
- ❏ **VIDEO POSTER:** Encounter at Farpoint video release in Britain,
color promotional, 20" x 32", 1989 $10-15

- ❏ **Zimmerman, Herman:** Klingon Birds of Prey (3) near Qo'nos,
art by Tsuneo Sanda, 24" x 36", limited edition, 1995 $25-30

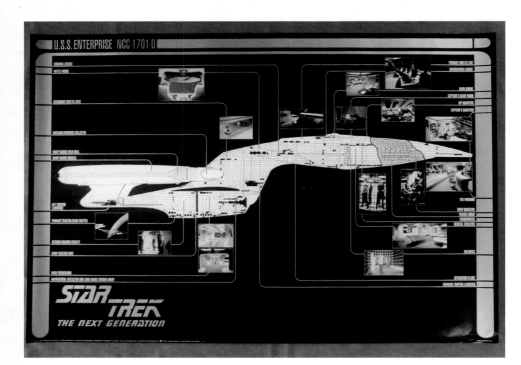

The U.S.S. Enterprise NCC-1701-D. 1991. 27" x 40".
Courtesy of the Collection of Jeff Maynard — New Eye Studio

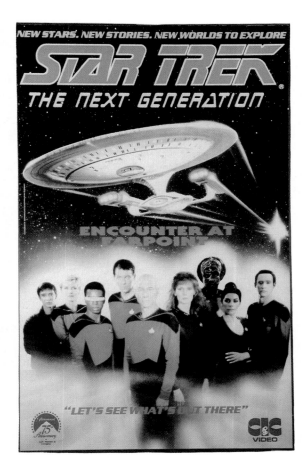

New Stars. New Stories. New Worlds To Explore. Star Trek: The Next Generation.
CIC Video promotional poster in Britain. 1989. *Courtesy of the Collection of Jeff Maynard — New Eye Studio*

Boldly Go. Star Trek: Generations teaser movie poster,
1994. 39 1/2" x 26 1/2". *Courtesy of the Collection of Jeff Maynard — New Eye Studio*

Star Trek: Generations

❑ **Boldly Go:** Generations one-sheet movie poster with
Enterprise-D & delta shield, 39 1/2" x 26 1/2", 1994 $12-14

❑ **Two Captains. One Destiny.:** one-sheet movie poster with
Kirk & Picard faces & delta shield, 39 1/2" x 27", 1994 $12-14

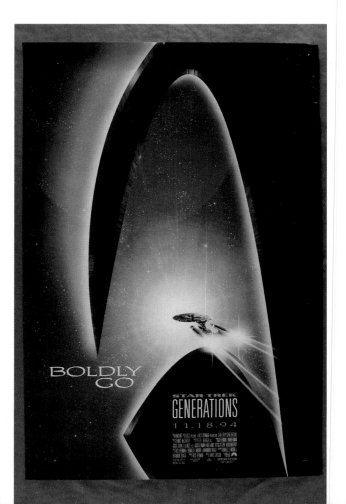

Poster Books / Magazines

Star Trek: The Next Generation. The Official Poster Magazine.
Fold out posters sold in an eight sheet magazine format. The poster, unfolded, measures 34" x 22". Articles appear on the back of the posters with color photos. Popular in England, rarely seen in the United States. To date there have been over 80 issues available.
- ❑ #1: Poster of the Enterprise-D, Encounter at Farpoint
  Episode, Article provides a guided tour of the Enterprise-D. $12-14
- ❑ #2-82 $4-6

PROPS and PROP REPRODUCTIONS

High quality reproductions which may be found in the market today produced by fans and through kits.

Analyzers (updated Tricorders)
- ❑ Next Generation Standard Analyzer Kit: solid cast resin kit
  with instructions $50-55
- ❑ Next Generation Standard Science Analyzer: solid cast
  non-functioning, with flip up cover & detachable scanner $95-105

Data Recorders
- ❑ Next Generation Large Data Recorder: flat, non-
  functioning, detailed & painted with displays, 8" x 6" $55-60
- ❑ Next Generation Small Data Recorder: flat, non-
  functioning, detailed & painted with displays, 4" x 6" $45-50
- ❑ Next Generation Data Recorder Kits: large & small,
  graphics for screen, paint, instructions, flat pad, 8" x
  6" or 4" x 6" $25-28

Dr. Crusher's Medical Equipment
- ❑ Next Generation series "Medicine" Applicator: removable
  medicine vial, non-functioning, solid cast $60-65
- ❑ Next Generation series Medical Analyzer: solid cast,
  non-functioning unit with flip open panel, removable
  machined metal scanner (small, oblong, hand unit) $150-175
- ❑ Next Generation Medical Scanner: small, cylindrical hand
  unit, 360 degree LED light scan, red LED sensor tip,
  sound effects $150-175
- ❑ Next Generation Medical Analyzer Kit: resin kit, opens
  & closes, non-functioning $65-75

Phasers
- ❑ Next Generation Early Phaser: wide-mouth "dustbuster"
  design, solid cast, non-functioning, painted & detailed $85-100
- ❑ Next Generation Cobra Phaser: with hand grip, non-
  functioning, detailed & painted $110-130
- ❑ Next Generation Cobra Phaser: later design, features
  high intensity LED beam, sound, hand polished cast
  aluminum $99-110
- ❑ Next Generation Cobra Phaser Kit: solid cast resin $60-66
- ❑ Next Generation Type 1 Phaser: hand unit, non-
  functioning, finished & painted $45-50

PROMOTIONAL ITEMS

The Next Generation
- ❑ Advance Brochure: "Captain's Log" metal folder, complete
  with spiral-bound demographics book of original series
  & a 20th anniversary T-shirt, 1986 $400-500
- ❑ 1989 Promotional Pack: colorful folder for TV executives
  and other VIPs, featuring a view of the Enterprise-D
  bridge with a rotating wheel showing different space
  scenes on the bridge viewscreen. Includes a photo
  pack & printed material. $200-220
- ❑ 1992 Promotional Pack: Aluminum document holder with
  spring lock hinge & custom brass engraving of the
  Next Generation name plate; contains photos &
  printed material. $300-330

Star Trek: Generations
Theater Lobby Cards (11" x 14") & Stills (8" x 10")
Star Trek: Generations: $10-12
- ❑ Cards
- ❑ Stills

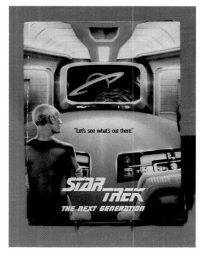

Star Trek: The Next Generation "Let's see what's out there." 1989 Promotional pack for television executives. Wheel on folder revolves bridge viewscreen space scene. Complete with photo pack and printed material inside. *Courtesy of the Collection of Jeff Maynard — New Eye Studio*

Star Trek: The Next Generation:
- ❑ Cards: Fifth Anniversary Special Collector's
  Edition, 12 cards $15-17

Press Books & Kits
Star Trek: Generations: market value
- ❑ Book
- ❑ Kit

Standees
- ❑ Star Trek: Generations   market value

Program Books
- ❑ Star Trek: Generations   market value

PUZZLES

F.X. SCHMID — 1993
- ❑ Star Trek: The Next Generation Puzzle: color art of
  crew & aliens, the Enterprise-D, & a Romulan
  Warbird, 1000 pieces $15-17

Star Trek: The Next Generation Puzzle featuring portraits of the crew, aliens, the Enterprise-D, & a Romulan Warbird, by F. X. Schmid, 1993. *Courtesy of the Collection of Jeff Maynard — New Eye Studio*

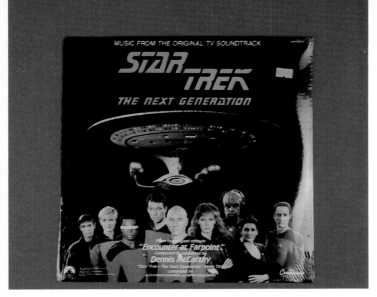

Star Trek: The Next Generation Original TV Soundtrack score by GNP Crescendo Records. *Courtesy of the Collection of Jeff Maynard — New Eye Studio*

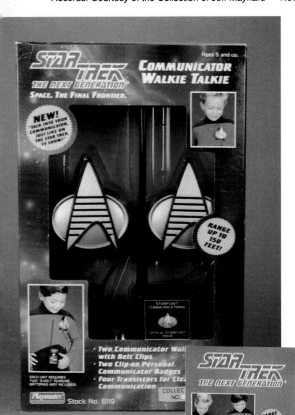

Star Trek: The Next Generation Communicator Walkie-Talkie by Playmates, 1993. *Courtesy of the Collection of Jeff Maynard — New Eye Studio*

- ❑ U.S.S. Enterprise NCC-1701-D Magnetic Holographic Puzzle: 29 piece holographic view of the ship as seen from the front from below — $10-11

RECORDS, TAPES, and COMPACT DISCS

Audio Novels

SIMON & SCHUSTER Audio Novels
Based on Star Trek novels by Pocket Books and narrated by cast members. Recorded on tape only.

- ❑ All Good Things — $17-19
- ❑ Contamination — $17-19
- ❑ Dark Mirror — $17-19
- ❑ The Devil's Heart: McFadden — $17-19
- ❑ Gulliver's Fugitives: Jonathan Frakes, 1990 — $10-12
- ❑ Imzadi: Frakes — $17-19
- ❑ Q-In-Law: Barrett & De Lancie — $12-14
- ❑ Q-Squared — $17-19
- ❑ Relics — $17-19
- ❑ Reunion — $16-18
- ❑ Star Trek: Generations: De Lancie — $17-19
- ❑ Christmas Carol: by Charles Dickens, dramatic narration by Patrick Stewart, CD or cassette — $15-20

Klingon Audio Books on Tape

- ❑ Conversational Klingon — $12-14
- ❑ Power Klingon — $12-14

"Captain, I have an incoming transmission...badly garbled!" Star Trek Personalities Sing

- ❑ Ol' Yellow Eyes is Back: Brent Spiner (Data) sings with full orchestral accompaniment, CD or cassette — $12-22

Soundtracks & Themes

- ❑ Encounter at Farpoint: Next Generation Volume I arranged from Next Generation episode score, 12" LP album, CD or cassette by GNP Crescendo Records — $22-24
- ❑ Both Worlds: Next Generation Volume II arranged from Next Generation Borg episode Part I & II, Ron Jones composed & conducted, CD or cassette by GNP Crescendo Records — $22-24
- ❑ Yesterdays Enterprise, Unification, & Hollow Pursuits: Next Generation Volume III, arranged from Next Generation series episodes, CD or cassette by GNP Crescendo Records — $22-24
- ❑ Star Trek: The Next Generation: Next Generation series soundtrack, Dennis McCarthy composed & conducted, in 12" LP album, CD or cassette by GNP Crescendo Records — $22-24

TOYS and CRAFTS

From the Quartermaster: Communicators, Phasers, and Tricorders

Communicators
- ❑ "Communicator Walkie Talkie": two walkie talkies with belt clip receivers with antennae, clip on communicator badges (gold & silver), by Playmates, 1993 — $40-45
- ❑ "Personal Communicator": gold & silver plastic with light & sound effects from the series, by Playmates, 1995 — $10-11

Phasers

- ❑ Phaser: gray plastic Next Generation TV series hand phaser with light & sound, by Galoob, 1988 $50-55
- ❑ Phaser: gray & black, hand grip cobra Next Generation series design with three white push buttons, sound effects, & lights, by Playmates, 1992 $20-22
- ❑ Phaser: gray plastic Next Generation series hand phaser with lights & three sound effects with gold & silver buttons, by Playmates, 1994 $20-22
- ❑ "Type II Phaser Mini Playset": Innerspace Series phaser toy, plastic, opens for alien planet play scene with three miniature articulated Next Generation action figures, by Playmates, 1995 $15-17
- ❑ "Klingon Disruptor": red & black plastic Next Generation disruptor with lights & sound effects, Klingon symbol on the grip, by Playmates, 1995 $15-17
- ❑ "Bajoran Phaser": brown & black plastic, light-up beam emitter & sound effects, by Playmates, 1995 $20-22

Tricorders

- ❑ "Star Trek: The Next Generation Tricorder: unfolding grey plastic with interior decals, lights, & sound effects, clips to belt, 6" x 3" x 1 1/2" thick when open, by Playmates, 1993 $15-17
- ❑ "Star Trek: The Next Generation Innerspace Series Medical Tricorder Mini Playset": gray plastic, opens out into the Next Generation sick bay with decals and three articulated miniature action figures, by Playmates, 1995 $15-17
- ❑ "Bajoran Tricorder": brown plastic, light-up viewscreen, flashing analysis indicators, three sound effects, by Playmates, 1995 $20-22

Star Trek: The Next Generation Personal Communicator toy by Playmates, 1992. *Courtesy of the Collection of Jeff Maynard — New Eye Studio*

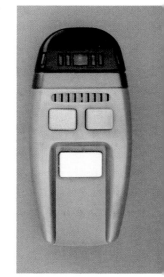

Next Generation hand phaser by Playmate Toys, 1994. Different sounds and lights with each gold button pressed. The silver button "fires" the phaser. *Courtesy of the Collection of John E. Balbach*

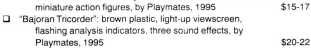
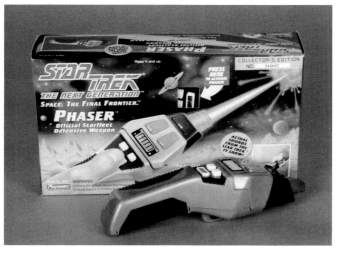

Star Trek: The Next Generation Phaser toy by Playmates, 1992. *Courtesy of the Collection of Jeff Maynard — New Eye Studio*

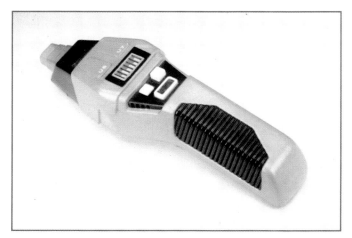

Playmates Next Generation toys hand phaser with grip, 1992, 8" long. *Courtesy of the Collection of Bob Hoag*

This is the colorful box front of the Type II Phaser Mini Playset. The back of the box may be seen on the following page. *Courtesy of the Collection of Jeff Maynard — New Eye Studio*

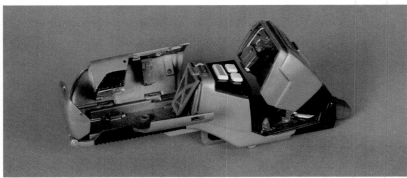

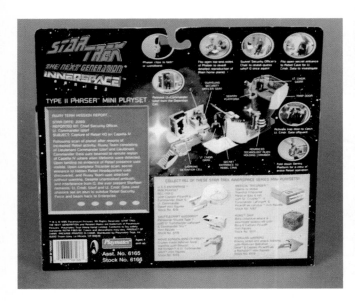

Star Trek: The Next Generation Innerspace Series Type II Phaser Mini Playset by Playmates, 1995. *Courtesy of the Collection of Jeff Maynard — New Eye Studio*

Star Trek: The Next Generation Klingon Disruptor toy by Playmates, 1995. *Courtesy of the Collection of Jeff Maynard — New Eye Studio*

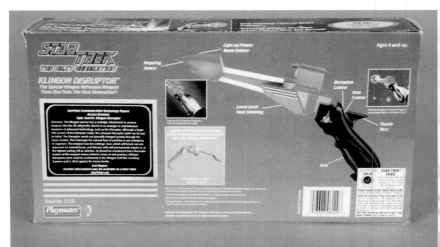

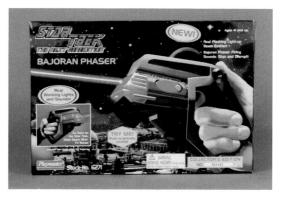

Star Trek: The Next Generation Bajoran Phaser toy with lights & sound effects by Playmates, 1995. *Courtesy of the Collection of Jeff Maynard — New Eye Studio*

Star Trek: The Next Generation Tricorder with lights and sound effects by Playmates, 1993. 6" x 3" x 1 1/2" thick when open. Clips to belt. *Courtesy of the Collection of Bob Hoag*

Star Trek: The Next Generation Innerspace Medical Tricorder Mini Playset by Playmates, 1995. *Courtesy of the Collection of Jeff Maynard — New Eye Studio*

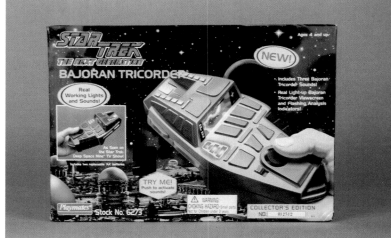

Star Trek: The Next Generation Bajoran Tricorder toy by Playmates, 1995. *Courtesy of the Collection of Jeff Maynard — New Eye Studio*

From the Space Dock: Starships and Their Interiors

Star Trek: The Next Generation Bridge Playset by Playmates, 1993. *Courtesy of the Collection of Jeff Maynard — New Eye Studio*

On The Bridge
❑ "Bridge Playset. The Control Center for the Starship
Enterprise": plastic reproduction of the Enterprise-D
bridge with eight sound effects, light up viewscreen, &
a technical blueprint. Connects with other Playmates
playsets. For use with Playmates Next Generation
action figures, by Playmates, 1993 $210-230

Engineering
❑ "Star Trek: Generations. Engineering Playset": plastic
engineering panels with decals, hinged reactor core
chamber with power-up dilithium crystal, lights, & three
sound effects. For play with Playmates Next Generation
action figures, by Playmates, 1994 $40-45

In the Transporter Room
❑ "Star Trek: The Next Generation Transporter Playset":
plastic transporter pad with decals & sound effects. Put
the Playmates action figure within & "transports" away.
By Playmates, 1994 $40-45

Ships of the Line & Vessels of Alien Races
❑ Enterprise-D: General Mills' 4" plastic cereal premium, the
first Next Generation collectible, 1987 $50-55
❑ Enterprise-D: die-cast Next Generation starship in light
blue, by Galoob, 1987 (sold with their Next Generation
action figures) $45-50
❑ Enterprise-D: Next Generation Starship Enterprise with lights
in the engine nacelles, four sound effects, & a technical
blueprint, 15" in length, by Playmates, 1992 $40-45
❑ Enterprise-D Glider: detailed 18" glider by Playmates, 1993 $15-17
❑ "Shuttlecraft Galileo. Captain's Armed Auxiliary Ship!": hinged
gullwing side hatches, hinged back hatch, pop-up sensor
unit, slide out phaser cannons, holds 6 Galoob Next
Generation action figures, by Galoob, 1989 $35-60
❑ "Shuttlecraft Goddard. Official Starfleet Transport Craft": white
plastic with light up thrusters, sound effects, & room for 3
Playmates action figures, by Playmates $40-45
❑ Borg Ship: square plastic vessel with sound effects, lights
in interior, & display stand, by Playmates $40-45
❑ Klingon Attack Cruiser: green plastic ship with light up
engines, 4 sound effects, & a technical blueprint, by
Playmates, 1993 $40-45
❑ Klingon Bird-of-Prey: green plastic ship with light up engine
exhaust & torpedo launchers, sound effects, & display
stand, by Playmates, 1995 $40-45

Star Trek: Generations Engineering Playset by Playmates, 1994. *Courtesy of the Collection of Jeff Maynard — New Eye Studio*

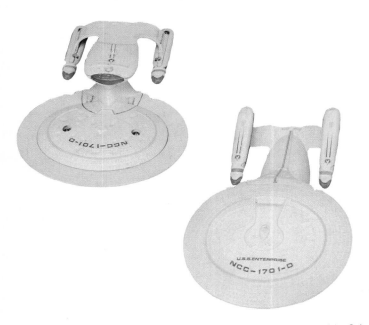

Galoob die-cast Enterprise-D, 1987, 5 3/4" long, 4 1/2" wide. *Courtesy of the Collection of Bob Hoag*

Starship Enterprise by Playmates, from The Next Generation series, with lights and sound effects. *Courtesy of the Collection of Bob Hoag*

Star Trek: The Next Generation Starship Enterprise toy by Playmates, 1992. *Courtesy of the Collection of Jeff Maynard — New Eye Studio*

Star Trek: The Next Generation Starship Enterprise Glider by Playmates, 1993. *Courtesy of the Collection of Jeff Maynard — New Eye Studio*

Star Trek: The Next Generation Shuttlecraft Galileo by Galoob, 1989. *Courtesy of the Collection of Jeff Maynard — New Eye Studio*

Playmates Shuttlecraft Goddard, with opening hatches fore and aft, lights, and sound effects. *Courtesy of the Collection of Bob Hoag*

Star Trek: The Next Generation Klingon Attack Cruiser toy by Playmates, 1993. *Courtesy of the Collection of Jeff Maynard — New Eye Studio*

❑ Romulan Warbird: gray/green plastic ship with light up engines, 4 sound effects, & a technical blueprint, by Playmates, 1993 .... $40-45

❑ Ferengi Fighter: orange & black plastic ship with fold-up phaser weapons, opening canopy, wingtip phaser cannons, & holds 2 Galoob Next Generation action figures, by Galoob, 1989 .... $100-110

Innerspace Series Mini Playsets by Playmates:

❑ U.S.S. Enterprise Mini Playset NCC-1701-D: plastic ship with hinged oversized saucer section, opens to bridge interior play area with three miniature articulated action figures, small shuttlecraft, & decals, 1995 .... $24-27

❑ Shuttlecraft Goddard Mini Playset: plastic personal shuttle type 7, opens to shuttlecraft's interior with two miniature articulated action figures $8-9

❑ Borg Ship Mini Playset: plastic ship, opens to Borg Bio-Lab &

Regeneration Station, with two miniature articulated action figures $8-9

❑ Klingon Bird of Prey Mini Playset: plastic cruiser class ship, opens to the main bridge, & three miniature articulated action figures $8-9

❑ Romulan Warbird Mini Playset: opens to Romulan bridge, with two miniature articulated action figures, 1994 .... $8-9

MicroMachines Star Trek Space Series by Galoob

❑ Star Trek: The Next Generation #1: includes Klingon Vor'cha Attack Cruiser, U.S.S. Enterprise NCC-1701-D, Romulan Scout Ship $8-9

❑ Star Trek: The Next Generation #2: Borg Ship, Ferengi Marauder, U.S.S. Enterprise NCC-1701-C $8-9

❑ Star Trek: The Next Generation #3: Romulan Warbird, Shuttlecraft, U.S.S. Stargazer $8-9

❑ Star Trek: Generations: Klingon Bird-of-Prey, Enterprise-B, Enterprise-D $8-9

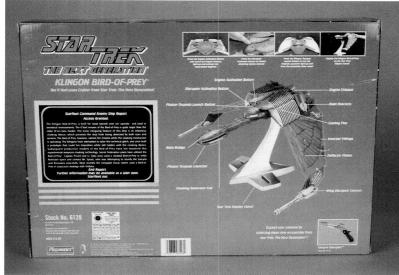

Star Trek: The Next Generation Klingon Bird of Prey toy by Playmates, 1995. *Courtesy of the Collection of Jeff Maynard — New Eye Studio*

Star Trek: The Next Generation Romulan Warbird toy by Playmates, 1993. *Courtesy of the Collection of Jeff Maynard — New Eye Studio*

Star Trek: The Next Generation Ferengi Fighter toy by Galoob, 1989. *Courtesy of the Collection of Jeff Maynard — New Eye Studio*

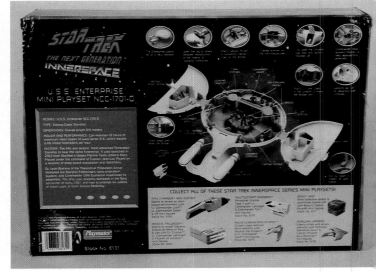

Star Trek: The Next Generation Innerspace Series, U.S.S. Enterprise Mini Playset NCC-1701-D by Playmates, 1995. *Courtesy of the Collection of Jeff Maynard — New Eye Studio & Courtesy of the Collection of Michael W. Snyder*

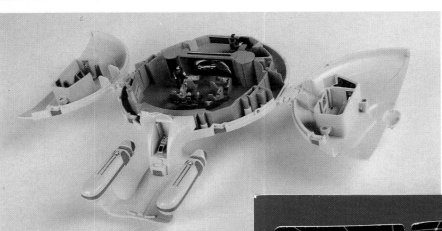

The Original MicroMachines Scale Miniatures, Star Trek: The Next Generation ships by Galoob. Left: Collection # 4 featuring the Ferengi Maurauder, Borg Ship & Shuttlecraft: right: Collection #3, Klingon Vor'Cha Attack Cruiser, U.S.S. Enterprise NCC 1701-D, and Romulan Warbird. *Courtesy of the Collection of Bob Hoag*

Toys, Crafts, and the Twenty-fourth Century: Miscellany

❑ "Space Age Crystal Growing Kit": Next Generation version of magic rocks, grows 14 crystals 6" long, by Kristal Corporation, 1995 $30-33

Star Trek: The Next Generation Space Age Crystal Growing Kit by Kristal Corp., 1995. *Courtesy of the Collection of Jeff Maynard — New Eye Studio*

146

Deep Space Nine Crew
These vinyl dolls range from $10-12 each
- ❏ Kira
- ❏ Odo
- ❏ Quark
- ❏ Sisko

BOOKS

Childrens' Books

Deep Space Nine Junior Paperbacks
- ❏ #1 *Star Ghost* $4-5
- ❏ #2 *Stowaways* $4-5
- ❏ #3 *Prisoners of Peace* $4-5

Pocket Books Star Trek: Deep Space Nine Paperback Novels
Each of these books are organized by number from the first to the most recent release rather than by alphabetical title listing. Deep Space Nine was first aired during the 1992-1993 season.
- ❏ The Search: novelization of the premiere, unnumbered. $6-7
- ❏ #1 *Emmisary* $6-7
- ❏ #2 *The Seige* $6-7
- ❏ #3 *Blood Letter* $6-7
- ❏ #4 *Big Game* $6-7
- ❏ #5 *Fallen Heroes* $6-7
- ❏ #6 *Betrayal* $6-7
- ❏ #7 *Warchild* $6-7
- ❏ #8 *Antimatter* $6-7
- ❏ #9 *Proud Helios* $6-7
- ❏ #10 *Valhalla* $6-7
- ❏ #11 *Devil in the Sky* $6-7
- ❏ #12 *The Laertian Gamble* $6-7

References, Manuals and Memoirs
- ❏ *Deep Space Crew Book* by James Van Hise $15-17
- ❏ *Deep Space Nine: A Celebration*, James Van Hise editor $15-17
- ❏ *The Making of Star Trek Deep Space Nine* by Judith & Garfield Reeves-Stevens, Pocket Books $15-17

CALENDARS
- ❏ 1994 Pocket Books: Star Trek: Deep Space Nine with series stills within $10-11
- ❏ 1995 Pocket Books: Star Trek: Deep Space Nine with series stills within $11-12
- ❏ 1996 Pocket Books: Star Trek: Deep Space Nine with cast on cover. $12-14

CERAMICS

Collector's Plates, Dining and Serving Wares

Hamilton Commemorative Plates
Deep Space Nine Commemorative plates, individually numbered.
- ❏ #1 Commander Sisko $35-40
- ❏ #2 Chief Odo $35-40
- ❏ #3 Major Kira Nerys $35-40
- ❏ #4 Deep Space Nine Space Station $35-40

PFALTZGRAFF
Bajoran Bone China
Pfaltzgraff has a Bajoran offering featuring the insignia of the Bajor Sector. The plates have a distinctive triangular shape.
Bajor Sector Bone China Buffet Dinner Set
Each set includes three pieces. $150-175
- ❏ Dinner plate
- ❏ Cup
- ❏ Saucer
- ❏ Mug: an additional large Bajoran Sector mug was produced. $50-55

Mugs

Magic Mugs
- ❏ Deep Space Nine Appearing Worm Home: the worm hole appears in space when the mug is warm to the right of the space station. $12-14

Star Trek: Deep Space Nine "Bajor Sector" bone china mug by Pfaltzgraff, 1993. *Courtesy of the Collection of Jeff Maynard — New Eye Studio*

Applause Inc. — 1994
Star Trek Figural Mugs: Sculpted three dimensional busts of characters from Star Trek, ST:TNG, & DS9. The entire bust is hollow and open at the top of the head, forming the mug.
- ❏ Quark $15-17

Quark's Bar Mug — 1995: white mug with transferred image of DS9's most popular Ferengi with a bottle in front of his bar shelves and bottles; emblazoned with "Quark's Bar" on opposite side.
- ❏ Quark's Bar Mug $15-17

CLOTHING and ACCESSORIES

Tee Shirts

Tee shirts are produced quickly, cheaply, and in large quantities. Licensed and unlicensed Star Trek tee shirts abound. Silkscreening allows small runs of many different designs. With this situation there has been an eye-popping proliferation of tee shirts over the past thirty years of Star Trek. By in large, tee shirts will never become great collectibles and, as such, they will not be covered here.

COMICS

Both DC and Malibu Comics have brought Star Trek: Deep Space Nine into the comics.

DC & MALIBU COMICS
Deep Space Nine/Star Trek: The Next Generation
- ❏ In October 1994, these two comic companies introduced a collaborative four part mini-series combining charactors from both series in the Deep Space Nine setting with original stories. $3-10 each

MALIBU COMICS
Star Trek: Deep Space Nine
- ❏ Comic series introduced in December 1994 by Malibu. Based on the characters and concepts from the series. This is an ongoing series as of this printing. $3-10 each

COSTUMES, PATTERNS, and MAKEUP KITS

Bajoran nosepiece: light flesh colored.
- ❏ small nose piece $7-8
- ❏ large nose piece $8-9

Star Trek PVC Masks
Colorful masks with elastic cords to hold them in place, designed for children. Masks made for characters from both The Next Generation and Deep Space Nine.
- ❏ Sisko $4-5
- ❏ Odo $4-5
- ❏ Quark $4-5

Star Trek: Deep Space Nine costume, men's uniform shirt. *Courtesy of the Collection of Jeff Maynard — New Eye Studio*

Carafe seen on Star Trek: Deep Space Nine, by BMF of Germany. *Courtesy of the Collection of Jeff Maynard — New Eye Studio*

Star Trek: Deep Space Nine Costumes:
Commander Sisko Red Uniform Shirt
- Adult Shirt $48-53
- Child's Jump suit $30-33

Deluxe Engineering Gold Uniform Shirt
- Adult Shirt $48-53
- Child's Jumpsuit $30-33

Deluxe Crew Teal Uniform Shirt
- Men's Shirt $48-53
- Women's Jump suit $60-70
- Child's Jump suit $30-33

Major Kira Deluxe Jump Suit Uniform
- Adult Jump suit (includes belt) $60-70
- Child's Jump suit (includes belt) $30-33

Quark Full Deluxe Uniform
- Adult (all include pants & jacket with inset shirt) $50-55
- Child $30-33

Odo Full Deluxe Uniform
- Adult (all include pants & shirts) $50-55
- Child $30-33

Simplicity
Patterns for various Deep Space Nine uniforms
- Men's Jump suit $11-12
- Women's Jump suit $11-12
- Odo's Security Uniform $12-13
- Major Kira's Uniform $12-13

DECALS and STICKERS

A.H. Prismatic
- Star Trek Hologram Stickers: nine scenes from Deep Space Nine in a cartoon format $6-7

FILM & VIDEO

See Crossover Products.

HOUSEHOLD WARES
Around the House

Computer Mousepads: with art and scenes from the original series, the first six films, The Next Generation television series, the Generations movie and Deep Space Nine.
- Deep Space Nine Space Station $15-17

In The Kitchen
- **Carafe** seen in Quark's bar on Deep Space Nine by BMF of Germany $40-45

JEWELRY
Cloisonne, Enamel, and Polychrome Pins
HOLLYWOOD COMMEMORATIVE PIN COMPANY
- Bajoran Ear Clip: for pierced ears or clip ons, 1993 .... $10-11
- Bajoran Communicator Pin: gold with black enamel, 1993 .... $10-11
- Star Trek: Deep Space Nine: rectangular title pin, 1993 .... $8-9
- Star Trek: Deep Space Nine 1993: triangular pin with space station, 1992 .... $8-9
- Deep Space Nine Cast & Crew 1, 1992-1993: 1993 .... $6-7
- Deep Space Nine Runabout: cutout $10-11

Pendants
SILVER DEER
Producers of crystal collectibles, manufactured "Starcatchers," beveled disks displaying gold central images, complete with neck cord.
- Bajoran Symbol $8-9
- Cardassian Symbol $8-9

FILM and VIDEO

- ☐ Star Trek-The Beginnings: includes the first episodes of the original Star Trek, The Next Generation, and Deep Space Nine on videocassette. $20-30

GLASSWARES and TANKARDS

Frosted glassware:
- ☐ shot glass with UFP symbol in gold & "United Federation of Planets" around the gold trim, 1994 $6-7
- ☐ tumbler with UFP symbol in gold & "United Federation of Planets" around the gold trim, 1994 $12-14
- ☐ mug with UFP symbol, the Enterprise-D, DS9 space station, the DS9 Runabout, & original Enterprise, 1994 $15-17

HOUSEHOLD WARES

Around the House

Computer Mousepads: with art and scenes from the original series, the first six films, The Next Generation television series, the Generations movie and Deep Space Nine.
- ☐ Three Enterprises: the original, the movie, and The Next Generation vessels $11-13

TOYS and CRAFTS

Ships of the Line & Vessels of Alien Races
- ☐ MicroMachines Star Trek Collector's Set: with ships from the original series, the first six films, & The Next Generation, by Galoob, 1993 $25-28
- ☐ MicroMachines Limited Edition Collector's Set: with ships from the original series, the movies, The Next Generation, & Deep Space Nine, by Galoob, 1993 $35-40

Endnotes

1. This list was based, in part, upon the listings in Cornwell & Kott. *The Official Price Guide: Star Trek And Star Wars Collectibles.* The listings throughout this book have been greatly expanded by the continued rapid outpouring of new Star Trek collectibles.
2. ibid. 21.
3. Keven Stevens. "The Top 25 Star Trek Collectibles of All Time." *Star Trek® Communicator.™ The Magazine of Star Trek: The Official Fan Club.* #100 Dec/Jan. 94/95. 76-79.
4. Cornwell & Kott. *The Official Price Guide: Star Trek And Star Wars Collectibles.* 22.
5. ibid. 22.
6. Logan. "The Magnificent Seven." 20.
7. Cornwell & Kott. *The Official Price Guide: Star Trek And Star Wars Collectibles.* 23-25.
8. Boorstin. *The Americans.* 444-445.

Frosted Star Trek glassware: shot glass with gold UFP symbol; tumbler with UFP symbol, & mug with UFP symbol & Star Trek: The Next Generation Enterprise-D, Star Trek: Deep Space Nine Station, Star Trek: Deep Space Nine Runabout & original series Enterprise, 1994. *Courtesy of the Collection of Jeff Maynard — New Eye Studio*

Star Trek Collector's Set MicroMachines K-Mart exclusive by Galoob, 1993. Ships from the original series, the movies, and The Next Generation. *Courtesy of the Collection of Jeff Maynard — New Eye Studio*

Star Trek Limited Edition Collector's Set MicroMachines, a larger set by Galoob, 1993. Ships from the original series, the movies, The Next Generation, and Deep Space Nine. *Courtesy of the Collection of Jeff Maynard — New Eye Studio*

159